Renaissance Poetry

ENGLISH MASTERPIECES · AN ANTHOLOGY OF IMAGINATIVE LITERATURE FROM CHAUCER TO T. S. ELIOT · UNDER THE GENERAL EDITORSHIP OF MAYNARD MACK, YALE UNIVERSITY

Renaissance Poetry

edited by

LEONARD DEAN

Professor of English, University of Connecticut

Second Edition

PRENTICE-HALL, INC.

Englewood Cliffs, N. J.

TO THE READER

These volumes present a carefully proportioned collection of writings in English, from Chaucer to the present, which are primarily valuable as literary works of art. Writings in the less imaginative modes have been almost entirely excluded, and complete works have been preferred to excerpts. Where cutting or selection was necessary, an effort has been made to preserve what is crucial for an understanding of the artistic value of the whole piece. Since novels cannot be condensed or excerpted satisfactorily, they have been omitted. Separate reprints of prose fiction may be used to supplement the last two volumes of this set. The introductions try to focus the reader's attention on what is imaginatively interesting and valuable in the various selections. If they succeed, they will at the same time provide the justification for this anthology and distinguish it from the many other anthologies that are available.

© 1950, 1961, BY PRENTICE-HALL, INC. ALL RIGHTS RESERVED.
PRINTED IN THE UNITED STATES OF AMERICA

LIBRARY OF CONGRESS
CATALOG CARD No. 61-9352

Current printing (last digit):
17   16   15   14   13   12   11

28137-C

Contents

v

EDMUND SPENSER

CHRISTOPHER MARLOWE

SIR WALTER RALEGH

FULKE GREVILLE

MICHAEL DRAYTON

WILLIAM SHAKESPEARE

JOHN DONNE

BEN JONSON

ROBERT HERRICK

THOMAS CAREW

GEORGE HERBERT

Renaissance Poetry

This volume contains some three hundred poems, exclusive of Milton's, written in English between Chaucer and Dryden. Since they were chosen for their basic literary value, they should be largely available to any good reader without elaborate introduction. The modern perspective, however, is likely to need historical correction in one way. Renaissance poetry is more formal, less autobiographical and less directly related to experience than much poetry of later periods. From essays on poetry like Sidney's and from the actual poems, it is clear that Renaissance poets were careful to distinguish themselves from historians and biographers, and to seek instead the formal excellence appropriate to the various kinds of poetry. A love poem was not an essay in autobiography, and even poems for special occasions like some of those by Jonson, Donne, and Marvell were not composed as historical documents. The prime aim, to use the Renaissance term, was to make an imitation. This act had two aspects: first the poet sought to grasp the essential meaning and value of experience, and secondly he tried to express that insight in a recognized and appropriate literary form. The more detailed suggestions that follow, therefore, are focused on those formal excellences of Renaissance poetry that may be misjudged or undervalued by the modern reader.

Elizabethan Courtly Love Poems

Anthologies like this one frequently include, for its historical interest, the following sonnet by Sir Thomas Wyatt.

I

The lover compareth his state to a ship in
perilous storm on the sea

My galley chargèd with forgetfulness
Through sharp seas, in winter nights, doth pass
'Tween rock and rock; and eke my foe, alas,
That is my lord, steereth with cruelness;
And every oar a thought in readiness,
As though that death were light in such a case.
An endless wind doth tear the sail apace,
Of forcèd sighs and trusty fearfulness;
A rain of tears, a cloud of dark disdain,
Have done the wearied cords great hinderance;
Wreathèd with error and with ignorance,
The stars be hid that led me to this pain;
Drowned is reason, that should be my comfort,
And I remain despairing of the port.

Our first reaction is likely to be that *My galley* is a poor love poem because it sounds insincere, and the case will appear to be closed when it is known that the sonnet was not spontaneously original but was actually translated from Petrarch. An Elizabethan's reaction would almost certainly be different. Sidney, it is true, admonishes himself (in Sonnet 1) to look into his heart and write, but he is not really arguing for less artificiality and more spontaneity; he is rather paying an ingenious, even artificial, compliment to Stella. In Sonnet 3 he says that, since in Stella nature and perfection are one, "then all my deed/But copying is, what in her Nature writes." Other poets, that is, have to prettify their subjects artificially because they have to write about girls who are not perfect to start with; but since Stella is naturally perfect already, the poet who writes about her must simply report what he sees and feels. She is the single miraculously golden thing in a brazen world. Only about Stella, says Sidney cleverly, can one be spontaneous and candid. It is improbable, then, that Sidney or any other Elizabethan writer would attribute the insincere effect of *My galley* to the fact that Wyatt was not reporting an actual experience. Sidney would more likely point out that *My galley* is badly written, as we can easily see on a second reading. Although the poem sounds artificial, it is relatively simple in construction. It contains only one device, an extended comparison of the speaker to a storm-tossed ship. The comparison does suggest in a general way the pain of unrequited love; but what, for example, is the lover in the first line forgetful of? Himself, because he is lost in love? Everything except thought of the port? And what is the port? His mistress's arms? Or a haven to which he can escape from love? On examination these and other details prove to be puzzling rather than illuminating, and consequently the poem gives the immediate impression of being "insincere."

My galley does have historical interest, however, because it comes close to being formula-writing; and it is in formula-writing of course that a literary convention or dominant literary type is most clearly visible. We are conscious of the presence of a literary convention when we notice that it compels the attention of the majority of writers of a given period. The dominant type that compelled the attention of many Elizabethan love poets was the so-called courtly love sonnet or lyric, which appears clearly in such a formula-poem as *My galley* and which Wyatt helped to introduce into England through his translations from Italian poetry. In the conventional courtly love poem, the man is pictured as pleading with a girl to return his love. He catalogues the symptoms of his lovesickness and the charms of the girl, and he argues that she can be even more perfect by taking pity on his plight. This conventional situation does have the merit of helping the poet organize experience, but the better poets wanted to say things about love and personal relationships that were not possible within such a pattern, at least in the stereotyped form of that pattern. As a result, although they could not ignore it completely, they modified the courtly love formula or combined it with other traditions and attitudes.

An early example of this interweaving of traditions (Chaucerian and Italian among them) is Wyatt's *They flee from me,* in which a man who has known a different kind of love tries to adjust himself to the behavior of a "new-fangled" mistress. Our first reaction to this poem may be that it sounds more "sincere" than *My galley.* It does so, however, not because it is truer biographically, but because it is more successfully artful and because it organizes a more complex and permanently interesting interpretation of love. The first stanza, for example, is not a factual statement about the girls that the speaker used to know; it is a carefully chosen comparison of a girl and an animal. The animal is not named, but it is certainly not ample and domestic like a cow, nor is it altogether wild like a tiger. It is more probably a doe—graceful, curious, and skittish. The comparison suggests the mixed feelings of the speaker, and it influences our reaction to the second stanza, which employs another means of arousing and controlling emotion—a dramatic scene. The details of the scene are selected to emphasize the delicate seductiveness of the doe-like girl, who is disturbingly attractive in submission because the very act shows her untamableness. "Dear heart, how like you this?"

is obviously not a request for information. She puts herself in danger (from Latin *dominus*—master) to prove her own mastery. In the last stanza the speaker discusses his predicament with the reader. "It was no dream," he begins: "it doesn't seem possible now but she really did hold me in her arms. I soon found out, however, that I was the one who had been tamed; my 'gentleness' was real, her 'goodness' was pretended. Now that I have been served so kindly, I should like to know what she deserves." The speaker would like to be rigidly severe, but he is a helpless male. "Kindly" (which the printer Tottle weakened to "unkindly") sums up his dilemma. It means both "unkindly" (cruelly) and "naturally" (according to her nature). The speaker is at once sarcastic and wrily resigned. It's the nature of the beast. Girls are that way, but what can you do about it, and would you have them any different?

Closer to the Petrarchan formula is Sidney's *With how sad steps, oh moon,* in which the lovesick speaker assumes that the pale moon must be lovesick too. The transfer of symptoms suggests, however, that the speaker is capable of some amused detachment about his own plight; the hint of self-consciousness makes him seem more real. Sidney partly accepts, and partly toys with, the conventional situation. Drayton, in *Since there's no help,* presents a speaker who pretends to give up the courtly love formula entirely, and to accept the girl's refusal as final. She is pictured as being so shocked that she clings uncharacteristically to the man, who pushes her aside: "Nay, I have done, you get no more of me." The delight and surprise of the reader is largely dependent upon his, too, being accustomed to the usual situation. The speaker proceeds coolly to congratulate himself on the completeness of the break and to instruct the girl, irritatingly, how they should behave now that they are just friends. It is a fresh approach, but of course he is only pretending to be fresh, and his problem is to recover the girl now that she has been shaken out of her fashionable position by his unconventional treatment. Since an about-face on his part would be unstrategic, he works more subtly by taking advantage of another aspect of the conventional courtly love sonnet, its formal diction and rhythm. In the first nine lines the language and rhythm are that of ordinary conversation; at line ten the language becomes heavy with alliteration, personified abstractions, and successive strong accents. The change in style demands a bombastic tone of voice, one through which the speaker can continue to make fun of the conventional protestations of love and at the same time admit his own real feelings. Even more directly satiric of the courtly love formula is Shakespeare's Sonnet 130. The man speaking acknowledges that his mistress does not have the fashionable charms:

her eyes are not like the sun, her lips are not so red as coral, and so on. I grant, he says finally with a straight face, that I never saw a goddess go—I am a simple person; but although my mistress is not divine like other poets' mistresses, she does have one useful virtue: she is alive, she can go.

While the courtly love pattern is a useful approach to many Elizabethan love poems, it is finally, as might be expected, too narrow a concept for the understanding of major poems by such writers as Spenser, Marlowe, Shakespeare, and Donne.

~

Edmund Spenser

Two obstacles to a clearer view of Spenser's real merits as a poet have been the widespread notions that he is a poet's poet and that *The Faeric Queene's* structure and meaning are adequately described in his famous letter to Ralegh. Lamb's phrase "the poet's poet" has apparently meant for many editors and readers a kind of ineffectual and unimportant prettiness, something so purely poetical that it is all sweetness without sense. The letter to Ralegh has suggested furthermore that Spenser began *The Faerie Queene* with a clearly formulated plan, that he wrote straight through to where the work breaks off in Book VI, that the structure and meaning are solely those of such a continuous allegorical narrative, and that descriptive sections (like some of those included in this volume) were meant as digressive examples of unusually "poetical" poetry. Recent studies have shown, however, that the plan described in the letter to Ralegh of 1590 is not an accurate account of the composition of *The Faerie Queene*. It was, for example, not Book I but perhaps a part or version of Book III that Spenser showed to Gabriel Harvey in 1580. Apparently, then, Spenser was experimentally interweaving a variety of descriptive and narrative materials in an effort to develop several related philosophical themes. From this view, sections like The Bower of Bliss are not purple passages but functional, and the methods employed in them are not mysteriously and quintessentially poetic but the normal ones available to a writer of Spenser's time and temperament.

The Bower of Bliss, to be more particular, has seemed basically contradictory to readers who believed in the idea of the poet's poet. They have felt that it betrays a conflict between what they consider Spenser's essential love of lushness and the explicit allegorical argument of the passage against physical pleasure. The Bower is revealed to be something quite different, as C. S. Lewis has shown, when it is closely examined without any preconceptions about Spenser's subconscious aims. It comes at the end of Book II, after the central character Sir Guyon has passed through a series of experiences designed to clarify the quality of temperance. The meaning of this final experience is defined by Spenser's careful selection of details in his description of The Bower, a perfectly normal poetic method. Inspection will show that the lushness of the foliage is really artificial and metallic, that the bathing girls are strip teasers rather than lovers, and that the men are Peeping Toms. When Guyon destroys The Bower, then, he in effect rejects in the name of temperance a life of futile and irresponsible titillation and debauchery in favor of natural fruition.

This point is clearer, as C. S. Lewis has further shown, when The Bower of Bliss is contrasted with The Garden of Adonis, which appears in Book III. The heroine of this Book is Britomart, who represents chaste affection, a vigorous, healthful, and fruitfully disciplined love. Her nature is defined through a series of contrasts in which she is distinguished from characters who are deficient or excessive or maladjusted with respect to love. Her last adventure is the rescue of Amoret, who had been immaculately conceived and born, adopted by Venus, and reared in The Garden of Adonis as the companion of Pleasure, the daughter of Cupid. The Garden, in contrast to The Bower, is all that is natural and fecund. It "is the first semenarie of all things," the seed-bed of the actual world. Here all growth is natural self-development. It is an Eden of life as it might be, freed from the mortal limitation of Time, which all "glory to the ground downe flings." Love here is spontaneous and naturally good: "Franckly each paramour his leman knows." Venus possesses her dear Adonis, "and of his sweetness takes her fill"; Cupid lays aside his "sad darts" and is reconciled to Psyche. In this environment, with its promise of eternal fruitfulness in the midst of change and decay, Amoret is "trained up in true feminitee . . . To be th' ensample of true love alone,/And Lodestarre of all chaste affectione,/To all faire Ladies, that doe live on ground." The association of Britomart and Amoret completes the definition of "chaste affection."

The dance of the Graces works similarly to point toward the essential spirit of courtesy, the theme of Book VI. Calidore, in love with Pastorella, leaves his quest for the Blatant Beast (malice or slander) and turns from the vain shadows of court to the "perfect pleasures" of the country. In this idealized pastoral land, as in the fields where Lycidas once piped happily with his friend, and as in the Garden of Adonis, there "was gathered . . . all that ever was by natures skill/Devised to work delight." We enter this land to the sound of music, and hesitate amidst the ever fruitful trees on the edge of a natural amphitheater. From this point in the poet's symbolic fiction, midway between the actual world behind us and the vision of perfect value before us, we watch "An hundred naked maidens lilly white,/All raunged in a ring, and dauncing in delight" around three others who honored one set in the center like "a precious gemme." At our approach, the dancers vanish and we are left with the shepherd Colin Clout, who explains that the three Graces, divinely born, bestow on men "all gracious gifts, . . . all the complements of curtesie." With the name of Colin Clout, Spenser's own pastoral disguise as a poet, and with the comparison of the central Grace to the sun and then to Gloriana and so to Queen Elizabeth, we are recalled to the actual world and to the tension that exists between it and the pastoral world of ideally ordered grace. The passage, then, far from being descriptive decoration, is felt to be a carefully devised conclusion to the definition of courtesy, safeguarding it from sermonizing or from mere politeness, and attaching it to the realm of infinite possibility.

A comparable pattern, finally, may be seen in the House of Holiness and the Vision of the New Jerusalem from Book I, which traces man's passage through temptation and sin to blessedness. In the House of Holiness the Red Cross Knight passes through his culminating religious experience guided by Faith, Hope, and Love, and then ascends the hill of Contemplation from whence he has a vision of the Heavenly City, where "the blessed angels . . . in gladsome companee . . . wend,/As commonly as friend does with friend." This vision, like that of the Graces of Courtesy, enlarges and idealizes the theme of the Book; and after it, likewise, we are brought back to the actual world and to our inescapable responsibilities, but now inspired by the vision to perform them in the light of the ideal.

There has been less temptation, of course, to read Spenser's marriage poems as the work of a rather mechanical allegorist and poet's poet, and more tendency to see him here as a poet interested in deepening the theme of love through an intricately allusive and symbolic style. The *Prothalamion* opens, like the vision of the Graces of Courtesy, with a passage from the "empty shaddowes" of court to a pastoral scene where a delicate tension can be maintained between the idealized existence described and hoped for and the shifting fortunes of actual life, "Olde woes" which "here fits not well to tell." In this poem and in the *Epithalamion* an ordered, ceremonial structure works with the selective details to suggest a pattern of things as they should be. This in turn is reinforced by allusions and echoes, often mythological and Biblical, that extend and direct the meaning. The bride in *Epithalamion,* for example, is associated first with the sun through Phoebus and with the bridegroom in the Psalms who "rejoiceth like a mighty man to run his race"; and later with the moon, Cynthia, her love for Endymion; and finally the bride of Christ.

∾

Christopher Marlowe

An obstacle to a clearer view of *Hero and Leander,* an Ovidian erotic narrative in a tradition that includes Shakespeare's *Venus and Adonis,* has been the assumption that it should tell a simple tragic story like its source, a 340-line poem by Musaeus of the fifth century A.D. Working from this assumption, many readers have found *Hero and Leander* to be full of inconsistencies in form, characterization, and tone. Working from the evidence in the poem, however, and looking for its ambition, which is the legitimate one, we do not find a poet or speaker who is trying to imitate Musaeus but rather one with a variety of interests which combine to form a very probable Renaissance character, and it is this which gives the poem its real unity. One such interest may even be that of violating the effect of Musaeus's poem, as Sidney deliberately violates in his nightingale song the pathos of Ovid's account of the rape of Philomela. It may be felt, in fact, that the speaker's general attitude toward the basic story is one of amused and sophisticated detachment. He makes Hero and Leander perform so as to provide a large amount of sheer sexual titillation. Their inexpertness in love-making ("And as a brother with his sister toyed,/Supposing nothing else was to be done") spices a familiar act for the worldly speaker and reader. At the same time it is in character for the speaker, though not for Leander, to know the fashionable philosophizing about love and the sequence of arguments (like those used by Comus) against coyness or chastity. Appropriate to the speaker, also, are the luxurious descriptions and the contrasting witty style (foreshadowing *The Rape of the Lock*) with its satirical ambiguities and its deliberately too-neat couplets that almost take the heart out of the truisms they express.

∾

Shakespeare's Sonnets

While some of Shakespeare's sonnets deal with fashionable themes and are largely comprehensible in terms of literary conventions like that of courtly love, they have impressed most readers as being uncontainable by any convention, as being not even about love but about life itself. An attempt has been made to account for this impression of range and intensity by supposing that the sonnets reflect some equally intense experience of the author's, but there is no external evidence for such a supposition. The sonnets make the impression they do because they actually treat a considerable variety of personal relationships, which are frequently explored with unusual profundity, and which are related to a large context not only explicitly but indirectly through the comparative terms of metaphors and other figures.

Anyone will approve complimentary statements about Shakespeare, but he may think privately after a first honest reading of such a sonnet as 30 ("When to the sessions of sweet silent thought") that it is mainly an exercise in cleverness, that Shakespeare wrote the plain sense with one hand while playing only roughly parallel verbal tricks with the other. This centers attention on the important critical problem, the usefulness of the sonnet's language and imagery. What is gained by the intricate alliteration, repetition, and balance, and by the consistent use of comparisons to banking? Here are some possible answers. (1) The wittiness helps to characterize the speaker as mentally quick and self-possessed; it is such a speaker rather than a soft-headed enjoyer of the blues who makes the final avowal to his friend. (2) The intricacy of the first twelve lines verbally represents the confined, unhealthy, fruitlessly repetitive brooding of the speaker. (3) The banking terms help to define the speaker's emotion by bringing in such feelings as worry over debts, the urgency and finality of business contracts, the relief at the payment of debts—which here have to be repaid over and over as in a nightmare. (4) The whole effect intensifies the miraculousness of the relief (costless and uncomplicated) afforded by the friend; he is the opposite of the world of which the banking terms are one sign; he alone can free one from its time-bound perverseness. (5) The stylistic pattern (intricacy to neat conclusiveness in the last couplet, elaboration of metaphor to its resolution) parallels the psychological pattern (frustration to release and consummation).

A first honest reading of such a sonnet as 33, on the other hand, may produce the reaction that it is straightforward enough, except perhaps for the last two lines, but that it is mainly pretty and even trite. There seems at first glance to be nothing notable about the comparison between alternate sunny and cloudy weather and the uneven course of a friendship. A second reading will show, however, that the language or imagery is much more precise and alive than that. This first becomes evident, perhaps, when we discover that the commonest meaning of "flatter" (the toadying of a yes-man) will not work. The context of "glorious," "sovereign," "kissing," "gilding," "alchemy" forces us to reinterpret "flatter" to mean "bring out the good points of," "inspire with hope," "caress and smooth." The flatterer is not a fawning subordinate, but a majestic, even divine power that benevolently and almost impersonally brings out the best in everything it looks on, that miraculously increases the value of what is imperfect and earthy. Even so, says the speaker in an effort to make us understand what has happened to him and how he feels about it, did "my sun" (my friend) shine on me. We are obliged to see that this is more than the usual sunshine-to-tears-but-I-love-him-still sort of thing. The effect of the friend on the speaker has been like that of the sun on the earth; it has made him almost saint-like, with a halo of splendor on his brow. Furthermore, just as one does not criticize the sun for allowing itself to be cut off by a dark cloud (its absolute value makes such criticism irrelevant; it is not in the realm of longer or shorter working hours or exchange of services), so the speaker can not react to the absence of his friend with the usual posturing of the piqued lover. The courtly love situation is in the background again, but close inspection shows something more than conventional sonneteering.

❧

John Donne

When we pass from Spenser and Shakespeare to Donne, we may feel that his poetry is more *logical* than theirs. Since *logical* is an inexact term (*witty, strong, metaphysical* are others that have been tried since the seventeenth century), a definition through analysis may help to clarify some of Donne's typical methods and effects.

Although many of Donne's poems begin like Drayton's *Since there's no help* with an abrupt, colloquial violation of the conventional attitudes toward their subjects, Donne is likely to proceed not with a dramatic scene but with a chain of arguments. The sonnet *Death,* for example, opens with the unorthodox assertion that death is not mighty and dreadful, and then goes on with a reasoned defense of that thesis. The conclusion, though, is drawn not from the reasoning, but from the nonrational idea of immortality. The conclusion is emphasized in part by being stated as a paradox ("Death, thou shalt die"), but it is also emphatic because it at last gives open expression to our growing dissatisfaction with the preceding argument. There had been no chance, for instance, to speak out against the pseudological syllogism that since the best men die, death should not be feared; the seemingly logical surface of the argument had kept our uneasiness underground, where it grew so strong that it wanted no more of this kind of logic and welcomed the super-rational conclusion. This method is to use logic, or more accurately, a pseudological sequence, to prepare for a conclusion beyond logic.

In terms of content rather than of technique, this interest in logic and value may appear as social comedy, as the situation of two lovers against the world and the superiority of their relationship to approved conduct. In *The Sun Rising* Donne presents a man and his mistress still in bed after the start of the day's routine business. Like Falstaff, the man takes the offensive; instead of waiting to be lectured about his idleness and lack of character, the speaker attacks the sun (and any punctual person) as a pedantic busybody, as, of all things, "unruly." This is a typical method of comedy: the upsetting of accepted estimates and categories in order to get a fresh hearing for the essential spirit of things. The logic established by respectability is shown to be illogical and superficial; the behavior we are conventionally asked to imitate is shown to have no value at all except as it imitates what it scorns: "Nothing else is./Princes do but play us; compared to this,/All honor's mimic, all wealth alchemy." *The Canonization* reveals a similar pattern. "For God's sake hold your tongue, and let us love," exclaims the speaker to his respectable critic. He goes on to anticipate the critic's moralizing (chide my palsy, gout, falling hair, and ruined fortune if that makes you feel virtuous), and he urges him sarcastically to work harder than ever at being proper and successful (make money, take courses in Culture, set a course and go straight to your goal). Our love, adds the speaker, does not interfere with the folly of the world: soldiers still find wars in which to die, and lawyers still get fees from petty quarrels. The poem ends like the preceding one with the assertion that in time the lovers' secret value will be worshipped and desired by their critics, who will have found only unhappiness in their own seeming success. In these and similar poems, what appears at first to be merely a defense of sensual pleasure becomes a manifesto for more basic and inclusive values. The intellectual tone of these poems may spring in part from their paradoxical nature, from their seeming to be only plausible arguments for the weak position. Ultimately, though, the paradox takes the form of fundamental redefinition and revaluation. It is this serious kind of paradox that distinguishes the best love poems (like *The Ecstasy*) and the best religious poems, and keeps them from being merely clever.

A related method is the use of a logical structure as an analytical instrument or to give us the impression that we are experiencing a search for truth. The method is seemingly comparable to the scientist's, in which an initial hypothesis is submitted to a series of searching tests with the result that the conclusion has the appearance of being incontestably true. The organization of *The Prohibition,* for example, is that of two propositions ("Take heed of loving me"; "Take heed of hating me") so examined as to necessitate the deductive concluding request for a tension of love and hate. In other poems this method may produce a tone of mock-painstakingness or problem-solving, which acts as a solvent of excessive or sentimental emotion. In *The Broken Heart* the speaker argues that a lover's heartbreak, unlike other griefs, is necessarily complete, and then he goes on in the manner of a person "scientifically" reconstructing his actions so as to account for an inexplicable loss: "I brought a heart into the room,/But from the room I carried none with me."

This impression of going through a process is frequently the result of a theme being developed in an elaborated comparison. While the extended metaphor is not Donne's only figure of speech, still it is more frequent in his poetry than in, say, Shakespeare's sonnets, where one finds characteristically a diffused sequence of images, such as the montage of boughs, birds, choirs, and ruined cathedrals in Sonnet 73. In *The Flea,* for example, the man argues his suit through a developed identification: "This flea is you and I, and this/ Our marriage bed and temple is." The comparison has been condemned as bad taste, and it has been defended as wit (a striking conjunction of incongruities). Both reactions testify to the effectiveness of the comparison in forcing the reader to enter the character of the speaker. We react strongly because we actually experience the speaker's values and mental processes. The characteristic danger of the extended metaphor is that it may not in every detail be appropriate and illuminating. In the third stanza of *A Lecture upon the Shadow,* for example, the comparative term of the metaphor goes its own way and no longer coalesces with the central term or theme.

The extended metaphor is most successful when it serves as a pervasive body for an abstract theme rather than as a blueprint. This is illustrated in *The First Anniversary,* where the death of an actual person (Elizabeth Drury, daughter of Donne's patron) becomes the occasion and symbol for an "anatomy of the world," an examination of the moral predicament of fallen mankind. The death or withdrawal of Elizabeth Drury is equated with the incoming of evil, formlessness, mortal limitation. Since life or original perfection cannot be recovered, the speaker "will try/What we may gain by thy anatomy" (59-60), by a knowledge of our ethical sickness. That sickness here, as in other poems by Donne, is the overthrow of the spirit by the letter. "The heart being perish'd, no part can be free" (186). "This world's general sickness doth not lie/In any humor or one certain part,/But, as thou saw'st it rotten at the heart" (240-242). In this condition relationships are only formal or nominal at best, and at worst, " 'Tis all in pieces, all coherence gone." Complete health, the verdure and luster of an "unvexed paradise" (363-4), the proportion of true beauty (306)—that cannot be recovered; but the memory of the symbolic Elizabeth Drury is at least "a glimmering light,/ A faint, weak love of virtue and of good" (70-1) by which one may become a "weedless paradise," free at least, that is, from self-engendered sin and more capable of estimating things at "their true worth" (90). As an essay in moral philosophy the *Anniversary* is admirable but not original. Donne himself thought of it, for several reasons, as a poem or a "song" (460-66). To see what that means in the fullest sense is to understand what is both characteristic and permanent in Donne's poetry.

∼

Ben Jonson

The usual words for Jonson's poetry are *lucid, clear,* and *classical;* and they are likely to seem appropriate to the reader who turns to Jonson from the *strong* poetry of Donne. Such a reader, although he knows that Jonson was a deliberate craftsman, may even wish to add the word *artless.* Senses adjusted to Donne have difficulty in perceiving Jonson's methods and effects. The striking images, the dramatic situations, the sharp changes in diction and tone, the attention-compelling arguments are gone, and in their place is an apparently smooth surface. It is not impenetrable or artless, however, and actually a good deal is going on in a Jonsonian poem.

Some of the things that go on are easiest to see in the epigrams.

On something that walks somewhere has the form of a conundrum or riddle, where the neuter terms in the title and the pronoun *it* are a necessary part of the guessing game. We soon see, however, that the simple words are doing triple duty. The neuterness is also an insult and a definition. This is reinforced by the metaphor "buried," and by the controlled irregularities of rhythm in the last sentence. "Good Lord," because of the ambiguous accent, teeters between a conventional salutation and an exclamation of disgust and scorn; and the successive heavy accents on the monosyllables "walk dead still" emphasize the main point of the satire and suggest the motion of an automaton. Another example is the expression "I hope so" in *To my mere English censurer*. The chief effect, of course, comes from the twist which the expression gives to the preceding argument, but the effect is intensified by the heavy punctuation within the line on either side of the expression and by the fact that it is at the turning point in the epigram.

The values and devices in the epistles may be somewhat harder to see. *Inviting a Friend to Supper*, for example, may provoke the question: why should we spend time reading an old dinner invitation and menu? The question assumes that the occasional or ostensible subject is the real one. A closer look at the poem, however, shows that the subject is actually the definition of *liberty*, "The liberty that we'll enjoy to-night." The definition, further, is not a stenographic description of a particular night, but a delicate balance between what we all know particular nights or parties or human relationships are certain to be and what they might be. The *liberty* desired is partly the result of abiding by certain rules, yet it is not anything that can be defined in crudely insistent or regulatory fashion. It is more nearly the result of a subtle adjustment and discrimination among values. The poem does not state those values bluntly, but rather represents them through the character of the speaker; and his character is formed and projected through Jonson's careful use of language.

In the lyrics the effects are seemingly the most artless of all. *Queen and huntress*, for example, is apparently about the moon or Diana, and then very gently it becomes symbolic. The over-all tone is that of the prayer or charm—a prayer for something chaste, fair, ceremonial, bright, and excellent, and a charm against the earth, the darkness of a moonless night, and the tension of the mortal hunt. In whatever form, however, epigram, epistle, elegy, or lyric, the chief thing is the controlled play of language, which is none the less alive for being subtle.

Viewing the poetry in this volume as a whole, one may generalize that it deals with human nature rather than with external nature, with love, religion, and personal relationships rather than with social problems, and that its values, despite the growth of science and secularism, are basically Christian. But it is perhaps in terms of style that the diverse poems in this volume can be most clearly related and distinguished from surrounding periods. The richly metaphorical language of Renaissance poetry, which the next age was inclined to regard as imprecise, provided the necessary means for giving body and order to experience in a world that was both medieval and modern.

Popular Ballads

SIR PATRICK SPENS

The king sits in Dumferling toune,
    Drinking the blude-reid wine:
"O whar will I get guid sailor,
    To sail this schip of mine?"

Up and spak an eldern knicht,   5
    Sat at the kings richt kne:
"Sir Patrick Spens is the best sailor,
    That sails upon the se."

The king has written a braid letter,
    And signd it wi his hand,   10
And sent it to Sir Patrick Spence,
    Was walking on the sand.

The first line that Sir Patrick red,
    A loud lauch lauched he;
The next line that Sir Patrick red,   15
    The teir blinded his ee.

"O wha is this has don this deid,
    This ill deid don to me,
To send me out this time o' the yeir,
    To sail upon the se!   20

"Mak hast, mak haste, my mirry men all,
    Our guid schip sails the morne":

SIR PATRICK SPENS: 9. *braid:* broad, official. 14. *lauch:* laugh.

16

"O say na sae, my master deir,
 For I feir a deadlie storme.

"Late, late yestreen I saw the new moone,   25
 Wi the auld moon in hir arme,
And I feir, I feir, my deir master,
 That we will cum to harme."

O our Scots nobles wer richt laith
 To weet their cork-heild schoone;   30
Bot lang owre a' the play wer playd,
 Thair hats they swam aboone.

O lang, lang may their ladies sit,
 Wi thair fans into their hand,
Or eir they se Sir Patrick Spence   35
 Cum sailing to the land.

O lang, lang may the ladies stand,
 Wi thair gold kems in their hair,
Waiting for thair ain deir lords,
 For they'll se thame na mair.   40

Haf owre, haf owre to Aberdour,
 It's fiftie fadom deip,
And thair lies guid Sir Patrick Spence,
 Wi the Scots lords at his feit.

∾

JOHNIE ARMESTRONG

There dwelt a man in faire Westmerland,
 Jonne Armestrong men did him call,
He had nither lands nor rents coming in,
 Yet he kept eight score men in his hall.

He had horse and harness for them all,   5
 Goodly steeds were all milke-white;
O the golden bands an about their necks,
 And their weapons, they were all alike.

---

29. *richt laith:* right loath. 31. *owre:* ere, before. 32. *aboone:* above.

Newes then was brought unto the king
   That there was sicke a won as hee,   10
That lived lyke a bold out-law,
   And robbed all the north country.

The king he writt an a letter then,
   A letter which was large and long;
He signed it with his owne hand,   15
   And promised to doe him no wrong.

When this letter came Jonne untill,
   His heart it was as blythe as birds on the tree:
"Never was I sent for before any king,
   My father, my grandfather, nor none but mee.   20

"And if wee goe the king before,
   I would we went most orderly;
Every man of you shall have his scarlet cloak,
   Laced with silver laces three.

"Every won of you shall have his velvett coat,   25
   Laced with sillver lace so white;
O the golden bands an about your necks,
   Black hatts, white feathers, all alyke."

By the morrow morninge at ten of the clock,
   Towards Edenburough gon was hee,   30
And with him all his eight score men;
   Good lord, it was a goodly sight for to see!

When Jonne came befower the king,
   He fell downe on his knee;
"O pardon, my soveraine leige," he said,   35
   "O pardon my eight score men and mee!"

"Thou shalt have no pardon, thou traytor strong,
   For thy eight score men nor thee;
For to-morrow morning by ten of the clock,
   Both thou and them shall hang on the gallow-tree."   40

But Jonne looke'd over his left shoulder,
   Good Lord, what a grevious look looked hee!
Saying, "Asking grace of a graceles face—
   Why there is none for you nor me."

JOHNIE ARMSTRONG: 10. *sicke a won:* such a one.

But Jonne had a bright sword by his side,   45
   And it was made of the mettle so free,
That had not the king stept his foot aside,
   He had smitten his head from his faire bodde.

Saying, "Fight on, my merry men all,
   And see that none of you be taine;   50
For rather then men shall say we were hanged,
   Let them report how we were slaine."

Then, God wott, faire Eddenburrough rose,
   And so besett poore Jonne rounde,
That fowerscore and tenn of Jonnes best men   55
   Lay gasping all upon the ground.

Then like a mad man Jonne laide about,
   And like a mad man then fought hee,
Untill a falce Scot came Jonne behinde,
   And runn him through the faire boddee.   60

Saying, "Fight on, my merry men all,
   And see that none of you be taine;
And I will stand by and bleed but awhile,
   And then will I come and fight againe."

Newes then was brought to young Jonne Armestrong,   65
   As he stood by his nurses knee,
Who vowed if ere he lived for to be a man,
   O the treacherous Scots revengd hee'd be.

                              ❧

THE WIFE OF USHER'S WELL

There lived a wife at Usher's Well,
   And a wealthy wife was she;
She had three stout and stalwart sons,
   And sent them oer the sea.

They hadna been a week from her,   5
   A week but barely ane,
Whan word came to the carline wife
   That her three sons were gane.

THE WIFE OF USHER'S WELL: *7. carline wife*: old woman.

They hadna been a week from her,
   A week but barely three,   10
Whan word came to the carline wife
   That her sons she'd never see.

"I wish the wind may never cease,
   Nor fashes in the flood,
Till my three sons come hame to me,   15
   In earthly flesh and blood."

It fell about the Martinmass,
   When nights are lang and mirk,
The carline wife's three sons came hame,
   And their hats were o the birk.   20

It neither grew in syke nor ditch,
   Nor yet in ony sheugh;
But at the gates o Paradise,
   That birk grew fair eneugh.

"Blow up the fire, my maidens,   25
   Bring water from the well;
For a' my house shall feast this night,
   Since my three sons are well."

And she has made to them a bed,
   She's made it large and wide,
And she's taen her mantle her about,   30
   Sat down at the bed-side.

Up then crew the red, red cock,
   And up and crew the gray;
The eldest to the youngest said,   35
   "'T is time we were away."

The cock he hadna crawd but once,
   And clapped his wings at a',
When the youngest to the eldest said,
   "Brother, we must awa."   40

"The cock doth craw, the day doth daw,
   The channerin worm doth chide;

---

14. *fashes:* troubles. 17. *Martinmass:* November 11. 18. *mirk:* dark. 20. *birk:* birch. 21. *syke:* trench. 22. *sheugh:* furrow. 42. *channerin:* complaining.

Gin we be mist out o our place,
A sair pain we maun bide.

"Fare ye weel, my mother dear!   45
Fareweel to barn and byre!
And fare ye weel, the bonny lass
That kindles my mother's fire!"

❦

EDWARD

"Why dois your brand sae drap wi bluid,
   Edward, Edward,
Why dois your brand sae drap wi bluid,
   And why sae sad gang yee O?"
"O I hae killed my hauke sae guid,   5
   Mither, mither,
O I hae killed my hauke sae guid,
   And I had nae mair bot hee O."

"Your haukis bluid was nevir sae reid,
   Edward, Edward,   10
Your haukis bluid was never sae reid,
   My deir son I tell thee O."
"O I hae killed my reid-roan steid,
   Mither, mither,
O I hae killed my reid-roan steid,   15
   That erst was sae fair and frie O."

"Your steid was auld, and ye hae gat mair,
   Edward, Edward,
Your steid was auld, and ye hae gat mair,
   Sum other dule ye drie O."   20
"O I hae killed my fadir deir,
   Mither, mither,
O I hae killed my fadir deir,
   Alas, and wae is mee O!"

"And whatten penance wul ye drie for that, 25
   Edward, Edward,

---

43. *Gin:* if. 44. *maun bide:* must suffer. 46. *byre:* shed.
   EDWARD: 1. *brand:* sword. 20. *dule ye drie:* sorrow you suffer.

And whatten penance wul ye drie for that?
   My deir son, now tell me O."
"Ile set my feit in yonder boat,
     Mither, mither,   30
Ile set my feit in yonder boat,
   And Ile fare ovir the sea O."

"And what wul ye doe wi your towirs and your ha,
   Edward, Edward,
And what wul ye doe wi your towirs and your ha,   35
   That were sae fair to see O?"
"Ile let thame stand tul they down fa,
     Mither, mither,
Ile let thame stand tul they doun fa,
   For here nevir mair maun I bee O."   40

"And what wul ye leive to your bairns and your wife,
   Edward, Edward,
And what wul ye leive to your bairns and your wife,
   Whan ye gang ovir the sea O?"
"The warldis room, late them beg thrae life,   45
     Mither, mither,
The warldis room, late them beg thrae life,
   For thame nevir mair wul I see O."

"And what wul ye leive to your ain mither dear,
   Edward, Edward,   50
And what wul ye leive to your ain mither dear?
   My deir son, now tell me O."
"The curse of hell frae me sall ye beir,
     Mither, mither,
The curse of hell frae me sall ye beir,   55
   Sic counseils ye gave to me O."

❧

LORD RANDAL

"O where hae ye been, Lord Randal, my son?
O where hae ye been, my handsome young man?"
"I hae been to the wild wood; mother, make my bed soon,
For I'm weary wi hunting, and fain wald lie down."

33. *ha:* hall. 41. *bairns:* children. 45. *warldis:* world's.

"Where gat ye your dinner, Lord Randal, my son?   5
Where gat ye your dinner, my handsome young man?"
"I dined wi my true-love; mother, make my bed soon,
For I'm weary wi hunting, and fain wald lie down."

"What gat ye to your dinner, Lord Randal, my son?
What gat ye to your dinner, my handsome young man?"   10
"I gat eels boiled in broo; mother, make my bed soon,
For I'm weary wi hunting, and fain wald lie down."

"What became of your bloodhounds, Lord Randal, my son?
What became of your bloodhounds, my handsome young man?"
"O they swelld and they died; mother, make my bed soon,   15
For I'm weary wi hunting, and fain wald lie down."

"O I fear ye are poisond, Lord Randal, my son!
O I fear ye are poisond, my handsome young man!"
"O yes! I am poisond; mother, make my bed soon,
For I'm sick at the heart, and I fain wald lie down."   20

❧

BARBARA ALLAN

It was in and about the Martinmas time,
   When the green leaves were a falling,
That Sir John Graeme, in the West Country,
   Fell in love with Barbara Allan.

He sent his man down through the town,   5
   To the place where she was dwelling:
"O haste and come to my master dear,
   Gin ye be Barbara Allan."

O hooly, hooly rose she up,
   To the place where he was lying,   10
And when she drew the curtain by,
   "Young man, I think you're dying."

"O it's I'm sick, and very, very sick,
   And 't is a' for Barbara Allan:"
"O the better for me ye's never be,   15
   Tho your heart's blood were a spilling.

BARBARA ALLAN: 8. *Gin:* if. 9. *hooly:* softly.

"O dinna ye mind, young man," said she,
  "When ye was in the tavern a drinking,
That ye made the healths gae round and round,
  And slighted Barbara Allan?"   20

He turnd his face unto the wall,
  And death was with him dealing:
"Adieu, adieu, my dear friends all,
  And be kind to Barbara Allan."

And slowly, slowly raise she up,   25
  And slowly, slowly left him,
And sighing said, she coud not stay,
  Since death of life had reft him,

She had not gane a mile but twa,
  When she heard the dead-bell ringing,   30
And every jow that the dead-bell geid,
  It cry'd, Woe to Barbara Allan!

"O mother, mother, make my bed!
  O make it saft and narrow!
Since my love died for me to-day,   35
  I'll die for him to-morrow."

❧

THE TWA CORBIES

As I was walking all alane,
I heard twa corbies making a mane;
The tane unto the t'other say,
"Where sall we gang and dine to-day?"

"In behint yon auld fail dyke,   5
I wot there lies a new slain knight;
And naebody kens that he lies there,
But his hawk, his hound, and lady fair.

"His hound is to the hunting gane,
His hawk to fetch the wild-fowl hame,   10
His lady's ta'en another mate,
So we may mak our dinner sweet.

---

31. *jow:* stroke; *geid:* gave.
  THE TWA CORBIES: 2. *corbies:* ravens; *mane:* moan, complaint. 5. *fail dyke:*
sod wall. 7. *kens:* knows.

"Ye'll sit on his white hause-bane,
And I'll pike out his bonny blue een;
Wi ae lock o his gowden hair   15
We'll theek our nest when it grows bare.

"Mony a one for him makes mane,
But nane sall ken where he is gane;
Oer his white banes, when they are bare,
The wind sall blaw for evermair."   20

∽✣

THE THREE RAVENS

There were three ravens sat on a tree,
Downe a downe, hay downe, hay downe
There were three ravens sat on a tree,
   With a downe.
There were three ravens sat on a tree,   5
They were as blacke as they might be.
   With a downe derrie, derrie, derrie, downe, downe.

The one of them said to his mate,
"Where shall we our breakfast take?"

"Downe in yonder greene field,   10
There lies a knight slain under his shield.

"His hounds they lie downe at his feete,
So well they can their master keepe.

"His haukes they flie so eagerly,
There's no fowle dare him come nie."   15

Downe there comes a fallow doe,
As great with yong as she might goe.

She lift up his bloudy hed,
And kist his wounds that were so red.

She got him up upon her backe,   20
And carried him to earthen lake.

She buried him before the prime,
She was dead herselfe ere even-song time.

---

13. *hause-bane:* neck bone. 14. *een:* eyes. 16. *theek:* thatch.
THE THREE RAVENS: 21. *lake:* pit.

God send every gentleman,
Such haukes, such hounds, and such a leman.   25

❦

HELEN OF KIRCONNELL

I wish I were where Helen lies,
Night and day on me she cries;
O that I were where Helen lies,
    On fair Kirconnell lea!

Curst be the heart that thought the thought,   5
And curst the hand that fired the shot,
When in my arms burd Helen dropt,
    And died to succour me!

O think na ye my heart was sair,
When my Love dropp'd and spak nae mair!   10
There did she swoon wi' meikle care,
    On fair Kirconnell lea.

As I went down the water side,
None but my foe to be my guide,
None but my foe to be my guide,   15
    On fair Kirconnell lea;

I lighted down my sword to draw,
I hacked him in pieces sma',
I hacked him in pieces sma',
    For her sake that died for me.   20

O Helen fair, beyond compare!
I'll mak a garland o' thy hair,
Shall bind my heart for evermair,
    Until the day I die!

O that I were where Helen lies!   25
Night and day on me she cries;
Out of my bed she bids me rise,
    Says, "Haste, and come to me!"

O Helen fair! O Helen chaste!
If I were with thee, I'd be blest,   30

---

25. *leman:* sweetheart.
HELEN OF KIRCONNELL: 7. *burd:* maid. 11. *meikle:* great.

Where thou lies low and taks thy rest,
  On fair Kirconnell lea.

I wish my grave were growing green,
A winding-sheet drawn owre my e'en,
And I in Helen's arms lying,   35
  On fair Kirconnell lea.

I wish I were where Helen lies!
Night and day on me she cries;
And I am weary of the skies,
  For her sake that died for me.   40

                       ~✌

THE DEMON LOVER

"O where have you been, my long, long love,
  This long seven years and mair?"
"O I'm come to seek my former vows
  Ye granted me before."

"O hold your tongue of your former vows,   5
  For they will breed sad strife;
O hold your tongue of your former vows,
  For I am become a wife."

He turned him right and round about,
  And the tear blinded his ee: 10
"I wad never hae trodden on Irish ground,
  If it had not been for thee.

"I might hae had a king's daughter,
  Far, far beyond the sea;
I might have had a king's daughter,   15
  Had it not been for love o thee."

"If ye might have had a king's daughter,
  Yersel ye had to blame;
Ye might have taken the king's daughter,
  For ye kend that I was nane.   20

"If I was to leave my husband dear,
  And my two babes also,

THE DEMON LOVER: 20. *kend:* knew.

O what have you to take me to,
   If with you I should go?"

"I hae seven ships upon the sea—   25
   The eighth brought me to land—
With four-and-twenty bold mariners,
   And music on every hand."

She has taken up her two little babes,
   Kissd them baith cheek and chin: 30
"O fair ye weel, my ain two babes,
   For I'll never see you again."

She set her foot upon the ship,
   No mariners could she behold;
But the sails were o the taffetie,   35
   And the masts o the beaten gold.

She had not saild a league, a league,
   A league but barely three,
When dismal grew his countenance,
   And drumlie grew his ee.   40

They had not saild a league, a league,
   A league but barely three,
Until she espied his cloven foot,
   And she wept right bitterlie.

"O hold your tongue of your weeping," says he,   45
   "Of your weeping now let me be;
I will shew you how the lilies grow
   On the banks of Italy."

"O what hills are yon, yon pleasant hills,
   That the sun shines sweetly on?"   50
"O yon are the hills of heaven," he said,
   "Where you will never win."

"O whaten a mountain is yon," she said,
   "All so dreary wi frost and snow?"
"O yon is the mountain of hell," he cried,   55
   "Where you and I will go."

He strack the tap-mast wi his hand,
   The fore-mast wi his knee,
And he brake that gallant ship in twain,
   And sank her in the sea.   60

_____

40. *drumlie:* gloomy.

Elizabethan Lyrics

❦

Sir Thomas Wyatt

THEY FLEE FROM ME
(1557)

They flee from me that sometime did me seek,
  With naked foot stalking in my chamber.
I have seen them gentle, tame and meek,
  That now are wild and do not remember
That sometime they put themselves in danger   5
    To take bread at my hand; and now they range
    Busily seeking with a continual change.

Thankt be fortune, it hath been otherwise
  Twenty times better; but once, in special,
In thin array, after a pleasant guise,   10
  When her loose gown from her shoulders did fall,
  And she me caught in her arms long and small,
    Therewith all sweetly did me kiss,
    And softly said: "Dear heart, how like you this?"
It was no dream; I lay broad waking: 15
  But all is turned thorough my gentleness

THEY FLEE FROM ME: First printed in Tottell's *Songs and Sonnets* (1557) and altered as indicated from manuscript version printed above. See Introduction. 2. *in*) T. within. 3. *I have seen them*) T. Once I have seen them. 4. *remember*) T. once remember. 5. *they put themselves*) T. they have put themselves. 7. *with a*) T. in. 9. *in special*) T. especial. 11. *from . . . did*) T. did from. 13. *therewith . . . did*) T. And therewithal so sweetly did me kiss. 15. *I lay*) T. for I lay broad awaking. 16. *turned*) T. turned now.

Into a strange fashion of forsaking;
   And I have leave to go of her goodness;
   And she also to use new-fangleness.
     But since that I so kindely am served,   20
     I fain would know what she hath deserved.

John Lyly

CUPID AND MY CAMPASPE
(1632)

Cupid and my Campaspe played
At cards for kisses; Cupid paid.
He stakes his quiver, bow, and arrows,
His mother's doves and team of sparrows,
Loses them too; then down he throws   5
The coral of his lip, the rose
Growing on's cheek (but none knows how),
With these the crystal of his brow,
And then the dimple of his chin:
All these did my Campaspe win.   10
At last he set her both his eyes;
She won, and Cupid blind did rise.
   O Love! has she done this to thee?
   What shall, alas, become of me?

          From *Alexander and Campaspe*

Thomas Lodge

ROSALIND'S MADRIGAL
(1590)

Love in my bosom like a bee
   Doth suck his sweet;

---

17. *strange*) T. bitter. 20. *so kindely am served*) T. unkindly so am **served.**
21. *I . . . deserved*) T. How like you this, what hath she now deserved?

Now with his wings he plays with me,
  Now with his feet.
Within mine eyes he makes his nest, 5
His bed amidst my tender breast,
My kisses are his daily feast,
And yet he robs me of my rest—
  Ah, wanton, will ye?

And if I sleep, then percheth he 10
  With pretty flight,
And makes his pillow of my knee
  The livelong night.
Strike I my lute, he tunes the string,
He music plays if so I sing, 15
He lends me every lovely thing,
Yet cruel he my heart doth sting—
  Whist, wanton, still ye!

Else I with roses every day
  Will whip you hence, 20
And bind you, when you long to play,
  For your offence.
I'll shut mine eyes to keep you in,
I'll make you fast it for your sin,
I'll count your power not worth a pin; 25
Alas! what hereby shall I win
  If he gainsay me?

What if I beat the wanton boy
  With many a rod?
He will repay me with annoy, 30
  Because a god.
Then sit thou safely on my knee,
And let thy bower my bosom be,
Lurk in mine eyes, I like of thee.
O Cupid, so thou pity me, 35
  Spare not, but play thee!

Thomas Dekker

GOLDEN SLUMBERS KISS YOUR EYES
(1603)

Golden slumbers kiss your eyes,
Smiles awake you when you rise;
Sleep, pretty wantons, do not cry,
And I will sing a lullaby,
Rock them, rock them, lullaby.   5

Care is heavy, therefore sleep you,
You are care, and care must keep you;
Sleep, pretty wantons, do not cry,
And I will sing a lullaby,
Rock them, rock them, lullaby.   10

From *Pleasant Comedy of Patient Grissill*

❧

Robert Greene

SEPHESTIA'S SONG TO HER CHILD
(1589)

Weep not, my wanton, smile upon my knee,
When thou art old there's grief enough for thee.
    Mother's wag, pretty boy,
    Father's sorrow, father's joy,
    When thy father first did see   5
    Such a boy by him and me,
    He was glad, I was woe;
    Fortune changed made him so,
    When he left his pretty boy,
    Last his sorrow, first his joy.   10

Weep not, my wanton, smile upon my knee,
When thou art old there's grief enough for thee.

Streaming tears that never stint,
Like pearl-drops from a flint,
Fell by course from his eyes,   15
That one another's place supplies.
Thus he grieved in every part;
Tears of blood fell from his heart,
When he left his pretty boy,
Father's sorrow, father's joy.   20

Weep not, my wanton, smile upon my knee,
When thou art old there's grief enough for thee.
The wanton smiled, father wept,
Mother cried, baby leapt;
More he crowed, more we cried,   25
Nature could not sorrow hide.
He must go, he must kiss
Child and mother, baby bliss,
For he left his pretty boy,
Father's sorrow, father's joy.   30
Weep not, my wanton, smile upon my knee,
When thou art old there's grief enough for thee.

From *Menaphon*

～

THE SHEPHERD'S WIFE'S SONG

(1590)

Ah, what is love? It is a pretty thing,
As sweet unto a shepherd as a king—
        And sweeter too,
For kings have cares that wait upon a crown,
And cares can make the sweetest love to frown.   5
        Ah then, ah then,
If country loves such sweet desires do gain,
What lady would not love a shepherd swain?

His flocks once folded, he comes home at night
As merry as a king in his delight—   10
        And merrier too,
For kings bethink them what the state require,
Where shepherds careless carol by the fire.

Ah then, ah then,
If country loves such sweet desires gain,   15
What lady would not love a shepherd swain?

He kisseth first, then sits as blithe to eat
His cream and curds as doth the king his meat—
          And blither too,
For kings have often fears when they do sup,   20
Where shepherds dread no poison in their cup.
          Ah then, ah then,
If country loves such sweet desires gain,
What lady would not love a shepherd swain?

To bed he goes, as wanton then, I ween,   25
As is a king in dalliance with a queen—
          More wanton too,
For kings have many griefs, affects to move,
Where shepherds have no greater grief than love.
          Ah then, ah then,   30
If country loves such sweet desires gain,
What lady would not love a shepherd swain?

Upon his couch of straw he sleeps as sound
As doth the king upon his beds of down—
          More sounder too,   35
For cares cause kings full oft their sleep to spill,
Where weary shepherds lie and snort their fill.
          Ah then, ah then,
If country loves such sweet desires gain,
What lady would not love a shepherd swain?   40

Thus with his wife he spends the year, as blithe
As doth the king, at every tide or sithe—
          And blither too,
For kings have wars and broils to take in hand,
Where shepherds laugh and love upon the land.   45
          Ah then, ah then,
If country loves such sweet desires gain,
What lady would not love a shepherd swain?

From *Mourning Garment*

❧

THE SHEPHERD'S WIFE'S SONG: 42. *sithe:* time.

SWEET ARE THE THOUGHTS
(1591)

Sweet are the thoughts that savor of content,
    The quiet mind is richer than a crown;
Sweet are the nights in careless slumber spent,
    The poor estate scorns fortune's angry frown:
Such sweet content, such minds, such sleep, such bliss,   5
Beggars enjoy, when princes oft do miss.

The homely house that harbors quiet rest,
    The cottage that affords no pride nor care,
The mean that grees with country music best,
    The sweet consort of mirth and music's fare,   10
Obscurèd life sets down a type of bliss;
A mind content both crown and kingdom is.

                      From *Farewell to Folly*

George Peele

WHAT THING IS LOVE
(c. 1591)

What thing is love? for, well I wot, love is a thing.
It is a prick, it is a sting,
It is a pretty, pretty thing;
It is a fire, it is a coal,
Whose flame creeps in at ev'ry hole;   5
And as my wit doth best devise,
Love's dwelling is in ladies' eyes,
From whence do glance love's piercing darts
That make such holes into our hearts;
And all the world herein accord   10
Love is a great and mighty lord;
And when he list to mount so high,
With Venus he in heaven doth lie,

And evermore hath been a god
Since Mars and she played even and odd.   15

~e~

Sir Edward Dyer

MY MIND TO ME A KINGDOM IS
(1588)

My mind to me a kingdom is;
   Such perfect joy therein I find
That it excels all other bliss
   Which God or nature hath assigned.
Though much I want that most would have,   5
Yet still my mind forbids to crave.

No princely port, nor wealthy store,
   No force to win a victory,
No wily wit to salve a sore,
   No shape to win a loving eye;   10
To none of these I yield as thrall,—
For why? my mind despise them all.

I see that plenty surfeit oft,
   And hasty climbers soonest fall;
I see that such as are aloft   15
   Mishap doth threaten most of all.
These get with toil and keep with fear;
Such cares my mind can never bear.

I press to bear no haughty sway,
   I wish no more than may suffice,   20
I do no more than well I may,
   Look, what I want my mind supplies.
Lo! thus I triumph like a king,
My mind content with anything.

I laugh not at another's loss,   25
   Nor grudge not at another's gain;
No worldly waves my mind can toss;

I brook that is another's bane.
I fear no foe, nor fawn on friend,
I loathe not life, nor dread mine end.   30

My wealth is health and perfect ease,
    And conscience clear my chief defence;
I never seek by bribes to please,
    Nor by desert to give offence.
Thus do I live, thus will I die,—   35
Would all did so as well as I!

❧

Sir Henry Wotton

THE CHARACTER OF A HAPPY LIFE
(1651)

How happy is he born or taught
    That serveth not another's will,
Whose armor is his honest thought,
    And simple truth his highest skill;

Whose passions not his masters are;   5
    Whose soul is still prepared for death,
Untied unto the world with care
    Of princes' grace or vulgar breath;

Who envies none whom chance doth raise,
    Or vice; who never understood   10
The deepest wounds are given by praise,
    By rule of state but not of good;

Who hath his life from rumors freed,
    Whose conscience is his strong retreat,
Whose state can neither flatterers feed   15
    Nor ruins make accusers great;

Who God doth late and early pray
    More of his grace than goods to send,
And entertains the harmless day
    With a well-chosen book or friend.   20

This man is free from servile bands
    Of hope to rise or fear to fall,
Lord of himself, though not of lands,
    And having nothing, yet hath all.

Samuel Daniel

CARE-CHARMER SLEEP
(1592)

Care-charmer sleep, son of the sable night,
    Brother to death, in silent darkness born,
    Relieve my languish and restore the light;
    With dark forgetting of my care, return.
And let the day be time enough to mourn   5
    The shipwreck of my ill-adventured youth;
    Let waking eyes suffice to wail their scorn
    Without the torment of the night's untruth.
Cease, dreams, th' images of day-desires,
    To model forth the passions of the morrow;   10
    Never let rising sun approve you liars,
    To add more grief to aggravate my sorrow.
Still let me sleep, embracing clouds in vain,
And never wake to feel the day's disdain.

LET OTHERS SING
(1592)

Let others sing of knights and paladins
    In agèd accents and untimely words,
    Paint shadows in imaginary lines
    Which well the reach of their high wits records;
But I must sing of thee, and those fair eyes   5
    Authentic shall my verse in time to come,

LET OTHERS SING: 2. *untimely:* archaic.

When yet th' unborn shall say, Lo where she lies,
Whose beauty made him speak that else was dumb.
These are the arks, the trophies I erect,
   That fortify thy name against old age;   10
   And these thy sacred virtues must protect
   Against the dark and time's consuming rage.
Though th' error of my youth in them appear,
Suffice, they show I lived and loved thee dear.

∾

Thomas Campion

ROSE-CHEEKED LAURA
(1602)

Rose-cheeked Laura, come,
Sing thou smoothly with thy beauty's
Silent music, either other
   Sweetly gracing.

Lovely forms do flow   5
From concent divinely framèd;
Heav'n is music, and thy beauty's
   Birth is heavenly.

These dull notes we sing
Discords need for helps to grace them;   10
Only beauty purely loving
   Knows no discord,

But still moves delight,
Like clear springs renewed by flowing,
Ever perfect, ever in them-   15
   Selves eternal.

∾

ROSE-CHEEKED LAURA: 6. *concent:* harmony.

THERE IS A GARDEN IN HER FACE
(c. 1617)

There is a garden in her face,
Where roses and white lilies grow;
A heav'nly paradise is that place,
Wherein all pleasant fruits do flow.
There cherries grow which none may buy   5
Till cherry-ripe themselves do cry.

Those cherries fairly do enclose
Of orient pearl a double row,
Which when her lovely laughter shows,
They look like rosebuds filled with snow.   10
Yet them nor peer nor prince can buy,
Till cherry-ripe themselves do cry.

Her eyes like angels watch them still;
Her brows like bended bows do stand,
Threat'ning with piercing frowns to kill   15
All that attempt with eye or hand
Those sacred cherries to come nigh,
Till cherry-ripe themselves do cry.

❧

FOLLOW YOUR SAINT
(1601)

Follow your saint, follow with accents sweet;
Haste you, sad notes, fall at her flying feet.
There, wrapped in cloud of sorrow, pity move,
And tell the ravisher of my soul I perish for her love.
But if she scorns my never-ceasing pain,   5
Then burst with sighing in her sight and ne'er return again.

All that I sung still to her praise did tend,
Still she was first, still she my songs did end.
Yet she my love and music both doth fly,
The music that her echo is and beauty's sympathy.   10

Then let my notes pursue her scornful flight:
It shall suffice that they were breathed and died for her delight.

❧

WHEN THOU MUST HOME
(1601)

When thou must home to shades of underground,
   And there arrived, a new admirèd guest,
The beauteous spirits do engirt thee round,
   White Iope, blithe Helen, and the rest,
To hear the stories of thy finished love   5
From that smooth tongue whose music hell can move,

Then wilt thou speak of banqueting delights,
   Of masks and revels which sweet youth did make,
Of tourneys and great challenges of knights,
   And all these triumphs for thy beauty's sake;   10
When thou hast told these honors done to thee,
Then tell, O tell, how thou didst murder me.

❧

Thomas Nashe

LITANY IN TIME OF PLAGUE
(1600)

Adieu, farewell earth's bliss,
This world uncertain is;
Fond are life's lustful joys,
Death proves them all but toys,
None from his darts can fly.   5
I am sick, I must die.
     Lord, have mercy on us!

Rich men, trust not in wealth,
Gold cannot buy you health;

LITANY IN TIME OF PLAGUE: 3. *Fond:* foolish.

Physic himself must fade,   10
All things to end are made.
The plague full swift goes by;
I am sick, I must die.
    Lord, have mercy on us!

Beauty is but a flower   15
Which wrinkles will devour:
Brightness falls from the air,
Queens have died young and fair,
Dust hath closed Helen's eye.
I am sick, I must die.   20
        Lord, have mercy on us!

Strength stoops unto the grave,
Worms feed on Hector brave,
Swords may not fight with fate.
Earth still holds ope her gate;   25
Come! come! the bells do cry.
I am sick, I must die.
    Lord, have mercy on us!

Wit with his wantonness
Tasteth death's bitterness;   30
Hell's executioner
Hath no ears for to hear
What vain art can reply.
I am sick, I must die.
        Lord, have mercy on us!   35

Haste, therefore, each degree,
To welcome destiny.
Heaven is our heritage,
Earth but a player's stage;
Mount we unto the sky.   40
I am sick, I must die.
        Lord, have mercy on us!

❧

36. *degree:* social class.

Sir Philip Sidney

From ASTROPHEL AND STELLA

(1591)

I

Loving in truth, and fain in verse my love to show,
　That she, dear she, might take some pleasure of my pain,
　Pleasure might cause her read, reading might make her know,
　Knowledge might pity win, and pity grace obtain,—
I sought fit words to paint the blackest face of woe;　　　　　5
　Studying inventions fine, her wits to entertain,
　Oft turning others' leaves to see if thence would flow
　Some fresh and fruitful showers upon my sun-burned brain.
But words came halting forth, wanting invention's stay;
　Invention, nature's child, fled step-dame Study's blows,　　　10
　And others' feet still seemed but strangers in my way.
Thus, great with child to speak, and helpless in my throes,
　Biting my truant pen, beating myself for spite,
　Fool, said my muse to me, look in thy heart and write.

3

Let dainty wits cry on the sisters nine,
　That, bravely masked, their fancies may be told;
　Or Pindar's apes flaunt they in phrases fine,
　Enam'ling with pied flowers their thoughts of gold;
Or else let them in statelier glory shine,　　　　　5
　Ennobling new-found tropes with problems old;
　Or with strange similes enrich each line,
　Of herbs or beasts which Ind or Afric hold.
For me, in sooth, no Muse but one I know;
　Phrases and problems from my reach do grow,　　　10
　And strange things cost too dear for my poor sprites.

ASTROPHEL AND STELLA: SONNET I: 9. *stay:* support.
SONNET 3: 3. *apes:* imitators.

How then? even thus,—in Stella's face I read
  What love and beauty be, then all my deed
  But copying is, what in her Nature writes.

~

5

It is most true that eyes are formed to serve
  The inward light, and that the heavenly part
  Ought to be king, from whose rules who do swerve,
  Rebels to nature, strive for their own smart.
It is most true what we call Cupid's dart   5
  An image is which for ourselves we carve,
  And, fools, adore in temple of our heart
  Till that good god make church and churchman starve.
True, that true beauty virtue is indeed,
  Whereof this beauty can be but a shade,   10
  Which elements with mortal mixture breed.
True, that on earth we are but pilgrims made,
  And should in soul up to our country move;
  True, and yet true that I must Stella love.

~

7

When nature made her chief work, Stella's eyes,
  In color black why wrapped she beams so bright?
  Would she in beamy black, like painter wise,
  Frame daintiest luster mixed of shades and light?
Or did she else that sober hue devise   5
  In object best to knit and strength our sight,
  Lest, if no veil these brave gleams did disguise,
  They, sunlike, should more dazzle than delight?
Or would she her miraculous power show,
  That, whereas black seems beauty's contrary,   10
  She even in black doth make all beauties flow?
Both so, and thus,—she, minding Love should be
  Placed ever there, gave him this mourning weed
  To honor all their deaths who for her bleed.

~

15

You that do search for every purling spring
  Which from the ribs of old Parnassus flows,
  And every flower, not sweet perhaps, which grows
  Near thereabouts into your poesy wring;
You that do dictionary's method bring   5
  Into your rhymes, running in rattling rows;
  You that poor Petrarch's long-deceasèd woes
  With new-born sighs and denizened wit do sing;
You take wrong ways, those far-fet helps be such
  As do bewray a want of inward touch,   10
  And sure at length stol'n goods do come to light.
But if, both for your love and skill, your name
  You seek to nurse at fullest breasts of Fame,
  Stella behold, and then begin to endite.

24

Rich fools there be whose base and filthy heart
  Lies hatching still the goods wherein they flow,
  And damning their own selves to Tantal's smart,
  Wealth breeding want, more blest, more wretched grow.
Yet to those fools heaven such wit doth impart,   5
  As what their hands do hold, their heads do know;
  And knowing, love; and loving, lay apart
  As sacred things, far from all danger's show.
But that rich fool, who by blind fortune's lot
  The richest gem of love and life enjoys,   10
  And can with foul abuse such beauties blot,
Let him, deprived of sweet but unfelt joys,
  Exiled for aye from those high treasures which
  He knows not, grow in only folly rich!

SONNET 15: 9. *far-fet:* far-fetched. 10. *bewray:* betray.
SONNET 24: 9. *rich:* play on the name of Lord Rich, husband of Stella
(Penelope Devereux, daughter of the Earl of Essex).

28

You that with allegory's curious frame
  Of others' children changelings use to make,
  With me those pains, for God's sake, do not take;
  I list not dig so deep for brazen fame.
When I say Stella, I do mean the same   5
  Princess of beauty for whose only sake
  The reins of love I love, though never slake,
  And joy therein, though nations count it shame.
I beg no subject to use eloquence,
  Nor in hid ways do guide philosophy;   10
  Look at my hands for no such quintessence,
But know that I in pure simplicity
  Breathe out the flames which burn within my heart,
  Love only reading unto me this art.

31

With how sad steps, O moon, thou climb'st the skies!
  How silently, and with how wan a face!
  What! may it be that even in heav'nly place
  That busy archer his sharp arrows tries?
Sure, if that long-with-love-acquainted eyes   5
  Can judge of love, thou feel'st a lover's case;
  I read it in thy looks,—thy languished grace
  To me, that feel the like, thy state descries.
Then, ev'n of fellowship, O moon, tell me,
  Is constant love deemed there but want of wit?   10
  Are beauties there as proud as here they be?
Do they above love to be loved, and yet
  Those lovers scorn whom that love doth possess?
  Do they call virtue there ungratefulness?

35

What may words say, or what may words not say,
  Where truth itself must speak like flattery?

SONNET 28: 1. *curious:* overly ingenious. 7. *slake:* slack.

Within what bounds can one his liking stay,
   Where nature doth with infinite agree?
What Nestor's counsel can my flames allay,   5
   Since reason's self doth blow the coal in me?
   And ah, what hope that hope should once see day,
   Where Cupid is sworn page to chastity?
Honor is honored, that thou dost possess
   Him as thy slave, and now long-needy Fame   10
   Doth even grow rich, naming my Stella's name.
Wit learns in thee perfection to express,
   Not thou by praise, but praise in thee is raised;
   It is a praise to praise, when thou art praised.

39

Come sleep! O sleep, the certain knot of peace,
   The baiting place of wit, the balm of woe,
   The poor man's wealth, the prisoner's release,
   Th' indifferent judge between the high and low;
With shield of proof shield me from out the prease   5
   Of those fierce darts despair at me doth throw;
   O make in me those civil wars to cease;
   I will good tribute pay, if thou do so.
Take thou of me smooth pillows, sweetest bed,
   A chamber deaf to noise and blind to light,   10
   A rosy garland and a weary head;
And if these things, as being thine by right,
   Move not thy heavy grace, thou shalt in me,
   Livelier than elsewhere, Stella's image see.

41

Having this day my horse, my hand, my lance
   Guided so well that I obtained the prize,
   Both by the judgment of the English eyes
   And of some sent from that sweet enemy, France;
Horsemen my skill in horsemanship advance,   5
   Town-folks my strength; a daintier judge applies

SONNET 39: 2. *baiting:* feeding and resting. 5. *prease:* press.

His praise to sleight which from good use doth rise;
   Some lucky wits impute it but to chance;
Others, because of both sides I do take
   My blood from them who did excel in this,   10
   Think nature me a man of arms did make.
How far they shot awry! The true cause is,
   Stella looked on, and from her heav'nly face
   Sent forth the beams which made so fair my race.

54

Because I breathe not love to every one,
   Nor do not use set colors for to wear,
   Nor nourish special locks of vowèd hair,
   Nor give each speech a full point of a groan,
The courtly nymphs, acquainted with the moan   5
   Of them who in their lips Love's standard bear,
   What, he! say they of me, Now I dare swear
   He cannot love; no, no, let him alone.
And think so still, so Stella know my mind;
   Profess indeed I do not Cupid's art;   10
   But you, fair maids, at length this true shall find,
That his right badge is but worn in the heart;
   Dumb swans, not chatt'ring pies, do lovers prove;
   They love indeed who quake to say they love.

63

O grammar-rules, O now your virtues show;
   So children still read you with awful eyes,
   As my young dove may, in your precepts wise,
   Her grant to me by her own virtue know;
For late, with heart most high, with eyes most low,   5
   I craved the thing which ever she denies;
   She, lightning Love displaying Venus' skies,
   Lest once should not be heard, twice said, No, No!
Sing then, my muse, now Io Paean sing;
   Heav'ns envy not at my high triumphing,   10

But grammar's force with sweet success confirm;
For grammar says,—oh this, dear Stella, weigh,—
  For grammar says,—to grammar who says nay?—
  That in one speech two negatives affirm!

71

Who will in fairest book of Nature know
How virtue may best lodged in beauty be,
Let him but learn of love to read in thee,
Stella, those fair lines which true goodness show.
There shall he find all vices' overthrow,   5
Not by rude force, but sweetest sovereignty
Of reason, from whose light those night birds fly,
That inward sun in thine eyes shineth so.
And, not content to be perfection's heir
Thyself, dost strive all minds that way to move,   10
Who mark in thee what is in thee most fair.
So while thy beauty draws the heart to love,
  As fast thy virtue bends that love to good.
  But, ah, Desire still cries, "Give me some food."

74

I never drank of Aganippe well,
Nor ever did in shade of Tempe sit,
And Muses scorn with vulgar brains to dwell;
Poor layman I, for sacred rites unfit.
Some do I hear of poets' fury tell,   5
But, God wot, wot not what they mean by it;
And this I swear by blackest brook of hell,
I am no pick-purse of another's wit.
How falls it then that with so smooth an ease
My thoughts I speak; and what I speak doth flow   10
In verse, and that my verse best wits doth please?
Guess we the cause. What, is it thus? Fie, no.

SONNET 74: 1. *Aganippe well:* at the foot of Mt. Helicon, sacred to the
Muses. 2. *Tempe:* valley sacred to Apollo.

Or so? Much less. How then? Sure thus it is:
My lips are sweet, inspired with Stella's kiss.

⤳

THE NIGHTINGALE
(1598)

The nightingale, as soon as April bringeth
  Unto her rested sense a perfect waking,
While late bare earth, proud of new clothing, springeth,
  Sings out her woes, a thorn her song-book making,
  And mournfully bewailing,   5
Her throat in tunes expresseth
What grief her breast oppresseth
  For Tereus' force on her chaste will prevailing.
O Philomela fair, O take some gladness,
That here is juster cause of plaintful sadness: 10
Thine earth now springs, mine fadeth;
Thy thorn without, my thorn my heart invadeth.

Alas, she hath no other cause of anguish
  But Tereus' love, on her by strong hand wroken,
Wherein she suffering, all her spirits languish;   15
  Full womanlike complains her will was broken.
  But I, who daily craving,
Cannot have to content me,
Have more cause to lament me,
  Since wanting is more woe than too much having.   20
O Philomela fair, O take some gladness,
That here is juster cause of plaintful sadness:
Thine earth now springs, mine fadeth;
Thy thorn without, my thorn my heart invadeth.

⤳

THE NIGHTINGALE: 8. *Tereus:* King of Thrace who brutally violated his
sister-in-law, Philomela, and cut out her tongue. She and her sister, Queen
Procne, avenged themselves and escaped Tereus with the help of the gods,
who metamorphosed one into a nightingale and the other into a swallow.

THOU BLIND MAN'S MARK
(1598)

Thou blind man's mark, thou fool's self-chosen snare,
Fond fancy's scum, and dregs of scattered thought;
Band of all evils, cradle of causeless care;
Thou web of will, whose end is never wrought;
Desire, desire! I have too dearly bought,   5
With price of mangled mind, thy worthless ware;
Too long, too long, asleep thou hast me brought,
Who should my mind to higher things prepare.
But yet in vain thou hast my ruin sought;
In vain thou madest me to vain things aspire;   10
In vain thou kindlest all thy smoky fire;
For virtue hath this better lesson taught,—
    Within myself to seek my only hire,
    Desiring nought but how to kill desire.

LEAVE ME, O LOVE
(1598)

Leave me, O love which reachest but to dust;
And thou, my mind, aspire to higher things;
Grow rich in that which never taketh rust,
Whatever fades but fading pleasure brings.
Draw in thy beams, and humble all thy might   5
To that sweet yoke where lasting freedoms be;
Which breaks the clouds and opens forth the light,
That doth both shine and give us sight to see.
O take fast hold; let that light be thy guide
In this small course which birth draws out to death,   10
And think how evil becometh him to slide,
Who seeketh heav'n, and comes of heav'nly breath.
    Then farewell, world; thy uttermost I see;
    Eternal Love, maintain thy life in me.

    Splendidis longum valedico nugis.

LEAVE ME, O LOVE: 15. *Splendidis . . . nugis:* a long farewell to glittering trifles.

Edmund Spenser

THE BOWER OF BLISS

(*The Faerie Queene*, Book II, Canto xii)

(1590)

42

Thence passing forth, they shortly do arrive,
   Whereas the Bowre of *Blisse* was situate;
   A place pickt out by choice of best alive,
   That natures worke by art can imitate:
   In which what ever in this worldly state   5
   Is sweet, and pleasing unto living sense,
   Or that may dayntiest fantasie aggrate,
   Was poured forth with plentiful dispence,
And made there to abound with lavish affluence.

43

Goodly it was enclosèd round about,   10
   Aswell their entred guests to keepe within,
   As those unruly beasts to hold without;
   Yet was the fence thereof but weake and thin;
   Nought feard their force, that fortilage to win,
   But wisedomes powre, and temperaunces might,   15
   By which the mightiest things efforced bin:
   And eke the gate was wrought of substaunce light,
Rather for pleasure, then for battery or fight.

44

Yt framèd was of precious yvory,
   That seemed a worke of admirable wit;   20
   And therein all the famous history
   Of *Jason* and *Medæa* was ywrit;

THE BOWER OF BLISS: 6. *aggrate:* delight.

Her mighty charmes, her furious loving fit,
His goodly conquest of the golden fleece,
His falsèd faith, and love too lightly flit,   25
The wondred *Argo,* which in venturous peece
First through the *Euxine* seas bore all the flowr of *Greece.*

45

Ye might have seene the frothy billowes fry
  Under the ship, as thorough them she went,
  That seemd the waves were into yvory,   30
  Or yvory into the waves were sent;
  And other where the snowy substaunce sprent
  With vermell, like the boyes bloud therein shed,
  A piteous spectacle did represent,
  And otherwhiles with gold besprinkelèd;   35
Yt seemd th'enchaunted flame, which did *Creüsa* wed.

46

All this, and more might in that goodly gate
  Be red; that ever open stood to all,
  Which thither came: but in the Porch there sate
  A comely personage of stature tall,
  And semblaunce pleasing, more then naturall,   40
  That travellers to him seemd to entize;
  His looser garment to the ground did fall,
  And flew about his heeles in wanton wize,
Not fit for speedy pace, or manly exercize.   45

47

They in that place him *Genius* did call:
  Not that celestiall powre, to whom the care
  Of life, and generation of all
  That lives, pertaines in charge particulare,
  Who wondrous things concerning our welfare,   50
  And straunge phantomes doth let us oft forsee,
  And oft of secret ill bids us beware:
  That is our Selfe, whom though we do not see,
Yet each doth in him selfe it well perceive to bee.

---

32. *sprent:* sprinkled.

48

Therefore a God him sage Antiquity   55
  Did wisely make, and good *Agdistes* call:
  But this same was to that quite contrary,
  The foe of life, that good envyes to all,
  That secretly doth us procure to fall,
  Through guilefull semblaunts, which he makes us see.   60
  He of this Gardin had the governall,
  And Pleasures porter was devizd to bee,
Holding a staffe in hand for more formalitee.

49

With diverse flowres he daintily was deckt,
  And strowed round about, and by his side   65
  A mighty mazer bowle of wine was set,
  As if it had to him bene sacrifide;
  Wherewith all new-come guests he gratifide:
  So did he eke Sir *Guyon* passing by:
  But he his idle curtesie defide,   70
  And overthrew his bowle disdainfully;
And broke his staffe, with which he charmèd semblants sly.

50

Thus being entred, they behold around
  A large and spacious plaine, on every side
  Strowed with pleasauns, whose faire grassy ground   75
  Mantled with greene, and goodly beautifide
  With all the ornaments of *Floraes* pride,
  Wherewith her mother Art, as halfe in scorne
  Of niggard Nature, like a pompous bride
  Did decke her, and too lavishly adorne,   80
When forth from virgin bowre she comes in th'early morne.

51

Thereto the heavens alwayes joviall,
  Lookt on them lovely, still in stedfast state,
  Ne suffred storme nor frost on them to fall,
  Their tender buds or leaves to violate,   85
  Nor scorching heat, nor cold intemperate
  T'afflict the creatures, which therein did dwell,
  But the milde aire with season moderate

66. *mazer:* hard wood. 72. *charmèd semblants sly:* magically produced deceiving spirits.

Gently attempred, and disposd so well,
That still it breathèd forth sweet spirit and holesome smell.   90

52

More sweet and holesome, then the pleasaunt hill
  Of *Rhodope,* on which the Nimphe, that bore
  A gyaunt babe, her selfe for griefe did kill;
  Or the Thessalian *Tempe,* where of yore
  Faire *Daphne Phœbus* hart with love did gore;   95
  Or *Ida,* where the Gods lov'd to repaire,
  When ever they their heavenly bowres forlore;
  Or sweet *Parnasse,* the haunt of Muses faire;
Or *Eden* selfe, if ought with *Eden* mote compaire.

53

Much wondred *Guyon* at the faire aspect   100
  Of that sweet place, yet suffred no delight
  To sincke into his sence, nor mind affect,
  But passèd forth, and lookt still forward right,
  Bridling his will, and maistering his might:
  Till that he came unto another gate;   105
  No gate, but like one, being goodly dight
  With boughes and braunches, which did broad dilate
Their clasping armes, in wanton wreathings intricate.

54

So fashionèd a porch with rare device,
  Archt over head with an embracing vine,   110
  Whose bounches hanging downe, seemed to entice
  All passers by, to tast their lushious wine,
  And did themselves into their hands incline,
  As freely offering to be gatherèd:
  Some deepe empurpled as the *hyacint,*   115
  Some as the rubine, laughing sweetly red,
Some like faire emeraudes, not yet well ripenèd.

55

And them amongst, some were of burnisht gold,
  So made by art, to beautifie the rest,
  Which did themselves emongst the leaves enfold,   120
  As lurking from the vew of covetous guest,
  That the weake bowes, with so rich load opprest,

Did bow adowne, as over-burdenèd.
Under that porch a comely dame did rest,
Clad in faire weedes, but fowle disorderèd,   125
And garments loose, that seemd unmeet for womanhed.

56

In her left hand a cup of gold she held,
And with her right the riper fruit did reach,
Whose sappy liquor, that with fulnesse sweld,
Into her cup she scruzd, with daintie breach   130
Of her fine fingers, without fowle empeach,
That so faire wine-presse made the wine more sweet:
Thereof she usd to give to drinke to each,
Whom passing by she happenèd to meet:
It was her guise, all straungers goodly so to greet.   135

57

So she to *Guyon* offred it to tast;
Who taking it out of her tender hond,
The cup to ground did violently cast,
That all in peeces it was broken fond,
And with the liquor stainèd all the lond: 140
Whereat *Excesse* exceedingly was wroth,
Yet no'te the same amend, ne yet withstond,
But suffered him to passe, all were she loth;
Who nought regarding her displeasure forward goth.

58

There the most daintie paradise on ground,   145
It selfe doth offer to his sober eye,
In which all pleasures plenteously abound,
And none does others happinesse envye:
The painted flowres, the trees upshooting hye,
The dales for shade, the hilles for breathing space,   150
The trembling groves, the christall running by;
And that, which all faire workes doth most aggrace,
The art, which all that wrought, appearèd in no place.

59

One would have thought, (so cunningly, the rude,
And scornèd parts were mingled with the fine,)   155

---

131. *empeach:* injury. 142. *no'te:* might not.

That nature had for wantonesse ensude
Art, and that art at nature did repine;
So striving each th' other to undermine,
Each did the others worke more beautifie;
So diff'ring both in willes, agreed in fine: 160
So all agreed through sweete diversitie,
This Gardin to adorne with all varietie.

60

And in the midst of all, a fountaine stood,
Of richest substaunce, that on earth might bee,
So pure and shiny, that the silver flood   165
Through every channell running one might see;
Most goodly it with curious imageree
Was over-wrought, and shapes of naked boyes,
Of which some seemd with lively jollitee,
To fly about, playing their wanton toyes,   170
Whilest others did them selves embay in liquid joyes.

61

And over all, of purest gold was spred,
A trayle of yvie in his native hew:
For the rich mettall was so colourèd,
That wight, who did not well avis'd it vew,   175
Would surely deeme it to be yvie trew:
Low his lascivious armes adown did creepe,
That themselves dipping in the silver dew,
Their fleecy flowres they tenderly did steepe,
Which drops of christall seemd for wantones to weepe.   180

62

Infinit streames continually did well
Out of this fountaine, sweet and faire to see,
The which into an ample laver fell,
And shortly grew to so great quantitie,
That like a little lake it seemd to bee;   185
Whose depth exceeded not three cubits hight,
That through the waves one might the bottom see,
All pav'd beneath with jaspar shining bright,
That seemd the fountaine in that sea did sayle upright.

---

156. *ensude:* imitated. 160. *fine:* aim, end.

63

And all the margent round about was set,   190
  With shady laurell trees, thence to defend
  The sunny beames, which on the billowes bet,
  And those which therein bathèd, mote offend.
  As *Guyon* hapned by the same to wend,
  Two naked damzelles he therein espyde,   195
  Which therein bathing, seemèd to contend,
  And wrestle wantonly, ne car'd to hyde,
Their dainty parts from vew of any, which them eyde.

64

Sometimes the one would lift the other quight
  Above the waters, and then downe againe   200
  Her plong, as over maisterèd by might,
  Where both awhile would coverèd remaine,
  And each the other from to rise restraine;
  The whiles their snowy limbes, as through a vele,
  So through the christall waves appearèd plaine: 205
  Then suddeinly both would themselves unhele,
And th'amarous sweet spoiles to greedy eyes revele.

65

As that faire starre, the messenger of morne,
  His deawy face out of the sea doth reare:
  Or as the *Cyprian* goddesse, newly borne   210
  Of th'Oceans fruitfull froth, did first appeare:
  Such seemèd they, and so their yellow heare
  Christalline humour droppèd downe apace.
  Whom such when *Guyon* saw, he drew him neare,
  And somewhat gan relent his earnest pace,   215
His stubborne brest gan secret pleasaunce to embrace.

66

The wanton maidens him espying, stood
  Gazing a while at his unwonted guise;
  Then th'one her selfe low duckèd in the flood,
  Abasht, that her a straunger did avise: 220
  But th'other rather higher did arise,
  And her two lilly paps aloft displayd,

---

206. *unhele:* uncover.

And all, that might his melting hart entise
  To her delights, she unto him bewrayd:
The rest hid underneath, him more desirous made.   225

67

With that, the other likewise up arose,
  And her faire lockes, which formerly were bownd
  Up in one knot, she low adowne did lose:
  Which flowing long and thick, her cloth'd arownd,
  And th'yvorie in golden mantle gownd: 230
  So that faire spectacle from him was reft,
  Yet that, which reft it, no lesse faire was fownd:
  So hid in lockes and waves from lookers theft,
Nought but her lovely face she for his looking left.

68

Withall she laughèd, and she blusht withall,   235
  That blushing to her laughter gave more grace,
  And laughter to her blushing, as did fall:
  Now when they spide the knight to slacke his pace,
  Them to behold, and in his sparkling face
  The secret signes of kindled lust appeare,   240
  Their wanton meriments they did encreace,
  And to him beckned, to approch more neare,
And shewd him many sights, that courage cold could reare.

69

On which when gazing him the Palmer saw,
  He much rebukt those wandring eyes of his,   245
  And counseld well, him forward thence did draw.
  Now are they come nigh to the *Bowre of blis*
  Of her fond favorites so nam'd amis:
  When thus the Palmer; Now Sir, well avise;
  For here the end of all our travell is: 250
  Here wonnes *Acrasia,* whom we must surprise,
Else she will slip away, and all our drift despise.

70

Eftsoones they heard a most melodious sound,
  Of all that mote delight a daintie eare,

---

251. *wonnes:* dwells. 252. *drift:* scheme.

Such as attonce might not on living ground,   255
Save in this paradise, be heard elswhere:
Right hard it was, for wight, which did it heare,
To read, what manner musicke that mote bee:
For all that pleasing is to living eare,
Was there consorted in one harmonee,   260
Birdes, voyces, instruments, windes, waters, all agree.

71

The joyous birdes shrouded in chearefull shade,
Their notes unto the voyce attempred sweet;
Th'angelicall soft trembling voyces made
To th'instruments divine respondence meet: 265
The silver sounding instruments did meet
With the base murmure of the waters fall:
The waters fall with difference discreet,
Now soft, now loud, unto the wind did call:
The gentle warbling wind low answered to all.   270

72

There, whence that musick seemèd heard to bee,
Was the faire witch her selfe now solacing,
With a new lover, whom through sorceree
And witchcraft, she from farre did thither bring:
There she had him now layd a slombering,   275
In secret shade, after long wanton joyes:
Whilst round about them pleasauntly did sing
Many faire ladies, and lascivious boyes,
That ever mixt their song with light licentious toyes.

73

And all that while, right over him she hong,   280
With her false eyes fast fixèd in his sight,
As seeking medicine, whence she was stong,
Or greedily depasturing delight:
And oft inclining downe with kisses light,
For feare of waking him, his lips bedewd,   285
And through his humid eyes did sucke his spright,
Quite molten into lust and pleasure lewd;
Wherewith she sighèd soft, as if his case she rewd.

---

268. *discreet:* distinct. 279. *toyes:* love play.

74

The whiles some one did chaunt this lovely lay;
  Ah see, who so faire thing doest faine to see,   290
  In springing flowre the image of thy day;
  Ah see the virgin rose, how sweetly shee
  Doth first peepe forth with bashfull modestee,
  That fairer seemes, the lesse ye see her may;
  Lo see soone after, how more bold and free   295
  Her barèd bosome she doth broad display;
Loe see soone after, how she fades, and falles away.

75

So passeth, in the passing of a day,
  Of mortall life the leafe, the bud, the flowre,
  Ne more doth flourish after first decay,   300
  That earst was sought to decke both bed and bowre,
  Of many a ladie, and many a paramowre:
  Gather therefore the rose, whilest yet is prime,
  For soone comes age, that will her pride deflowre:
  Gather the rose of love, whilest yet is time,   305
Whilest loving thou mayst lovèd be with equall crime.

76

He ceast, and then gan all the quire of birdes
  Their diverse notes t'attune unto his lay,
  As in approvance of his pleasing words.
  The constant paire heard all, that he did say,   310
  Yet swarvèd not, but kept their forward way,
  Through many covert groves, and thickets close,
  In which they creeping did at last display
  That wanton ladie, with her lover lose,
Whose sleepie head she in her lap did soft dispose.   315

77

Upon a bed of roses she was layd,
  As faint through heat, or dight to pleasant sin,
  And was arayd, or rather disarayd,
  All in a vele of silke and silver thin,
  That hid no whit her alablaster skin,   320
  But rather shewd more white, if more might bee:

---

306. *crime:* judgment.

More subtile web *Arachne* cannot spin,
  Nor the fine nets, which oft we woven see
Of scorched deaw, do not in th'aire more lightly flee.

78

Her snowy brest was bare to readie spoyle   325
  Of hungry eies, which n'ote therewith be fild,
  And yet through languour of her late sweet toyle,
  Few drops, more cleare then nectar, forth distild,
  That like pure orient perles adowne it trild,
  And her faire eyes sweet smyling in delight,   330
  Moystened their fierie beames, with which she thrild
  Fraile harts, yet quenchèd not; like starry light
Which sparckling on the silent waves, does seeme more bright.

79

The young man sleeping by her, seemed to bee
  Some goodly swayne of honorable place,   335
  That certes it great pittie was to see
  Him his nobilitie so foule deface;
  A sweet regard, and amiable grace,
  Mixèd with manly sternnesse did appeare
  Yet sleeping, in his well proportiond face,   340
  And on his tender lips the downy heare
Did now but freshly spring, and silken blossomes beare.

80

His warlike armes, the idle instruments
  Of sleeping praise, were hong upon a tree,
  And his brave shield, full of old moniments,   345
  Was fowly ra'st, that none the signes might see;
  Ne for them, ne for honour carèd hee,
  Ne ought, that did to his advauncement tend,
  But in lewd loves, and wastfull luxuree,
  His dayes, his goods, his bodie he did spend: 350
O horrible enchantment, that him so did blend.

81

The noble Elfe, and c refull Palmer drew
  So nigh them, minding nought, but lustfull game,

---

345. *moniments:* records of knightly deeds. 351. *blend:* blind.

That suddein forth they on them rusht, and threw
A subtile net, which onely for the same   355
The skilfull Palmer formally did frame.
So held them under fast, the whiles the rest
Fled all away for feare of fowler shame.
The faire enchauntresse, so unwares opprest,
Tryde all her arts, and all her sleights, thence out to wrest.   360

82

And eke her lover strove: but all in vaine;
    For that same net so cunningly was wound,
    That neither guile, nor force might it distraine.
    They tooke them both, and both them strongly bound
    In captive bandes, which there they readie found: 365
    But her in chaines of adamant he tyde;
    For nothing else might keepe her safe and sound;
    But *Verdant* (so he hight) he soone untyde,
And counsell sage in steed thereof to him applyde.

83

But all those pleasant bowres and pallace brave,   370
    Guyon broke downe, with rigour pittilesse;
    Ne ought their goodly workmanship might save
    Them from the tempest of his wrathfulnesse,
    But that their blisse he turn'd to balefulnesse:
    Their groves he feld, their gardins did deface,   375
    Their arbers spoyle, their cabinets suppresse,
    Their banket houses burne, their buildings race,
And of the fairest late, now made the fowlest place.

84

Then led they her away, and eke that knight
    They with them led, both sorrowfull and sad: 380
    The way they came, the same retourn'd they right,
    Till they arrivèd, where they lately had
    Charm'd those wild-beasts, that rag'd with furie mad.
    Which now awaking, fierce at them gan fly,
    As in their mistresse reskew, whom they lad;   385
    But them the Palmer soone did pacify.
Then *Guyon* askt, what meant those beastes, which there did ly.

---

376. *cabinets:* bowers.

85

Said he, These seeming beasts are men indeed,
 Whom this enchauntresse hath transformèd thus,
 Whylome her lovers, which her lusts did feed,   390
 Now turnèd into figures hideous,
 According to their mindes like monstruous.
 Sad end (quoth he) of life intemperate,
 And mournefull meed of joyes delicious:
 But Palmer, if it mote thee so aggrate,   395
Let them returnèd be unto their former state.

86

Streight way he with his vertuous staffe them strooke,
 And streight of beasts they comely men became;
 Yet being men they did unmanly looke,
 And starèd ghastly, some for inward shame,   400
 And some for wrath, to see their captive dame:
 But one above the rest in speciall,
 That had an hog beene late, hight *Grille* by name,
 Repinèd greatly, and did him miscall,
That had from hoggish forme him brought to naturall.   405

87

Said *Guyon,* See the mind of beastly man,
 That hath so soone forgot the excellence
 Of his creation, when he life began,
 That now he chooseth, with vile difference,
 To be a beast, and lacke intelligence.   410
 To whom the Palmer thus, The donghill kind
 Delights in filth and foule incontinence:
 Let *Grill* be *Grill,* and have his hoggish mind,
But let us hence depart, whilest wether serves and wind.

❧

---

404. *miscall:* abuse.

THE GARDEN OF ADONIS
(*The Faerie Queene*, Book III, Canto vi)
(1590)

26

To search the god of love, her nymphes she sent
   Throughout the wandring forrest every where:
   And after them her selfe eke with her went
   To seeke the fugitive, both farre and nere,
   So long they sought, till they arrivèd were   5
   In that same shadie covert, whereas lay
   Faire *Crysogone* in slombry traunce whilere:
   Who in her sleepe (a wondrous thing to say)
Unwares had borne two babes, as faire as springing day.

27

Unwares she them conceiv'd, unwares she bore: 10
   She bore withouten paine, that she conceivèd
   Withouten pleasure: ne her need implore
   Lucinaes aide: which when they both perceivèd,
   They were through wonder nigh of sense bereavèd,
   And gazing each on other, nought bespake: 15
   At last they both agreed, her seeming grievèd
   Out of her heavy swowne not to awake,
But from her loving side the tender babes to take.

28

Up they them tooke, each one a babe uptooke,
   And with them carried, to be fosterèd;   20
   Dame *Phœbe* to a nymph her babe betooke,
   To be upbrought in perfect maydenhed,
   And of her selfe her name *Belphœbe* red:
   But *Venus* hers thence farre away convayd,
   To be upbrought in goodly womanhed,   25
   And in her litle loves stead, which was strayd,
Her *Amoretta* cald, to comfort her dismayd.

THE GARDEN OF ADONIS: I. *she:* Venus.

29

She brought her to her joyous paradize,
    Where most she wonnes, when she on earth does dwel.
    So faire a place, as Nature can devize: 30
    Whether in *Paphos,* or *Cytheron* hill,
    Or it in *Gnidus* be, I wote not well;
    But well I wote by tryall, that this same
    All other pleasant places doth excell,
    And callèd is by her lost lovers name,   35
The *Gardin* of *Adonis,* farre renownd by fame.

30

In that same Gardin all the goodly flowres,
    Wherewith dame Nature doth her beautifie,
    And decks the girlonds of her paramoures,
    Are fetcht: there is the first seminarie   40
    Of all things, that are borne to live and die,
    According to their kindes. Long worke it were,
    Here to account the endlesse progenie
    Of all the weedes, that bud and blossome there;
But so much as doth need, must needs be counted here.   45

31

It sited was in fruitfull soyle of old,
    And girt in with two walles on either side;
    The one of yron, the other of bright gold,
    That none might thorough breake, nor overstride:
    And double gates it had, which opened wide,   50
    By which both in and out men moten pas;
    Th'one faire and fresh, the other old and dride:
    Old *Genius* the porter of them was,
Old *Genius,* the which a double nature has.

32

He letteth in, he letteth out to wend,   55
    All that to come into the world desire;
    A thousand thousand naked babes attend
    About him day and night, which doe require,
    That he with fleshly weedes would them attire:
    Such as him list, such as eternall fate   60
    Ordainèd hath, he clothes with sinfull mire,
    And sendeth forth to live in mortall state,
Till they againe returne backe by the hinder gate.

33

After that they againe returnèd beene,
  They in that Gardin plantèd be againe;   65
  And grow afresh, as they had never seene
  Fleshly corruption, nor mortall paine.
  Some thousand yeares so doen they there remaine;
  And then of him are clad with other hew,
  Or sent into the chaungefull world againe,   70
  Till thither they returne, where first they grew:
So like a wheele around they runne from old to new.

34

Ne needs there gardiner to set, or sow,
  To plant or prune: for of their owne accord
  All things, as they created were, doe grow,   75
  And yet remember well the mightie word,
  Which first was spoken by th'Almightie lord,
  That bad them to increase and multiply:
  Ne doe they need with water of the ford,
  Or of the clouds to moysten their roots dry;   80
For in themselves eternall moisture they imply.

35

Infinite shapes of creatures there are bred,
  And uncouth formes, which none yet ever knew,
  And every sort is in a sundry bed
  Set by it selfe, and ranckt in comely rew: 85
  Some fit for reasonable soules t'indew,
  Some made for beasts, some made for birds to weare,
  And all the fruitfull spawne of fishes hew
  In endlesse rancks along enraungèd were,
That seem'd the *Ocean* could not containe them there.   90

36

Daily they grow, and daily forth are sent
  Into the world, it to replenish more;
  Yet is the stocke not lessenèd, nor spent,
  But still remaines in everlasting store,
  As it at first created was of yore.   95
  For in the wide wombe of the world there lyes,

---

81. *imply:* contain. 83. *uncouth:* unfamiliar.

In hatefull darkenesse and in deepe horrore,
   An huge eternall *Chaos,* which supplyes
The substances of natures fruitfull progenyes.

37

All things from thence doe their first being fetch,   100
   And borrow matter, whereof they are made,
   Which when as forme and feature it does ketch,
   Becomes a bodie, and doth then invade
   The state of life, out of the griesly shade.
   That substance is eterne, and bideth so,   105
   Ne when the life decayes, and forme does fade,
   Doth it consume, and into nothing go,
But chaungèd is, and often altred to and fro.

38

The substance is not chaunged, nor alterèd,
   But th'only forme and outward fashion;   110
   For every substance is conditionèd
   To change her hew, and sundry formes to don,
   Meet for her temper and complexion:
   For formes are variable and decay,
   By course of kind, and by occasion;   115
   And that faire flowre of beautie fades away,
As doth the lilly fresh before the sunny ray.

39

Great enimy to it, and to all the rest,
   That in the *Gardin* of *Adonis* springs,
   Is wicked *Time,* who with his scyth addrest,   120
   Does mow the flowring herbes and goodly things,
   And all their glory to the ground downe flings,
   Where they doe wither, and are fowly mard:
   He flyes about, and with his flaggy wings
   Beates downe both leaves and buds without regard,   125
Ne ever pittie may relent his malice hard.

40

Yet pittie often did the gods relent,
   To see so faire things mard, and spoylèd quight:
   And their great mother *Venus* did lament

_____
111. *conditionèd:* bound.

The losse of her deare brood, her deare delight: 130
Her hart was pierst with pittie at the sight,
When walking through the Gardin, them she spyde,
Yet no'te she find redresse for such despight.
For all that lives, is subject to that law:
All things decay in time, and to their end do draw.   135

41

But were it not, that *Time* their troubler is,
  All that in this delightfull Gardin growes,
  Should happie be, and have immortall blis:
  For here all plentie, and all pleasure flowes,
  And sweet love gentle fits emongst them throwes,   140
  Without fell rancor, or fond gealosie;
  Franckly each paramour his leman knowes,
  Each bird his mate, ne any does envie
Their goodly meriment, and gay felicitie.

42

There is continuall spring, and harvest there   145
  Continuall, both meeting at one time:
  For both the boughes doe laughing blossomes beare,
  And with fresh colours decke the wanton prime,
  And eke attonce the heavy trees they clime,
  Which seeme to labour under their fruits lode: 150
  The whiles the joyous birdes make their pastime
  Emongst the shadie leaves, their sweet abode,
And their true loves without suspition tell abrode.

43

Right in the middest of that paradise,
  There stood a stately mount, on whose round top   155
  A gloomy grove of mirtle trees did rise,
  Whose shadie boughes sharpe steele did never lop,
  Nor wicked beasts their tender buds did crop,
  But like a girlond compassèd the hight,
  And from their fruitfull sides sweet gum did drop,   160
  That all the ground with precious deaw bedight,
Threw forth most dainty odours, and most sweet delight.

---

140. *fits:* emotions. 148. *prime:* spring.

44

And in the thickest covert of that shade,
  There was a pleasant arbour, not by art,
  But of the trees owne inclination made,   165
  Which knitting their rancke braunches part to part,
  With wanton yvie twyne entrayld athwart,
  And eglantine, and caprifole emong,
  Fashiond above within their inmost part,
  That nether *Phœbus* beams could through them throng,   170
Nor *Aeolus* sharp blast could worke them any wrong.

45

And all about grew every sort of flowre,
  To which sad lovers were transformd of yore;
  Fresh *Hyacinthus, Phœbus* paramoure,
  And dearest love,   175
  Foolish *Narcisse,* that likes the watry shore,
  Sad *Amaranthus,* made a flowre but late,
  Sad *Amaranthus,* in whose purple gore
  Me seemes I see *Amintas* wretched fate,
To whom sweet poets verse hath given endlesse date.   180

46

There wont faire *Venus* often to enjoy
  Her deare *Adonis* joyous company,
  And reape sweet pleasure of the wanton boy;
  There yet, some say, in secret he does ly,
  Lappèd in flowres and pretious spycery,   185
  By her hid from the world, and from the skill
  Of *Stygian* gods, which doe her love envy;
  But she her selfe, when ever that she will,
Possesseth him, and of his sweetnesse takes her fill.

47

And sooth it seemes they say: for he may not   190
  For ever die, and ever buried bee
  In balefull night, where all things are forgot;
  All be he subject to mortalitie,
  Yet is eterne in mutabilitie,
  And by succession made perpetuall,   195

---

168. *caprifole:* honeysuckle.

Transformèd oft, and chaungèd diverslie:
For him the Father of all formes they call;
Therefore needs mote he live, that living gives to all.

48

There now he liveth in eternall blis,
  Joying his goddesse, and of her enjoyd: 200
  Ne feareth he henceforth that foe of his,
  Which with his cruell tuske him deadly cloyd:
  For that wilde bore, the which him once annoyd,
  She firmely hath emprisonèd for ay,
  That her sweet love his malice mote avoyd,   205
  In a strong rocky cave, which is they say,
Hewen underneath that mount, that none him losen may.

49

There now he lives in everlasting joy,
  With many of the gods in company,
  Which thither haunt, and with the wingèd boy   210
  Sporting himselfe in safe felicity:
  Who when he hath with spoiles and cruelty
  Ransackt the world, and in the wofull harts
  Of many wretches set his triumphes hye,
  Thither resorts, and laying his sad darts   215
Aside, with faire *Adonis* playes his wanton parts.

50

And his true love faire *Psyche* with him playes.
  Faire *Psyche* to him lately reconcyld,
  After long troubles and unmeet upbrayes,
  With which his mother *Venus* her revyld,   220
  And eke himselfe her cruelly exyld:
  But now in stedfast love and happy state
  She with him lives, and hath him borne a chyld,
  Pleasure, that doth both gods and men aggrate,
Pleasure, the daughter of *Cupid* and *Psyche* late.   225

51

Hither great *Venus* brought this infant faire,
  The younger daughter of *Chrysogonee,*
  And unto *Psyche* with great trust and care

---

219. *unmeet upbrayes:* unseemly reproaches.

Committed her, yfostrèd to bee,
And trainèd up in true feminitee: 230
Who no lesse carefully her tenderèd,
Then her owne daughter *Pleasure,* to whom shee
Made her companion, and her lessonèd
In all the lore of love, and goodly womanhead.

52

In which when she to perfect ripenesse grew,   235
Of grace and beautie noble paragone,
She brought her forth into the worldes vew,
To be th'ensample of true love alone,
And lodestarre of all chaste affectione,
To all faire ladies, that doe live on ground.   240
To Faery court she came, where many one
Admyrd her goodly haveour, and found
His feeble hart wide launched with loves cruell wound.

THE GRACES OF COURTESY
(*The Faerie Queene,* Book VI, Canto x)
(1596)

Calidore sees the Graces daunce,
To Colins melody:
The whiles his Pastorell is led
Into captivity.

I

Who now does follow the foule *Blatant Beast,*
Whilest *Calidore* does follow that faire mayd,
Unmyndfull of his vow and high beheast,
Which by the Faery Queene was on him layd,
That he should never leave, nor be delayd   5
From chacing him, till he had it attchievèd?
But now entrapt of love, which him betrayd,
He mindeth more, how he may be relievèd
With grace from her, whose love his heart hath sore engrievèd.

2

That from henceforth he meanes no more to sew 10
  His former quest, so full of toile and paine;
  Another quest, another game in vew
  He hath, the guerdon of his love to gaine:
  With whom he myndes for ever to remaine,
  And set his rest amongst the rusticke sort, 15
  Rather then hunt still after shadowes vaine
  Of courtly favour, fed with light report
Of every blaste, and sayling alwaies in the port.

3

Ne certes mote he greatly blamèd be,
  From so high step to stoupe unto so low. 20
  For who had tasted once (as oft did he)
  The happy peace, which there doth overflow,
  And prov'd the perfect pleasures, which doe grow
  Amongst poore hyndes, in hils, in woods, in dales,
  Would never more delight in painted show 25
  Of such false blisse, as there is set for stales,
T'entrap unwary fooles in their eternall bales.

4

For what hath all that goodly glorious gaze
  Like to one sight, which *Calidore* did vew?
  The glaunce whereof their dimmèd eies would daze, 30
  That never more they should endure the shew
  Of that sunne-shine, that makes them looke askew.
  Ne ought in all that world of beauties rare,
  (Save onely *Glorianaes* heavenly hew
  To which what can compare?) can it compare; 35
The which as commeth now, by course I will declare.

5

One day as he did raunge the fields abroad,
  Whilest his faire *Pastorella* was elsewhere,
  He chaunst to come, far from all peoples troad,
  Unto a place, whose pleasaunce did appere 40
  To passe all others, on the earth which were:
  For all that ever was by natures skill

THE GRACES OF COURTESY: 10. *sew:* pursue. 26. *stales:* snares. 27. *bales:* griefs. 39. *troad:* path.

Devized to worke delight, was gathered there,
And there by her were pourèd forth at fill,
As if this to adorne, she all the rest did pill. 45

6

It was an hill plaste in an open plaine,
That round about was bordered with a wood
Of matchlesse hight, that seem'd th'earth to disdaine,
In which all trees of honour stately stood,
And did all winter as in sommer bud, 50
Spredding pavilions for the birds to bowre,
Which in their lower braunches sung aloud;
And in their tops the soring hauke did towre,
Sitting like king of fowles in majesty and powre.

7

And at the foote thereof, a gentle flud 55
His silver waves did softly tumble downe,
Unmard with ragged mosse or filthy mud,
Ne mote wylde beastes, ne mote the ruder clowne
There to approch, ne filth mote therein drowne:
But nymphes and faeries by the bancks did sit, 60
In the woods shade, which did the waters crowne,
Keeping all noysome things away from it,
And to the waters fall tuning their accents fit.

8

And on the top thereof a spacious plaine
Did spred it selfe, to serve to all delight,
Either to daunce, when they to daunce would faine, 65
Or else to course about their bases light;
Ne ought there wanted, which for pleasure might
Desirèd be, or thence to banish bale:
So pleasauntly the hill with equall hight, 70
Did seeme to overlooke the lowly vale;
Therefore it rightly cleepèd was mount *Acidale.*

9

They say that *Venus,* when she did dispose
Her selfe to pleasaunce, usèd to resort

---

45. *pill:* rob. 58. *clowne:* rustic person.

Unto this place, and therein to repose   75
And rest her selfe, as in a gladsome port,
Or with the Graces there to play and sport;
That even her owne Cytheron, though in it
  She usèd most to keepe her royall court,
  And in her soveraine majesty to sit,   80
She in regard hereof refusde and thought unfit.

10

Unto this place when as the Elfin Knight
  Approcht, him seemèd that the merry sound
Of a shrill pipe he playing heard on hight,
And many feete fast thumping th'hollow ground,   85
That through the woods their eccho did rebound.
He nigher drew, to weete what mote it be;
  There he a troupe of ladies dauncing found
  Full merrily, and making gladfull glee,
And in the midst a shepheard piping he did see.   90

11

He durst not enter into th'open greene,
  For dread of them unwares to be descryde,
For breaking of their daunce, if he were seene;
But in the covert of the wood did byde,
Beholding all, yet of them unespyde.   95
There he did see, that pleasèd much his sight,
  That even he him selfe his eyes envyde,
  An hundred naked maidens lilly white,
All raungèd in a ring, and dauncing in delight.

12

All they without were raungèd in a ring,   100
  And dauncèd round; but in the midst of them
Three other ladies did both daunce and sing,
The whilest the rest them round about did hemme,
And like a girlond did in compasse stemme:
And in the middest of those same three, was placed   105
  Another damzell, as a precious gemme,
  Amidst a ring most richly well enchaced,
That with her goodly presence all the rest much graced.

---

104. *stemme:* encircle.

13

Looke how the crowne, which *Ariadne* wore
  Upon her yvory forehead that same day,   11&omsp;
  That *Theseus* her unto his bridale bore,
  When the bold *Centaures* made that bloudy fray,
  With the fierce *Lapithes,* which did them dismay;
  Being now placed in the firmament,
  Through the bright heaven doth her beams display,   115
  And is unto the starres an ornament,
Which round about her move in order excellent.

14

Such was the beauty of this goodly band,
  Whose sundry parts were here too long to tell:
  But she that in the midst of them did stand,   120
  Seem'd all the rest in beauty to excell,
  Crownd with a rosie girlond, that right well
  Did her beseeme. And ever, as the crew
  About her daunst, sweet flowres, that far did smell,
  And fragrant odours they uppon her threw;   125
But most of all, those three did her with gifts endew.

15

Those were the Graces, daughters of delight,
  Handmaides of *Venus,* which are wont to haunt
  Uppon this hill, and daunce there day and night:
  Those three to men all gifts of grace do graunt,   130
  And all, that *Venus* in her selfe doth vaunt,
  Is borrowed of them. But that faire one,
  That in the midst was placèd paravaunt,
  Was she to whom that shepheard pypt alone,
That made him pipe so merrily, as never none.   135

16

She was to weete that jolly shepheards lasse,
  Which pipèd there unto that merry rout,
  That jolly shepheard, which there pipèd, was
  Poore *Colin Clout* (who knowes not *Colin Clout?*)
  He pypt apace, whilest they him daunst about.   140
  Pype jolly shepheard, pype thou now apace

---

133. *paravaunt:* preëminently.

Unto thy love, that made thee low to lout:
Thy love is present there with thee in place,
Thy love is there advaunst to be another Grace.

17

Much wondred *Calidore* at this straunge sight,   145
  Whose like before his eye had never seene,
  And standing long astonishèd in spright,
  And rapt with pleasaunce, wist not what to weene;
  Whether it were the traine of beauties Queene,
  Or nymphes, or faeries, or enchaunted show,   150
  With which his eyes mote have deluded beene.
  Therefore resolving, what it was, to know,
Out of the wood he rose, and toward them did go.

18

But soone as he appearèd to their vew,
  They vanisht all away out of his sight,   155
  And cleane were gone, which way he never knew;
  All save the shepheard, who for fell despight
  Of that displeasure, broke his bag-pipe quight,
  And made great mone for that unhappy turne.
  But *Calidore,* though no lesse sory wight,   160
  For that mishap, yet seeing him to mourne,
Drew neare, that he the truth of all by him mote learne.

19

And first him greeting, thus unto him spake,
  Haile jolly shepheard, which thy joyous dayes
  Here leadest in this goodly merry make,   165
  Frequented of these gentle nymphes alwayes,
  Which to thee flocke, to heare thy lovely layes;
  Tell me, what mote these dainty damzels be,
  Which here with thee doe make their pleasant playes?
  Right happy thou, that mayst them freely see: 170
But why when I them saw, fled they away from me?

20

Not I so happy, answerd then that swaine,
  As thou unhappy, which them thence didst chace,
  Whom by no meanes thou canst recall againe,

---

142. *lout:* bow. 147. *spright:* spirit.

For being gone, none can them bring in place,   175
But whom they of them selves list so to grace.
Right sory I, (saide then Sir *Calidore,*)
That my ill fortune did them hence displace.
But since things passèd none may now restore,
Tell me, what were they all, whose lacke thee grieves so sore.   180

21

Tho gan that shepheard thus for to dilate;
   Then wote thou shepheard, whatsoever thou bee,
   That all those ladies, which thou sawest late,
   Are *Venus* damzels, all within her fee,
   But differing in honour and degree: 185
   They all are Graces, which on her depend,
   Besides a thousand more, which ready bee
   Her to adorne, when so she forth doth wend:
But those three in the midst, doe chiefe on her attend.

22

They are the daughters of sky-ruling Jove,   190
   By him begot of faire *Eurynome,*
   The Oceans daughter, in this pleasant grove,
   As he this way comming from feastfull glee,
   Of *Thetis* wedding with *Æacidee,*
   In sommers shade him selfe here rested weary.   195
   The first of them hight mylde *Euphrosyne,*
   Next faire *Aglaia,* last *Thalia* merry:
Sweete goddesses all three which me in mirth do cherry.

23

These three on men all gracious gifts bestow,
   Which decke the body or adorne the mynde,   200
   To make them lovely or well favoured show,
   As comely carriage, entertainement kynde,
   Sweete semblaunt, friendly offices that bynde,
   And all the complements of curtesie:
   They teach us, how to each degree and kynde   205
   We should our selves demeane, to low, to hie;
To friends, to foes, which skill men call civility.

---

184. *fee:* service.

24

Therefore they alwaies smoothly seeme to smile,
  That we likewise should mylde and gentle be,
  And also naked are, that without guile   210
  Or false dissemblaunce all them plaine may see,
  Simple and true from covert malice free:
  And eeke them selves so in their daunce they bore,
  That two of them still froward seem'd to bee,
  But one still towards shew'd her selfe afore;   215
That good should from us goe, then come in greater store.

25

Such were those goddesses, which ye did see;
  But that fourth mayd, which there amidst them traced,
  Who can aread, what creature mote she bee,
  Whether a creature, or a goddesse graced   220
  With heavenly gifts from heven first enraced?
  But what so sure she was, she worthy was,
  To be the fourth with those three other placed:
  Yet was she certes but a countrey lasse,
Yet she all other countrey lasses farre did passe.   225

26

So farre as doth the daughter of the day,
  All other lesser lights in light excell,
  So farre doth she in beautyfull array,
  Above all other lasses beare the bell,
  Ne lesse in vertue that beseemes her well,   230
  Doth she exceede the rest of all her race,
  For which the Graces that here wont to dwell,
  Have for more honor brought her to this place,
And gracèd her so much to be another Grace.

27

Another Grace she well deserves to be,   235
  In whom so many graces gathered are,
  Excelling much the meane of her degree;
  Divine resemblaunce, beauty soveraine rare,
  Firme chastity, that spight ne blemish dare;

---

221. *enraced:* implanted.

All which she with such courtesie doth grace,   240
That all her peres cannot with her compare,
But quite are dimmed, when she is in place.
She made me often pipe and now to pipe apace.

28

Sunne of the world, great glory of the sky,
That all the earth doest lighten with thy rayes,   245
Great *Gloriana,* greatest Majesty,
  Pardon thy shepheard, mongst so many layes,
  As he hath sung of thee in all his dayes,
  To make one minime of thy poore handmayd,
  And underneath thy feete to place her prayse,   250
  That when thy glory shall be farre displayd
To future age of her this mention may be made.

29

When thus that shepherd ended had his speach,
Sayd *Calidore;* Now sure it yrketh mee,
That to thy blisse I made this luckelesse breach,   255
As now the author of thy bale to be,
Thus to bereave thy loves deare sight from thee:
But gentle shepheard pardon thou my shame,
Who rashly sought that, which I mote not see.
Thus did the courteous knight excuse his blame,   260
And to recomfort him, all comely meanes did frame.

~❧~

THE HOUSE OF HOLINESS AND
THE NEW JERUSALEM
(*The Faerie Queene,* Book I, Canto x)
(1590)

Her faithfull knight faire Una brings
to house of Holinesse,
Where he is taught repentance, and
the way to heavenly blesse.

---

249. *minime:* note.

1

What man is he, that boasts of fleshly might,
  And vaine assurance of mortality,
  Which all so soone, as it doth come to fight,
  Against spirituall foes, yeelds by and by,
  Or from the field most cowardly doth fly?   5
  Ne let the man ascribe it to his skill,
  That thorough grace hath gainèd victory.
  If any strength we have, it is to ill,
But all the good is Gods, both power and eke will.

2

By that, which lately hapned, *Una* saw,   10
  That this her knight was feeble, and too faint;
  And all his sinews woxen weake and raw,
  Through long enprisonment, and hard constraint,
  Which he endurèd in his late restraint,
  That yet he was unfit for bloudie fight: 15
  Therefore to cherish him with diets daint,
  She cast to bring him, where he chearen might,
Till he recovered had his late decayèd plight.

3

There was an auntient house not farre away,
  Renowmd throughout the world for sacred lore,   20
  And pure unspotted life: so well they say
  It governd was, and guided evermore,
  Through wisedome of a matrone grave and hore;
  Whose onely joy was to relieve the needes
  Of wretched soules, and helpe the helplesse pore: 25
  All night she spent in bidding of her bedes,
And all the day in doing good and godly deedes.

4

Dame *Cœlia* men did her call, as thought
  From heaven to come, or thither to arise,
  The mother of three daughters, well upbrought   30
  In goodly thewes, and godly exercise:
  The eldest two most sober, chast, and wise,
  Fidelia and *Speranza* virgins were,

THE HOUSE OF HOLINESS: 31. *thewes:* habits. 33. *Fidelia* and *Speranza:*
Faith and Hope.

Though spousd, yet wanting wedlocks solemnize;
  But faire *Charissa* to a lovely fere   35
Was lincked, and by him had many pledges dere.

5

Arrivèd there, the dore they find fast lockt;
  For it was warely watchèd night and day,
  For feare of many foes: but when they knockt,
  The porter opened unto them streight way: 40
  He was an agèd syre, all hory gray,
  With lookes full lowly cast, and gate full slow,
  Wont on a staffe his feeble steps to stay,
Hight *Humiltá.* They passe in stouping low;
For streight and narrow was the way, which he did show.   45

6

Each goodly thing is hardest to begin,
  But entred in a spacious court they see,
  Both plaine, and pleasant to be walkèd in,
  Where them does meete a francklin faire and free.
  And entertaines with comely courteous glee,   50
  His name was *Zele,* that him right well became,
  For in his speeches and behaviour hee
  Did labour lively to expresse the same,
And gladly did them guide, till to the hall they came.

7

There fairely them receives a gentle squire,   55
  Of milde demeanure, and rare courtesie,
  Right cleanly clad in comely sad attire;
  In word and deede that shew'd great modestie,
  And knew his good to all of each degree,
  Hight *Reverence.* He them with speeches meet   60
  Does faire entreat; no courting nicetie,
  But simple true, and eke unfainèd sweet,
As might become a squire so great persons to greet.

8

And afterwards them to his dame he leades,
  That agèd dame, the ladie of the place: 65
  Who all this while was busie at her beades:

---

35. *Charissa:* Charity, Love; *fere:* mate. 36. *pledges:* children.
57. *sad:* sober.

Which doen, she up arose with seemely grace,
And toward them full matronely did pace.
Where when that fairest *Una* she beheld,
Whom well she knew to spring from heavenly race,   70
Her hart with joy unwonted inly sweld,
As feeling wondrous comfort in her weaker eld.

9

And her embracing said, O happie earth,
Whereon thy innocent feet doe ever tread,
Most vertuous virgin borne of heavenly berth,   75
That to redeeme thy woefull parents head,
From tyrans rage, and ever-dying dread,
Hast wandred through the world now long a day;
Yet ceasest not thy wearie soles to lead,
What grace hath thee now hither brought this way?   80
Or doen thy feeble feet unweeting hither stray?

10

Strange thing it is an errant knight to see
Here in this place, or any other wight,
That hither turnes his steps. So few there bee,
That chose the narrow path, or seeke the right: 85
All keepe the broad high way, and take delight
With many rather for to go astray,
And be partakers of their evill plight,
Then with a few to walke the rightest way;
O foolish men, why haste ye to your owne decay?   90

11

Thy selfe to see, and tyred limbs to rest,
O matrone sage (quoth she) I hither came,
And this good knight his way with me addrest,
Led with thy prayses and broad-blazèd fame,
That up to heaven is blowne. The auncient dame   95
Him goodly greeted in her modest guise,
And entertaynd them both, as best became,
With all the court'sies that she could devise,
Ne wanted ought, to shew her bounteous or wise.

12

Thus as they gan of sundry things devise,   100
Loe two most goodly virgins came in place,

Ylinkèd arme in arme in lovely wise,
With countenance demure, and modest grace,
They numbred even steps and equall pace:
Of which the eldest, that *Fidelia* hight,   105
Like sunny beames threw from her christall face,
That could have dazed the rash beholders sight,
And round about her head did shine like heavens light.

13

She was araièd all in lilly white,
And in her right hand bore a cup of gold,   110
With wine and water fild up to the hight,
In which a serpent did himselfe enfold,
That horrour made to all, that did behold;
But she no whit did chaunge her constant mood:
And in her other hand she fast did hold   115
A booke, that was both signd and seald with blood,
Wherein darke things were writ, hard to be understood.

14

Her younger sister, that *Speranza* hight,
Was clad in blew, that her beseemèd well;
Not all so chearefull seemèd she of sight,   120
As was her sister; whether dread did dwell,
Or anguish in her hart, is hard to tell:
Upon her arme a silver anchor lay,
Whereon she leanèd ever, as befell:
And ever up to heaven, as she did pray,   125
Her stedfast eyes were bent, ne swarvèd other way.

15

They seeing *Una,* towards her gan wend,
Who them encounters with like courtesie;
Many kind speeches they betwene them spend,
And greatly joy each other well to see: 130
Then to the knight with shamefast modestie
They turne themselves, at *Unaes* meeke request,
And him salute with well beseeming glee;
Who faire them quites, as him beseemèd best,
And goodly gan discourse of many a noble gest.   135

---

110. *cup of gold:* sacramental cup. 116. *booke:* New Testament. 135. *gest:* deed.

16

Then *Una* thus; But she your sister deare;
  The deare *Charissa* where is she become?
  Or wants she health, or busie is elsewhere?
  Ah no, said they, but forth she may not come:
  For she of late is lightned of her wombe,   140
  And hath encreast the world with one sonne more,
  That her to see should be but troublesome.
  Indeede (quoth she) that should her trouble sore.
But thankt be God, and her encrease so evermore.

17

Then said the aged *Cælia,* Deare dame,   145
  And you good sir, I wote that of your toyle,
  And labours long, through which ye hither came,
  Ye both forwearied be: therefore a whyle
  I read you rest, and to your bowres recoyle.
  Then callèd she a groome, that forth him led   150
  Into a goodly lodge, and gan despoile
  Of puissant armes, and laid in easie bed;
His name was meeke *Obedience* rightfully ared.

18

Now when their wearie limbes with kindly rest,
  And bodies were refresht with due repast,   155
  Faire *Una* gan *Fidelia* faire request,
  To have her knight into her schoolehouse plaste,
  That of her heavenly learning he might taste,
  And heare the wisedome of her words divine.
  She graunted, and that knight so much agraste,   160
  That she him taught celestiall discipline,
And opened his dull eyes, that light mote in them shine.

19

And that her sacred Booke, with bloud ywrit,
  That none could read, except she did them teach,
  She unto him disclosèd every whit,   165
  And heavenly documents thereout did preach,
  That weaker wit of man could never reach,
  Of God, of grace, of justice, of free will,

---

160. *agraste:* favored.

That wonder was to heare her goodly speach:
For she was able, with her words to kill,   170
And raise againe to life the hart, that she did thrill.

20

And when she list poure out her larger spright,
She would commaund the hastie sunne to stay,
Or backward turne his course from heavens hight;
Sometimes great hostes of men she could dismay,   175
Dry-shod to passe, she parts the flouds in tway;
And eke huge mountaines from their native seat
She would commaund, themselves to beare away,
And throw in raging sea with roaring threat.
Almightie God her gave such powre, and puissance great.   180

21

The faithfull knight now grew in litle space,
By hearing her, and by her sisters lore,
To such perfection of all heavenly grace,
That wretched world he gan for to abhore,
And mortall life gan loath, as thing forlore,   185
Greev'd with remembrance of his wicked wayes,
And prickt with anguish of his sinnes so sore,
That he desirde to end his wretched dayes:
So much the dart of sinfull guilt the soule dismayes.

22

But wise *Speranza* gave him comfort sweet,   190
And taught him how to take assurèd hold
Upon her silver anchor, as was meet;
Else had his sinnes so great, and manifold
Made him forget all that *Fidelia* told.
In this distressèd doubtfull agonie,   195
When him his dearest *Una* did behold,
Disdeining life, desiring leave to die,
She found her selfe assayld with great perplexitie.

23

And came to *Cœlia* to declare her smart,
Who well acquainted with that commune plight,   200
Which sinfull horror workes in wounded hart,
Her wisely comforted all that she might,
With goodly counsell and advisement right;

And streightway sent with carefull diligence,
To fetch a leach, the which had great insight   205
In that disease of grievèd conscience,
And well could cure the same; His name was *Patience*.

24

Who comming to that soule-diseasèd knight,
Could hardly him intreat, to tell his griefe:
Which knowne, and all that noyd his heavie spright   210
Well searcht, eftsoones he gan apply reliefe
Of salves and med'cines, which had passing priefe,
And thereto added words of wondrous might:
By which to ease he him recurèd briefe,
And much asswag'd the passion of his plight,   215
That he his paine endur'd, as seeming now more light.

25

But yet the cause and root of all his ill,
Inward corruption, and infected sin,
Not purg'd nor heald, behind remainèd still,
And festring sore did rankle yet within,   220
Close creeping twixt the marrow and the skin.
Which to extirpe, he laid him privily
Downe in a darkesome lowly place farre in,
Whereas he meant his corrosives to apply,
And with streight diet tame his stubborne malady.   225

26

In ashes and sackcloth he did array
His daintie corse, proud humors to abate,
And dieted with fasting every day,
The swelling of his wounds to mitigate,
And made him pray both earely and eke late: 230
And ever as superfluous flesh did rot
Amendment readie still at hand did wayt,
To pluck it out with pincers firie whot,
That soone in him was left no one corrupted jot.

27

And bitter *Penance* with an yron whip,   235
Was wont him once to disple every day:

212. *priefe:* proven value. 225. *streight:* strict. 236. *disple:* subject to penance.

And sharpe *Remorse* his hart did pricke and nip,
That drops of bloud thence like a well did play;
And sad *Repentance* used to embay
His bodie in salt water smarting sore,   240
The filthy blots of sinne to wash away.
So in short space they did to health restore
The man that would not live, but earst lay at deathes dore.

28

In which his torment often was so great,
That like a lyon he would cry and rore,   245
And rend his flesh, and his owne synewes eat.
His owne deare *Una* hearing evermore
His ruefull shriekes and gronings, often tore
Her guiltlesse garments, and her golden heare,
For pitty of his paine and anguish sore;   250
Yet all with patience wisely she did beare;
For well she wist, his crime could else be never cleare.

29

Whom thus recover'd by wise Patience,
And trew *Repentance* they to *Una* brought:
Who joyous of his cured conscience,   255
Him dearely kist, and fairely eke besought
Himselfe to chearish, and consuming thought
To put away out of his carefull brest.
By this *Charissa,* late in child-bed brought,
Was woxen strong, and left her fruitfull nest;   260
To her faire *Una* brought this unacquainted guest.

30

She was a woman in her freshest age,
Of wondrous beauty, and of bountie rare,
With goodly grace and comely personage,
That was on earth not easie to compare;   265
Full of great love, but *Cupids* wanton snare
As hell she hated, chast in worke and will;
Her necke and breasts were ever open bare,
That ay thereof her babes might sucke their fill;
The rest was all in yellow robes arayèd still.   270

31

A multitude of babes about her hong,
Playing their sports, that joyd her to behold,

Whom still she fed, whiles they were weake and young,
But thrust them forth still, as they wexed old:
And on her head she wore a tyre of gold,   275
Adornd with gemmes and owches wondrous faire,
Whose passing price uneath was to be told;
And by her side there sate a gentle paire
Of turtle doves, she sitting in an yvorie chaire.

32

The knight and *Una* entring, faire her greet,   280
And bid her joy of that her happie brood;
Who them requites with court'sies seeming meet,
And entertaines with friendly chearefull mood.
Then *Una* her besought, to be so good,
As in her vertuous rules to schoole her knight,   285
Now after all his torment well withstood,
In that sad house of *Penaunce,* where his spright
Had past the paines of hell, and long enduring night.

33

She was right joyous of her just request,
And taking by the hand that faeries sonne,   290
Gan him instruct in every good behest,
Of love, and righteousnesse, and well to donne,
And wrath, and hatred warely to shonne,
That drew on men Gods hatred, and his wrath,
And many soules in dolours had fordonne: 295
In which when him she well instructed hath,
From thence to heaven she teacheth him the ready path.

34

Wherein his weaker wandring steps to guide,
An auncient matrone she to her does call,
Whose sober lookes her wisedome well descride: 300
Her name was *Mercie,* well knowne over all,
To be both gratious, and eke liberall:
To whom the carefull charge of him she gave,
To lead aright, that he should never fall
In all his wayes through this wide worldes wave,   305
That Mercy in the end his righteous soule might save.

---

276. *owches:* jewels.

35

The godly matrone by the hand him beares
   Forth from her presence, by a narrow way,
   Scattred with bushy thornes, and ragged breares,
   Which still before him she remov'd away,   310
   That nothing might his ready passage stay:
   And ever when his feet encombred were,
   Or gan to shrinke, or from the right to stray,
   She held him fast, and firmely did upbeare,
As carefull nourse her child from falling oft does reare.   315

36

Eftsoones unto an holy hospitall,
   That was fore by the way, she did him bring,
   In which seven bead-men that had vowèd all
   Their life to service of high heavens king
   Did spend their dayes in doing godly thing: 320
   Their gates to all were open evermore,
   That by the wearie way were traveiling,
   And one sate wayting ever them before,
To call in commers-by, that needy were and pore.

37

The first of them that eldest was, and best,   325
   Of all the house had charge and governement,
   As guardian and steward of the rest:
   His office was to give entertainement
   And lodging, unto all that came, and went:
   Not unto such, as could him feast againe,   330
   And double quite, for that he on them spent,
   But such, as want of harbour did constraine:
Those for Gods sake his dewty was to entertaine.

38

The second was as almner of the place,
   His office was, the hungry for to feed,   335
   And thirsty give to drinke, a worke of grace:
   He feard not once him selfe to be in need,
   Ne car'd to hoord for those, whom he did breede:
   The grace of God he layd up still in store,
   Which as a stocke he left unto his seede;   340
   He had enough, what need him care for more?
And had he lesse. yet some he would give to the pore.

39

The third had of their wardrobe custodie,
  In which were not rich tyres, nor garments gay,
  The plumes of pride, and wings of vanitie,   345
  But clothes meet to keepe keene could away,
  And naked nature seemely to aray;
  With which bare wretched wights he dayly clad,
  The images of God in earthly clay;
  And if that no spare cloths to give he had,   350
His owne coate he would cut, and it distribute glad.

40

The fourth appointed by his office was,
  Poore prisoners to relieve with gratious ayd,
  And captives to redeeme with price of bras,
  From Turkes and Sarazins, which them had stayed;   355
  And though they faultie were, yet well he wayd,
  That God to us forgiveth every howre
  Much more then that, why they in bands were layd,
  And he that harrowd hell with heavie stowre,
The faultie soules from thence brought to his heavenly bowre.   360

41

The fift had charge sicke persons to attend,
  And comfort those, in point of death which lay;
  For them most needeth comfort in the end,
  When sin, and hell, and death do most dismay
  The feeble soule departing hence away.   365
  All is but lost, that living we bestow,
  If not well ended at our dying day.
  O man have mind of that last bitter throw;
For as the tree does fall, so lyes it ever low.

42

The sixt had charge of them now being dead,   370
  In seemely sort their corses to engrave,
  And deck with dainty flowres their bridall bed,
  That to their heavenly spouse both sweet and brave
  They might appeare, when he their soules shall save.
  The wondrous workemanship of Gods owne mould,   375
  Whose face he made, all beasts to feare, and gave
  All in his hand, even dead we honour should.
Ah dearest God me graunt, I dead be not defould.

43

The seventh now after death and buriall done,
  Had charge the tender orphans of the dead   380
  And widowes ayd, least they should be undone:
  In face of judgement he their right would plead,
  Ne ought the powre of mighty men did dread
  In their defence, nor would for gold or fee
  Be wonne their rightfull causes downe to tread: 385
  And when they stood in most necessitee,
He did supply their want, and gave them ever free.

44

There when the Elfin knight arrivèd was,
  The first and chiefest of the seven, whose care
  Was guests to welcome, towardes him did pas: 390
  Where seeing *Mercie,* that his steps up bare,
  And alwayes led, to her with reverence rare
  He humbly louted in meeke lowlinesse,
  And seemely welcome for her did prepare:
  For of their order she was patronesse,   395
Albe *Charissa* were their chiefest founderesse.

45

There she awhile him stayes, him selfe to rest,
  That to the rest more able he might bee:
  During which time, in every good behest
  And godly worke of almes and charitee   400
  She him instructed with great industree;
  Shortly therein so perfect he became,
  That from the first unto the last degree,
  His mortall life he learnèd had to frame
In holy righteousnesse, without rebuke or blame.   405

46

Thence forward by that painfull way they pas,
  Forth to an hill, that was both steepe and hy;
  On top whereof a sacred chappell was,
  And eke a litle hermitage thereby,
  Wherein an agèd holy man did lye,   410
  That day and night said his devotion,
  Ne other worldly busines did apply;
  His name was heavenly *Contemplation*;
Of God and goodnesse was his meditation.

47

Great grace that old man to him given had;   415
　For God he often saw from heavens hight,
　All were his earthly eyen both blunt and bad,
　And through great age had lost their kindly sight,
　Yet wondrous quick and persant was his spright,
　As eagles eye, that can behold the sunne: 420
　That hill they scale with all their powre and might,
　That his frayle thighes nigh wearie and fordonne
Gan faile, but by her helpe the top at last he wonne.

48

There they do finde that godly aged sire,
　With snowy lockes adowne his shoulders shed,   425
　As hoarie frost with spangles doth attire
　The mossy braunches of an oke halfe ded.
　Each bone might through his body well be red,
　And every sinew seene through his long fast:
　For nought he car'd his carcas long unfed;   430
　His mind was full of spirituall repast,
And pyn'd his flesh, to keepe his body low and chast.

49

Who when these two approching he aspide,
　At their first presence grew agrievèd sore,
　That forst him lay his heavenly thoughts aside;   435
　And had he not that dame respected more,
　Whom highly he did reverence and adore,
　He would not once have movèd for the knight.
　They him saluted standing far afore;
　Who well them greeting, humbly did requight,   440
And asked, to what end they clomb that tedious height.

50

What end (quoth she) should cause us take such paine,
　But that same end, which every living wight
　Should make his marke, high heaven to attaine?
　Is not from hence the way, that leadeth right   445
　To that most glorious house, that glistreth bright
　With burning starres, and everliving fire,

---

419. *persant:* piercing.

Whereof the keyes are to thy hand behight
By wise *Fidelia?* she doth thee require,
To shew it to this knight, according his desire.   450

51

Thrise happy man, said then the father grave,
  Whose staggering steps thy steady hand doth lead,
  And shewes the way, his sinfull soule to save.
  Who better can the way to heaven aread,
  Then thou thy selfe, that was both borne and bred   455
  In heavenly throne, where thousand angels shine?
  Thou doest the prayers of the righteous sead
  Present before the majestie divine,
And his avenging wrath to clemencie incline.

52

Yet since thou bidst, thy pleasure shalbe donne.   460
  Then come thou man of earth, and see the way,
  That never yet was seene of faeries sonne,
  That never leads the traveiler astray,
  But after labours long, and sad delay,
  Brings them to joyous rest and endlesse blis.   465
  But first thou must a season fast and pray,
  Till from her bands the spright assoilèd is,
And have her strength recur'd from fraile infirmitis.

53

That done, he leads him to the highest mount;
  Such one, as that same mighty man of God,   470
  That bloud-red billowes like a wallèd front
  On either side disparted with his rod,
  Till that his army dry-foot through them yod,
  Dwelt fortie dayes upon; where writ in stone
  With bloudy letters by the hand of God,   475
  The bitter doome of death and balefull mone
He did receive, whiles flashing fire about him shone.

54

Or like that sacred hill, whose head full hie,
  Adornd with fruitfull olives all arownd,
  Is, as it were for endlesse memory   480

---

473. *yod:* went.

Of that deare Lord, who oft thereon was fownd,
For ever with a flowring girlond crownd:
Or like that pleasaunt mount, that is for ay
Through famous poets verse each where renownd,
On which the thrise three learnèd ladies play   485
Their heavenly notes, and make full many a lovely lay.

55

From thence, far off he unto him did shew
  A litle path, that was both steepe and long,
  Which to a goodly citie led his vew;
  Whose wals and towres were builded high and strong   490
  Of perle and precious stone, that earthly tong
  Cannot describe, nor wit of man can tell;
  Too high a ditty for my simple song;
  The citie of the great king hight it well,
Wherein eternall peace and happinesse doth dwell.   495

56

As he thereon stood gazing, he might see
  The blessed angels to and fro descend
  From highest heaven, in gladsome companee,
  And with great joy into that citie wend,
  As commonly as frend does with his frend.   500
  Whereat he wondred much, and gan enquere,
  What stately building durst so high extend
  Her loftie towres unto the starry sphere,
And what unknowen nation there empeopled were.

57

Faire knight (quoth he) *Hierusalem* that is,   505
  The new *Hierusalem,* that God has built
  For those to dwell in, that are chosen his,
  His chosen people purg'd from sinfull guilt,
  With pretious bloud, which cruelly was spilt
  On cursèd tree, of that unspotted lam,   510
  That for the sinnes of all the world was kilt:
  Now are they saints all in that citie sam,
More deare unto their God, then younglings to their dam.

58

Till now, said then the knight, I weened well,
  That great *Cleopolis,* where I have beene,   515

In which that fairest *Faerie Queene* doth dwell,
The fairest citie was, that might be seene;
And that bright towre all built of christall cleene,
Panthea, seemd the brightest thing, that was:
But now by proofe all otherwise I weene;   520
For this great citie that does far surpas,
And this bright angels towre quite dims that towre of glas.

59

Most trew, then said the holy aged man;
  Yet is *Cleopolis* for earthly frame,
  The fairest peece, that eye beholden can: 525
  And well beseemes all knights of noble name,
  That covet in th'immortall booke of fame
  To be eternizèd, that same to haunt,
  And doen their service to that soveraigne dame,
  That glorie does to them for guerdon graunt: 530
For she is heavenly borne, and heaven may justly vaunt.

60

And thou faire ymp, sprong out from English race,
  How ever now accompted elfins sonne,
  Well worthy doest thy service for her grace,
  To aide a virgin desolate foredonne.
  But when thou famous victorie hast wonne,   535
  And high emongst all knights hast hong thy shield,
  Thenceforth the suit of earthly conquest shonne,
  And wash thy hands from guilt of bloudy field:
For bloud can nought but sin, and wars but sorrowes yield.   540

61

Then seeke this path, that I to thee presage,
  Which after all to heaven shall thee send;
  Then peaceably thy painefull pilgrimage
  To yonder same *Hierusalem* do bend,
  Where is for thee ordaind a blessed end: 545
  For thou emongst those saints, whom thou doest see,
  Shalt be a saint, and thine owne nations frend
  And patrone: thou Saint *George* shalt callèd bee,
Saint *George* of mery England, the signe of victoree.

62

Unworthy wretch (quoth he) of so great grace,   550
  How dare I thinke such glory to attaine?

These that have it attaind, were in like cace
(Quoth he) as wretched, and liv'd in like paine.
But deeds of armes must I at last be faine,
And ladies love to leave so dearely bought? 555
What need of armes, where peace doth ay remaine,
(Said he) and battailes none are to be fought?
As for loose loves are vaine, and vanish into nought.

63

O let me not (quoth he) then turne againe
Backe to the world, whose joyes so fruitlesse are; 560
But let me here for aye in peace remaine,
Or streight way on that last long voyage fare,
That nothing may my present hope empare.
That may not be (said he) ne maist thou yit
Forgo that royall maides bequeathèd care, 565
Who did her cause into thy hand commit,
Till from her cursèd foe thou have her freely quit.

64

Then shall I soone, (quoth he) so God me grace,
Abet that virgins cause disconsolate,
And shortly backe returne unto this place, 570
To walke this way in pilgrims poore estate.
But now aread, old father, why of late
Didst thou behight me borne of English blood,
Whom all a faeries sonne doen nominate?
That word shall I (said he) avouchen good, 575
Sith to thee is unknowne the cradle of thy brood.

65

For well I wote, thou springst from ancient race
Of *Saxon* kings, that have with mightie hand
And many bloudie battailes fought in place
High reard their royall throne in *Britane* land, 580
And vanquisht them, unable to withstand:
From thence a faerie thee unweeting reft,
There as thou slepst in tender swadling band,
And her base elfin brood there for thee left.
Such men do chaungelings call, so chaungd by faeries theft. 585

66

Thence she thee brought into this faerie lond,
And in an heapèd furrow did thee hyde,

Where thee a ploughman all unweeting fond,
As he his toylesome teme that way did guyde,
And brought thee up in ploughmans state to byde,   590
Whereof *Georgos* he thee gave to name;
Till prickt with courage, and thy forces pryde,
To faery court thou cam'st to seeke for fame,
And prove thy puissaunt armes, as seemes thee best became.

67

O holy sire (quoth he) how shall I quight   595
The many favours I with thee have found,
That hast my name and nation red aright,
And taught the way that does to heaven bound?
This said, adowne he lookèd to the ground,
To have returnd, but dazèd were his eyne,   600
Through passing brightnesse, which did quite confound
His feeble sence, and too exceeding shyne.
So darke are earthly things compard to things divine.

68

At last whenas himselfe he gan to find,
To *Una* back he cast him to retire;   605
Who him awaited still with pensive mind.
Great thankes and goodly meed to that good syre,
He thence departing gave for his paines hyre.
So came to *Una,* who him joyd to see,
And after litle rest, gan him desire,   610
Of her adventure mindfull for to bee.
So leave they take of *Cœlia,* and her daughters three.

EPITHALAMION
(1595)

Ye learnèd sisters which have oftentimes
Beene to me ayding, others to adorne,
Whom ye thought worthy of your gracefull rymes,
That even the greatest did not greatly scorne
To heare theyr names sung in your simple layes,   5
But joyèd in theyr prayse.
And when ye list your owne mishaps to mourne,
Which death, or love, or fortunes wreck did rayse,
Your string could soone to sadder tenor turne,
And teach the woods and waters to lament   10
Your dolefull dreriment.
Now lay those sorrowfull complaints aside,
And having all your heads with girland crownd,
Helpe me mine owne loves prayses to resound,
Ne let the same of any be envide: 15
So Orpheus did for his owne bride,
So I unto my selfe alone will sing,
The woods shall to me answer and my eccho ring.

Early before the worlds light giving lampe,
His golden beame upon the hils doth spred,   20
Having disperst the nights unchearefull dampe,
Doe ye awake, and with fresh lusty hed,
Go to the bowre of my belovèd love,
My truest turtle dove,
Bid her awake; for Hymen is awake,   25
And long since ready forth his maske to move,
With his bright tead that flames with many a flake,
And many a bachelor to waite on him,
In theyr fresh garments trim.
Bid her awake therefore and soone her dight,   30
For lo the wishèd day is come at last,
That shall for al the paynes and sorrowes past,
Pay to her usury of long delight:
And whylest she doth her dight,

EPITHALAMION: *Title:* wedding song. 25. *Hymen:* god of marriage. 27.
tead: processional torch.

Doe ye to her of joy and solace sing,   35
That all the woods may answer and your eccho ring.

Bring with you all the nymphes that you can heare
Both of the rivers and the forrests greene:
And of the sea that neighbours to her neare,
Al with gay girlands goodly wel beseene.   40
And let them also with them bring in hand,
Another gay girland
For my fayre love of lillyes and of roses,
Bound truelove wize with a blew silke riband.
And let them make great store of bridale poses,   45
And let them eeke bring store of other flowers
To deck the bridale bowers.
And let the ground whereas her foot shall tread,
For feare the stones her tender foot should wrong
Be strewed with fragrant flowers all along,   50
And diapred lyke the discolorèd mead.
Which done, doe at her chamber dore awayt,
For she will waken strayt,
The whiles doe ye this song unto her sing,
The woods shall to you answer and your eccho ring.   55

Ye nymphes of Mulla which with carefull heed,
The silver scaly trouts doe tend full well,
And greedy pikes which use therein to feed,
(Those trouts and pikes all others doo excell)
And ye likewise which keepe the rushy lake,   60
Where none doo fishes take,
Bynd up the locks the which hang scatterd light,
And in his waters which your mirror make,
Behold your faces as the christall bright,
That when you come whereas my love doth lie,   65
No blemish she may spie.
And eke ye lightfoot mayds which keepe the deere,
That on the hoary mountayne use to towre,
And the wylde wolves which seeke them to devoure,
With your steele darts doo chace from comming neer,   70
Be also present heere,
To helpe to decke her and to help to sing,
That all the woods may answer and your eccho ring.

---

51. *diapred:* ornamented.

Wake, now my love, awake; for it is time,
The rosy Morne long since left Tithones bed,   75
All ready to her silver coche to clyme,
And Phœbus gins to shew his glorious hed.
Hark how the cheerefull birds do chaunt theyr laies
And carrol of loves praise.
The merry larke hir mattins sings aloft,   80
The thrush replyes, the mavis descant playes,
The ouzell shrills, the ruddock warbles soft,
So goodly all agree with sweet consent,
To this dayes merriment.
Ah my deere love why doe ye sleepe thus long,   85
When meeter were that ye should now awake,
T'awayt the comming of your joyous make,
And hearken to the birds lovelearnèd song,
The deawy leaves among.
For they of joy and pleasance to you sing,   90
That all the woods them answer and theyr eccho ring.

My love is now awake out of her dreame,
And her fayre eyes like stars that dimmèd were
With darksome cloud, now shew theyr goodly beams
More bright then Hesperus his head doth rere.   95
Come now ye damzels, daughters of delight,
Helpe quickly her to dight,
But first come ye fayre houres which were begot
In Joves sweet paradice, of Day and Night,
Which doe the seasons of the yeare allot,   100
And al that ever in this world is fayre
Doe make and still repayre.
And ye three handmayds of the Cyprian Queene,
The which doe still adorne her beauties pride,
Helpe to addorne my beautifullest bride: 105
And as ye her array, still throw betweene
Some graces to be seene,
And as ye use to Venus, to her sing,
The whiles the woods shall answer and your eccho ring.

---

81. *mavis descant:* thrush melody. 82. *ouzell:* blackbird; *ruddock:* robin redbreast. 87. *make:* mate. 103. *handmayds:* the three Graces of brightness, joy, and bloom; *Cyprian Queene:* Venus.

Now is my love all ready forth to come,   110
Let all the virgins therefore well awayt,
And ye fresh boyes that tend upon her groome
Prepare your selves; for he is comming strayt.
Set all your things in seemely good aray
Fit for so joyfull day,   115
The joyfulst day that ever sunne did see.
Faire sun, shew forth thy favourable ray,
And let thy lifull heat not fervent be
For feare of burning her sunshyny face,
Her beauty to disgrace.   120
O fayrest Phœbus, father of the Muse,
If ever I did honour thee aright,
Or sing the thing, that mote thy mind delight,
Doe not thy servants simple boone refuse,
But let this day, let this one day be myne,   125
Let all the rest be thine.
Then I thy soverayne prayses loud wil sing,
That all the woods shal answer and theyr eccho ring.

Harke how the minstrels gin to shrill aloud
Their merry musick that resounds from far,   130
The pipe, the tabor, and the trembling croud,
That well agree withouten breach or jar.
But most of all the damzels doe delite,
When they their tymbrels smyte,
And thereunto doe daunce and carrol sweet,   135
That all the sences they doe ravish quite,
The whyles the boyes run up and downe the street,
Crying aloud with strong confusèd noyce,
As if it were one voyce.
Hymen io Hymen, Hymen they do shout,   140
That even to the heavens theyr shouting shrill
Doth reach, and all the firmament doth fill,
To which the people standing all about,
As in approvance doe thereto applaud
And loud advaunce her laud,   145
And evermore they Hymen, Hymen sing,
That al the woods them answer and theyr eccho ring.

Loe where she comes along with portly pace
Lyke Phœbe from her chamber of the East,

---

123. *mote:* might. 131. *croud:* early form of fiddle. 148. *portly:* queenly.

Arysing forth to run her mighty race,   150
Clad all in white, that seemes a virgin best.
So well it her beseemes that ye would weene
Some angell she had beene.
Her long loose yellow locks lyke golden wyre,
Sprinckled with perle, and perling flowres a tweene,   155
Doe lyke a golden mantle her attyre,
And being crownèd with a girland greene,
Seeme lyke some mayden queene.
Her modest eyes abashèd to behold
So many gazers, as on her do stare,   160
Upon the lowly ground affixèd are.
Ne dare lift up her countenance too bold,
But blush to heare her prayses sung so loud,
So farre from being proud.
Nathlesse doe ye still loud her prayses sing,   165
That all the woods may answer and your eccho ring.

Tell me ye merchants daughters did ye see
So fayre a creature in your towne before,
So sweet, so lovely, and so mild as she,
Adornd with beautyes grace and vertues store,   170
Her goodly eyes lyke saphyres shining bright,
Her forehead yvory white,
Her cheekes lyke apples which the sun hath rudded,
Her lips lyke cherryes charming men to byte,
Her brest like to a bowle of creame uncrudded,   175
Her paps lyke lyllies budded,
Her snowie necke lyke to a marble towre,
And all her body like a pallace fayre,
Ascending uppe with many a stately stayre,
To honors seat and chastities sweet bowre.   180
Why stand ye still ye virgins in amaze,
Upon her so to gaze,
Whiles ye forget your former lay to sing,
To which the woods did answer and your eccho ring.

But if ye saw that which no eyes can see,   185
The inward beauty of her lively spright,

---

150. *race:* cf. Psalms 19.5—"as a bridegroom coming out of his chamber,
and rejoiceth as a strong man to run a race." 175. *uncrudded:* uncurded.
177. *necke:* cf. Song of Solomon 7—"Thy neck is as a tower of ivory. . ."

Garnisht with heavenly guifts of high degree,
Much more then would ye wonder at that sight,
And stand astonisht lyke to those which red
Medusaes mazeful hed.   190
There dwels sweet love and constant chastity,
Unspotted fayth and comely womanhood,
Regard of honour and mild modesty,
There vertue raynes as queene in royal throne,
And giveth lawes alone.   195
The which the base affections doe obay,
And yeeld theyr services unto her will,
Ne thought of thing uncomely ever may
Thereto approch to tempt her mind to ill.
Had ye once seene these her celestial threasures,   200
And unrevealèd pleasures,
Then would ye wonder and her prayses sing,
That al the woods should answer and your echo ring.

Open the temple gates unto my love,
Open them wide that she may enter in,   205
And all the postes adorne as doth behove,
And all the pillours deck with girlands trim,
For to recyve this saynt with honour dew,
That commeth in to you.
With trembling steps and humble reverence,   210
She commeth in, before th'almighties vew,
Of her ye virgins learne obedience,
When so ye come into those holy places,
To humble your proud faces:
Bring her up to th'high altar, that she may   215
The sacred ceremonies there partake,
The which do endlesse matrimony make,
And let the roring organs loudly play
The praises of the Lord in lively notes,
The whiles with hollow throates   220
The choristers the joyous antheme sing,
That al the woods may answere and their eccho ring.

Behold whiles she before the altar stands
Hearing the holy priest that to her speakes
And blesseth her with his two happy hands,   225

---

189. *red:* looked at. 196. *affections:* passions. 204. *gates:* cf. Psalms 24.7—
"Lift up your heads, O ye gates . . . and the King of Glory shall come in."

How the red roses flush up in her cheekes,
And the pure snow with goodly vermill stayne,
Like crimsin dyde in grayne,
That even th'angels which continually,
About the sacred altare doe remaine,   230
Forget their service and about her fly,
Ofte peeping in her face that seemes more fayre,
The more they on it stare.
But her sad eyes still fastened on the ground,
Are governèd with goodly modesty,   235
That suffers not one looke to glaunce awry,
Which may let in a little thought unsownd.
Why blush ye love to give to me your hand,
The pledge of all our band?
Sing ye sweet angels, Alleluya sing,   240
That all the woods may answere and your eccho ring.

Now al is done; bring home the bride againe,
Bring home the triumph of our victory,
Bring home with you the glory of her gaine,
With joyance bring her and with jollity.   245
Never had man more joyfull day then this,
Whom heaven would heape with blis.
Make feast therefore now all this live long day,
This day for ever to me holy is,
Poure out the wine without restraint or stay,   250
Poure not by cups, but by the belly full,
Poure out to all that wull,
And sprinkle all the postes and wals with wine,
That they may sweat, and drunken be withall.
Crowne ye God Bacchus with a coronall,   255
And Hymen also crowne with wreathes of vine,
And let the Graces daunce unto the rest;
For they can doo it best:
The whiles the maydens doe theyr carroll sing,
To which the woods shal answer and theyr eccho ring.   260

Ring ye the bels, ye yong men of the towne,
And leave your wonted labors for this day:
This day is holy; doe ye write it downe,
That ye for ever it remember may.

---

228. *in grayne:* in fast color. 234. *sad:* modest. 239. *band:* bond.

This day the sunne is in his chiefest hight,   265
With Barnaby the bright,
From whence declining daily by degrees,
He somewhat loseth of his heat and light,
When once the Crab behind his back he sees.
But for this time it ill ordainèd was,   270
To chose the longest day in all the yeare,
And shortest night, when longest fitter weare:
Yet never day so long, but late would passe.
Ring ye the bels, to make it weare away,
And bonefiers make all day,   275
And daunce about them, and about them sing:
That all the woods may answer, and your eccho ring.

Ah when will this long weary day have end,
And lende me leave to come unto my love?
How slowly do the houres theyr numbers spend!   280
How slowly does sad Time his feathers move!
Hast thee O fayrest planet to thy home
Within the westerne fome:
Thy tyred steedes long since have need of rest.
Long though it be, at last I see it gloome,   285
And the bright evening star with golden creast
Appeare out of the East.
Fayre childe of beauty, glorious lampe of love
That all the host of heaven in rankes doost lead,
And guydest lovers through the nightes dread,   290
How chearefully thou lookest from above,
And seemst to laugh atweene thy twinkling light
As joying in the sight
Of these glad many which for joy doe sing,
That all the woods them answer and their echo ring.   295

Now ceasse ye damsels your delights forepast;
Enough is it, that all the day was youres:
Now day is doen, and night is nighing fast:
Now bring the bryde into the brydall boures.
Now night is come, now soone her disaray,   300
And in her bed her lay;
Lay her in lillies and in violets,
And silken courteins over her display,
And odourd sheetes, and Arras coverlets.

---

266. *Barnaby:* St. Barnabas' Day, the summer solstice.

Behold how goodly my faire love does ly   305
In proud humility;
Like unto Maia, when as Jove her tooke,
In Tempe, lying on the flowry gras,
Twixt sleepe and wake, after she weary was,
With bathing in the Acidalian brooke.   310
Now it is night, ye damsels may be gon,
And leave my love alone,
And leave likewise your former lay to sing:
The woods no more shal answere, nor your echo ring.

Now welcome night, thou night so long expected,   315
That long daies labour doest at last defray,
And all my cares, which cruell love collected,
Hast sumd in one, and cancellèd for aye:
Spread thy broad wing over my love and me,
That no man may us see,   320
And in thy sable mantle us enwrap,
From feare of perrill and foule horror free.
Let no false treason seeks us to entrap,
Nor any dread disquiet once annoy
The safety of our joy: 325
But let the night be calme and quietsome,
Without tempestuous storms or sad afray:
Lyke as when Jove with fayre Alcmena lay,
When he begot the great Tirynthian groome:
Or lyke as when he with thy selfe did lie,   330
And begot Majesty.
And let the mayds and yongmen cease to sing:
Ne let the woods them answer, nor theyr eccho ring.

Let no lamenting cryes, nor dolefull teares,
Be heard all night within nor yet without: 335
Ne let false whispers, breeding hidden feares,
Breake gentle sleepe with misconceivèd dout.
Let no deluding dreames, nor dreadful sights
Make sudden sad affrights;
Ne let housefyres, nor lightnings helpelesse harmes,   340
Ne let the pouke, nor other evill sprights,

---

307. *Maia:* the most beautiful of the Pleiades, was loved by Jove and bore Hermes. The Romans regarded her as a goddess of spring. 329. *Tirynthian groome:* Hercules. 330. *thy selfe:* Night.

Ne let mischivous witches with theyr charmes,
Ne let hob goblins, names whose sence we see not,
Fray us with things that be not.
Let not the shriech oule, nor the storke be heard: 345
Nor the night raven that still deadly yels,
Nor damnèd ghosts cald up with mighty spels,
Nor griesly vultures make us once affeard:
Ne let th'unpleasant quyre of frogs still croking
Make us to wish theyr choking. 350
Let none of these theyr drery accents sing;
Ne let the woods them answer, nor theyr eccho ring.

But let stil Silence trew night watches keepe,
That sacred peace may in assurance rayne,
And tymely sleep, when it is tyme to sleepe, 355
May poure his limbs forth on your pleasant playne,
The whiles an hundred little wingèd loves,
Like divers fethered doves,
Shall fly and flutter round about your bed,
And in the secret darke, that none reproves, 360
Their prety stealthes shal worke, and snares shal spread
To filch away sweet snatches of delight,
Conceald through covert night.
Ye sonnes of Venus, play your sports at will,
For greedy pleasure, carelesse of your toyes, 365
Thinks more upon her paradise of joyes,
Then what ye do, albe it good or ill.
All night therefore attend your merry play,
For it will soone be day:
Now none doth hinder you, that say or sing, 370
Ne will the woods now answer, nor your eccho ring.

Who is the same, which at my window peepes?
Or whose is that faire face, that shines so bright,
Is it not Cinthia, she that never sleepes,
But walkes about high heaven al the night? 375
O fayrest goddesse, do thou not envy
My love with me to spy:
For thou likewise didst love, though now unthought,
And for a fleece of woll, which privily,
The Latmian shephard once unto thee brought, 380
His pleasures with thee wrought.

---

380. *Latmian shephard:* Endymion.

Therefore to us be favorable now;
And sith of wemens labours thou hast charge,
And generation goodly dost enlarge,
Encline thy will t'effect our wishfull vow,   385
And the chast wombe informe with timely seed,
That may our comfort breed:
Till which we cease our hopefull hap to sing,
Ne let the woods us answere, nor our eccho ring.

And thou great Juno, which with awful might   390
The lawes of wedlock still dost patronize,
And the religion of the faith first plight
With sacred rites hast taught to solemnize:
And eeke for comfort often callèd art
Of women in their smart,   395
Eternally bind thou this lovely band,
And all thy blessings unto us impart.
And thou glad Genius, in whose gentle hand,
The bridale bowre and geniall bed remaine,
Without blemish or staine,   400
And the sweet pleasures of theyr loves delight
With secret ayde doest succour and supply,
Till they bring forth the fruitfull progeny,
Send us the timely fruit of this same night.
And thou fayre Hebe, and thou Hymen free,   405
Grant that it may so be.
Til which we cease your further prayse to sing,
Ne any woods shal answer, nor your eccho ring.

And ye high heavens, the temple of the gods,
In which a thousand torches flaming bright   410
Doe burne, that to us wretched earthly clods,
In dreadful darknesse lend desirèd light;
And all ye powers which in the same remayne,
More then we men can fayne,
Poure out your blessing on us plentiously,   415
And happy influence upon us raine,
That we may raise a large posterity,
Which from the earth, which they may long possesse,
With lasting happinesse,
Up to your haughty pallaces may mount,   420
And for the guerdon of theyr glorious merit

---

399. *geniall:* marriage.   421. *guerdon:* reward.

May heavenly tabernacles there inherit,
Of blessed saints for to increase the count.
So let us rest, sweet love, in hope of this,
And cease till then our tymely joyes to sing,   425
The woods no more us answer, nor our eccho ring.

Song made in lieu of many ornaments,
With which my love should duly have bene dect,
Which cutting off through hasty accidents,
Ye would not stay your dew time to expect,   430
But promist both to recompens,
Be unto her a goodly ornament,
And for short time an endlesse moniment.

❧

PROTHALAMION

(1596)

I

Calme was the day, and through the trembling ayre,
Sweete breathing *Zephyrus* did softly play
A gentle spirit, that lightly did delay
Hot *Titans* beames, which then did glyster fayre:
When I whom sullein care,   5
Through discontent of my long fruitlesse stay
In princes court, and expectation vayne
Of idle hopes, which still doe fly away,
Like empty shaddowes, did aflict my brayne,
Walkt forth to ease my payne   10
Along the shoare of silver streaming *Themmes,*
Whose rutty bancke, the which his river hemmes,
Was paynted all with variable flowers,
And all the meades adornd with daintie gemmes,
Fit to decke maydens bowres,   15
And crowne their paramours,
Against the brydale day, which is not long:
    Sweete *Themmes* runne softly, till I end my song.

PROTHALAMION: *Title:* spousal song, written in celebration of the double marriage of the daughters of the Earl of Worcester. 12. *rutty:* rooty.

2

There, in a meadow, by the rivers side,
A flocke of *nymphes* I chaunced to espy,   20
All lovely daughters of the flood thereby,
With goodly greenish locks all loose untyde,
As each had bene a bryde,
And each one had a little wicker basket,
Made of fine twigs entraylèd curiously,   25
In which they gathered flowers to fill their flasket:
And with fine fingers, cropt full feateously
The tender stalkes on hye.
Of every sort, which in that meadow grew,
They gathered some; the violet pallid blew,   30
The little dazie, that at evening closes,
The virgin lillie, and the primrose trew,
With store of vermeil roses,
To decke their bridegromes posies,
Against the brydale day, which was not long: 35
    Sweete *Themmes* runne softly, till I end my song.

3

With that, I saw two swannes of goodly hewe,
Come softly swimming downe along the Lee;
Two fairer birds I yet did never see:
The snow which doth the top of *Pindus* strew,   40
Did never whiter shew,
Nor *Jove* himselfe when he a swan would be
For love of *Leda,* whiter did appeare:
Yet *Leda* was they say as white as he,
Yet not so white as these, nor nothing neare;   45
So purely white they were,
That even the gentle streame, the which them bare,
Seem'd foule to them, and bad his billowes spare
To wet their silken feathers, least they might
Soyle their fayre plumes with water not so fayre,   50
And marre their beauties bright,
That shone as heavens light,
Against their brydale day, which was not long:
    Sweete *Themmes* runne softly, till I end my song.

---

27. *feateously:* neatly. 38. *Lee:* river flowing into the Thames.

4

Eftsoones the *nymphes,* which now had flowers their fill,   55
Ran all in haste, to see that silver brood,
As they came floating on the christal flood.
Whom when they sawe, they stood amazèd still,
Their wondring eyes to fill,
Them seem'd they never saw a sight so fayre,   60
Of fowles so lovely, that they sure did deeme
Them heavenly borne, or to be that same payre
Which through the skie draw *Venus* silver teeme,
For sure they did not seeme
To be begot of any earthly seede,   65
But rather angels or of angels breede:
Yet were they bred of *Somers-heat* they say,
In sweetest season, when each flower and weede
The earth did fresh aray,
So fresh they seem'd as day,   70
Even as their brydale day, which was not long:
    Sweete *Themmes* runne softly, till I end my song.

5

Then forth they all out of their baskets drew,
Great store of flowers, the honour of the field,
That to the sense did fragrant odours yeild,   75
All which upon those goodly birds they threw,
And all the waves did strew,
That like old *Peneus* waters they did seeme,
When downe along by pleasant *Tempes* shore
Scattred with flowres, through *Thessaly* they streeme,   80
That they appeare through lillies plenteous store,
Like a brydes chamber flore:
Two of those *nymphes,* meane while, two garlands bound,
Of freshest flowres which in that mead they found,
The which presenting all in trim array,   85
Their snowie foreheads therewithall they crownd,
Whil'st one did sing this lay,
Prepar'd against that day,
Against their brydale day, which was not long:
    Sweete *Themmes* runne softly, till I end my song.   90

---

55. *Eftsoones:* at once. 67. *Somers-heat:* play on Somerset, the maiden name of the brides. 78. *Peneus:* river in Thessaly, conventionally used in pastoral poetry.

6

Ye gentle birdes, the worlds faire ornament,
And heavens glorie, whom this happie hower
Doth leade unto your lovers blisfull bower,
Joy may you have and gentle hearts content
Of your loves couplement: 95
And let faire *Venus,* that is queene of love,
With her heart-quelling sonne upon you smile,
Whose smile they say, hath vertue to remove
All loves dislike, and friendships faultie guile
For ever to assoile.   100
Let endless peace your steadfast hearts accord,
And blessed plentie wait upon your bord,
And let your bed with pleasures chast abound,
That fruitfull issue may to you afford,
Which may your foes confound,   105
And make your joyes redound,
Upon your brydale day, which is not long:
   Sweete *Themme*s run softlie, till I end my song.

7

So ended she; and all the rest around
To her redoubled that her undersong,   110
Which said, their bridale daye should not be long.
And gentle Eccho from the neighbour ground,
Their accents did resound.
So forth those joyous birdes did passe along,
Adowne the Lee, that to them murmurde low,   115
As he would speake, but that he lackt a tong
Yeat did by signes his glad affection show,
Making his streame run slow.
And all the foule which in his flood did dwell
Gan flock about these twaine, that did excell   120
The rest, so far, as *Cynthia* doth shend
The lesser starres. So they enrangèd well,
Did on those two attend,
And their best service lend,
Against their wedding day, which was not long: 125
   Sweete *Themmes* run softly, till I end my song.

---

121. *shend:* surpass.

8

At length they all to mery *London* came,
To mery London, my most kyndly nurse,
That to me gave this lifes first native sourse:
Though from another place I take my name,   130
An house of auncient fame.
There when they came, whereas those bricky towres,
The which on *Themmes* brode agèd backe doe ryde,
Where now the studious lawyers have their bowers
There whylome wont the Templer Knights to byde,   135
Till they decayd through pride:
Next whereunto there standes a stately place,
Where oft I gaynèd giftes and goodly grace
Of that great lord, which therein wont to dwell,
Whose want too well now feeles my freendles case: 140
But Ah here fits not well
Olde woes but joyes to tell
Against the bridale daye, which is not long:
     Sweet *Themmes* runne softly, till I end my song.

9

Yet therein now doth lodge a noble peer,   145
Great *Englands* glory and the Worlds wide wonder,
Whose dreadfull name, late through all *Spaine* did thunder,
And *Hercules* two pillors standing neere,
Did make to quake and feare:
Faire branch of honor, flower of chevalrie,   150
That fillest *England* with thy triumphs fame,
Joy have thou of thy noble victorie,
And endlesse happinesse of thine owne name
That promiseth the same:
That through thy prowesse and victorious armes,   155
Thy country may be freed from forraine harmes:
And great *Elisaes* glorious name may ring
Through al the world, fil'd with thy wide alarmes,
Which some brave muse may sing
To ages following,   160
Upon the brydale day, which is not long:
     Sweete *Themmes* runne softly, till I end my song.

---

137. *place:* palace of Spenser's early patron, the Earl of Leicester. 145. *peer:*
Earl of Essex. 153. *name:* Devereux, with a play on *heureux,* "happy."
158. *alarmes:* call to arms.

10

From those high towers, this noble lord issuing,
Like Radiant *Hesper* when his golden hayre
In th'*Ocean* billowes he hath bathèd fayre,   165
Descended to the rivers open vewing,
With a great traine ensuing.
Above the rest were goodly to bee seene
Two gentle knights of lovely face and feature
Beseeming well the bower of anie queene,   170
With gifts of wit and ornaments of nature,
Fit for so goodly stature:
That like the twins of *Jove* they seem'd in sight,
Which decke the bauldricke of the Heavens bright.
They two forth pacing to the rivers side,   175
Received those two faire brides, their loves delight,
Which at th'appointed tyde,
Each one did make his bryde,
Against their brydale day, which is not long:
   Sweete *Themmes* runne softly, till I end my song.   180

❧

Christopher Marlowe

HERO AND LEANDER

(1598)

[*First Sestiad*]

On Hellespont, guilty of true love's blood,
In view, and opposite, two cities stood,
Sea-borderers, disjoined by Neptune's might;
The one Abydos, the other Sestos hight.

173. *twins:* Gemini, or Castor and Pollux, the sons of Jove (in the form of a swan) and Leda, and brothers of Helen from the same egg. Jove turned them into stars, the third sign of the zodiac, which the sun enters about May 21. They are commonly represented as riding white horses, and wearing egg-shaped helmets crowned with stars. 174. *bauldricke:* baldric, an ornamental belt worn over the shoulder; here the Milky Way, in which the Gemini are placed.
HERO AND LEANDER: *First Sestiad:* 4. *hight:* called.

At Sestos, Hero dwelt; Hero the fair,   5
Whom young Apollo courted for her hair,
And offered as a dower his burning throne,
Where she should sit for men to gaze upon.
The outside of her garments were of lawn,
The lining purple silk, with gilt stars drawn;   10
Her wide sleeves green, and bordered with a grove
Where Venus in her naked glory strove
To please the careless and disdainful eyes
Of proud Adonis, that before her lies;
Her kirtle blue, whereon was many a stain,   15
Made with the blood of wretched lovers slain.
Upon her head she ware a myrtle wreath,
From whence her veil reached to the ground beneath.
Her veil was artificial flowers and leaves,
Whose workmanship both man and beast deceives;   20
Many would praise the sweet smell as she passed,
When 'twas the odor which her breath forth cast;
And there for honey bees have sought in vain,
And, beat from thence, have lighted there again.
About her neck hung chains of pebble-stone,   25
Which, lightened by her neck, like diamonds shone.
She ware no gloves, for neither sun nor wind
Would burn or parch her hands, but to her mind,
Or warm or cool them, for they took delight
To play upon those hands, they were so white.   30
Buskins of shells all silvered, usèd she,
And branched with blushing coral to the knee,
Where sparrows perched, of hollow pearl and gold,
Such as the world would wonder to behold;
Those with sweet water oft her handmaid fills,   35
Which, as she went, would chirrup through the bills.
Some say, for her the fairest Cupid pined,
And, looking in her face, was strooken blind.
But this is true: so like was one the other,
As he imagined Hero was his mother;   40
And oftentimes into her bosom flew,
About her naked neck his bare arms threw,
And laid his childish head upon her breast,
And with still panting rocked, there took his rest.
So lovely fair was Hero, Venus' nun,   45
As nature wept, thinking she was undone,
Because she took more from her than she left

And of such wondrous beauty her bereft;
Therefore, in sign her treasure suffered wrack,
Since Hero's time hath half the world been black.   50
Amorous Leander, beautiful and young,
(Whose tragedy divine Musæus sung)
Dwelt at Abydos; since him dwelt there none
For whom succeeding times make greater moan.
His dangling tresses that were never shorn,   55
Had they been cut and unto Colchis borne,
Would have allured the vent'rous youth of Greece
To hazard more than for the Golden Fleece.
Fair Cynthia wished his arms might be her sphere;
Grief makes her pale, because she moves not there.   60
His body was as straight as Circe's wand;
Jove might have sipped out nectar from his hand.
Even as delicious meat is to the taste,
So was his neck in touching, and surpassed
The white of Pelops' shoulder. I could tell ye   65
How smooth his breast was, and how white his belly,
And whose immortal fingers did imprint
That heavenly path, with many a curious dint,
That runs along his back; but my rude pen
Can hardly blazon forth the loves of men,   70
Much less of powerful gods; let it suffice
That my slack muse sings of Leander's eyes,
Those orient cheeks and lips, exceeding his
That leapt into the water for a kiss
Of his own shadow, and despising many,   75
Died ere he could enjoy the love of any.
Had wild Hippolytus Leander seen,
Enamoured of his beauty had he been;
His presence made the rudest peasant melt,
That in the vast uplandish country dwelt;   80
The barbarous Thracian soldier, moved with nought,
Was moved with him, and for his favor sought.
Some swore he was a maid in man's attire,
For in his looks were all that men desire:
A pleasant smiling cheek, a speaking eye,   85

---

65. *Pelops' shoulder:* ivory one given him by Demeter after he had been
served to the gods and then restored to life. 73. *his:* Narcissus. 77. *Hippoly-tus:* son of Theseus and the Amazon, Hippolyta; he preferred hunting to
love.

A brow for love to banquet royally;
And such as knew he was a man, would say,
Leander, thou art made for amorous play;
Why art thou not in love, and loved of all?
Though thou be fair, yet be not thine own thrall.   90
   The men of wealthy Sestos every year,
For his sake whom their goddess held so dear,
Rose-cheeked Adonis, kept a solemn feast.
Thither resorted many a wand'ring guest
To meet their loves; such as had none at all,   95
Came lovers home from this great festival.
For every street, like to a firmament,
Glistered with breathing stars, who, where they went,
Frighted the melancholy earth, which deemed
Eternal heaven to burn, for so it seemed   100
As if another Phaeton had got
The guidance of the sun's rich chariot.
But, far above the loveliest, Hero shined,
And stole away th' enchanted gazer's mind;
For like sea-nymphs' inveigling harmony,   105
So was her beauty to the standers by.
Nor that night-wand'ring pale and wat'ry star
(When yawning dragons draw her thirling car
From Latmos' mount up to the gloomy sky,
Where, crowned with blazing light and majesty,   110
She proudly sits) more over-rules the flood,
Than she the hearts of those that near her stood.
Even as when gaudy nymphs pursue the chase,
Wretched Ixion's shaggy-footed race,
Incensed with savage heat, gallop amain   115
From steep pine-bearing mountains to the plain,
So ran the people forth to gaze upon her,
And all that viewed her were enamoured on her.
And as in fury of a dreadful fight,
Their fellows being slain or put to flight,   120
Poor soldiers stand with fear of death dead-strooken,
So at her presence all, surprised and tooken,
Await the sentence of her scornful eyes;
He whom she favors lives, the other dies.
There might you see one sigh, another rage,   125
And some, their violent passions to assuage,

---

108. *thirling:* hurtling.   114. *race:* Centaurs.

Compile sharp satires; but alas, too late,
For faithful love will never turn to hate.
And many, seeing great princes were denied,
Pined as they went, and thinking on her, died.   130
On this feast day, oh, cursed day and hour!
Went Hero thorough Sestos, from her tower
To Venus' temple, where unhappily,
As after chanced, they did each other spy.
So fair a church as this had Venus none;   135
The walls were of discolored jasper stone,
Wherein was Proteus carvèd, and o'erhead
A lively vine of green sea-agate spread,
Where by one hand light-headed Bacchus hung,
And with the other wine from grapes out-wrung.   140
Of crystal shining fair the pavement was;
The town of Sestos called it Venus' glass;
There might you see the gods in sundry shapes,
Committing heady riots, incest, rapes;
For know that underneath this radiant floor   145
Was Danaë's statue in a brazen tower;
Jove slyly stealing from his sister's bed
To dally with Idalian Ganymed,
And for his love Europa bellowing loud,
And tumbling with the rainbow in a cloud;   150
Blood-quaffing Mars heaving the iron net
Which limping Vulcan and his Cyclops set;
Love kindling fire to burn such towns as Troy;
Silvanus weeping for the lovely boy
That now is turned into a cypress tree,   155
Under whose shade the wood-gods love to be.
And in the midst a silver altar stood;
There Hero sacrificing turtles' blood,
Veiled to the ground, veiling her eyelids close,
And modestly they opened as she rose;   160
Thence flew love's arrow with the golden head,
And thus Leander was enamourèd.
Stone still he stood, and evermore he gazed,
Till with the fire that from his count'nance blazed,
Relenting Hero's gentle heart was strook;   165
Such force and virtue hath an amorous look.
   It lies not in our power to love or hate,

---

136. *discolored*: vari-colored. 158. *turtles'*: turtle doves'.

For will in us is over-ruled by fate.
When two are stripped, long ere the course begin
We wish that one should lose, the other win;   170
And one especially do we affect
Of two gold ingots, like in each respect.
The reason no man knows, let it suffice,
What we behold is censured by our eyes.
Where both deliberate, the love is slight;   175
Who ever loved, that loved not at first sight?
   He kneeled, but unto her devoutly prayed;
Chaste Hero to herself thus softly said:
Were I the saint he worships, I would hear him;
And as she spake these words, came somewhat near him.   180
He started up; she blushed as one ashamed;
Wherewith Leander much more was inflamed.
He touched her hand; in touching it she trembled;
Love deeply grounded hardly is dissembled.
These lovers parlèd by the touch of hands;   185
True love is mute, and oft amazèd stands.
Thus while dumb signs their yielding hearts entangled,
The air with sparks of living fire was spangled,
And night, deep drenched in misty Acheron,
Heaved up her head, and half the world upon   190
Breathed darkness forth (dark night is Cupid's day).
And now begins Leander to display
Love's holy fire with words, with sighs, and tears,
Which like sweet music entered Hero's ears;
And yet at every word she turned aside,   195
And always cut him off as he replied.
At last, like to a bold sharp sophister,
With cheerful hope thus he accosted her:
   Fair creature, let me speak without offence;
I would my rude words had the influence   200
To lead thy thoughts as thy fair looks do mine!
Then shouldst thou be his prisoner who is thine.
Be not unkind and fair; misshapen stuff
Are of behavior boisterous and rough.
Oh, shun me not, but hear me ere you go,   205
God knows I cannot force love, as you do.
My words shall be as spotless as my youth,
Full of simplicity and naked truth.
This sacrifice, whose sweet perfume descending
From Venus' altar to your footsteps bending,   210

Doth testify that you exceed her far,
To whom you offer, and whose nun you are.
Why should you worship her? her you surpass
As much as sparkling diamonds flaring glass.
A diamond set in lead his worth retains;   215
A heavenly nymph, beloved of human swains,
Receives no blemish, but ofttimes more grace;
Which makes me hope, although I am but base,
Base in respect of thee, divine and pure,
Dutiful service may thy love procure,   220
And I in duty will excel all other,
As thou in beauty dost exceed Love's mother.
Nor heaven, nor thou, were made to gaze upon;
As heaven preserves all things, so save thou one.
A stately builded ship, well rigged and tall,   225
The ocean maketh more majestical;
Why vowest thou then to live in Sestos here,
Who on love's seas more glorious would appear?
Like untuned golden strings all women are,
Which long time lie untouched, will harshly jar.   230
Vessels of brass, oft handled, brightly shine;
What difference betwixt the richest mine
And basest mold, but use? for both, not used,
Are of like worth. Then treasure is abused,
When misers keep it; being put to loan,   235
In time it will return us two for one.
Rich robes themselves and others do adorn;
Neither themselves nor others, if not worn.
Who builds a palace, and rams up the gate,
Shall see it ruinous and desolate.   240
Ah, simple Hero, learn thyself to cherish!
Lone women, like to empty houses, perish.
Less sins the poor rich man that starves himself
In heaping up a mass of drossy pelf,
Than such as you; his golden earth remains,   245
Which after his decease some other gains;
But this fair gem, sweet in the loss alone,
When you fleet hence, can be bequeathed to none.
Or if it could, down from th' enamelled sky
All heaven would come to claim this legacy,   250
And with intestine broils the world destroy,

214. *flaring:* glaring. 251. *intestine broils:* civil wars.

And quite confound nature's sweet harmony.
Well therefore by the gods decreed it is
We human creatures should enjoy that bliss.
One is no number; maids are nothing, then,   255
Without the sweet society of men.
Wilt thou live single still? one shalt thou be
Though never-singling Hymen couple thee.
Wild savages, that drink of running springs,
Think water far excels all earthly things,   260
But they that daily taste neat wine, despise it;
Virginity, albeit some highly prize it,
Compared with marriage, had you tried them both,
Differs as much as wine and water doth.
Base bullion for the stamp's sake we allow;   265
Even so for men's impression do we you,
By which alone, our reverend fathers say,
Women receive perfection every way.
This idol which you term virginity
Is neither essence subject to the eye,   270
No, nor to any one exterior sense,
Nor hath it any place of residence,
Nor is 't of earth or mould celestial,
Or capable of any form at all.
Of that which hath no being, do not boast;   275
Things that are not at all, are never lost.
Men foolishly do call it virtuous;
What virtue is it, that is born with us?
Much less can honor be ascribed thereto;
Honor is purchased by the deeds we do.   280
Believe me, Hero, honor is not won
Until some honorable deed be done.
Seek you, for chastity, immortal fame,
And know that some have wronged Diana's name?
Whose name is it, if she be false or not,   285
So she be fair, but some vile tongues will blot?
But you are fair, ay me, so wondrous fair,
So young, so gentle, and so debonair,
As Greece will think, if thus you live alone,
Some one or other keeps you as his own.   290
Then, Hero, hate me not, nor from me fly
To follow swiftly blasting infamy.

---

265. *stamp's:* coinage.

Perhaps thy sacred priesthood makes thee loath;
Tell me, to whom mad'st thou that heedless oath?
   To Venus, answered she, and as she spake,   295
Forth from those two tralucent cisterns brake
A stream of liquid pearl, which down her face
Made milk-white paths, whereon the gods might trace
To Jove's high court. He thus replied: The rites
In which love's beauteous empress most delights   300
Are banquets, Doric music, midnight revel,
Plays, masks, and all that stern age counteth evil.
Thee as a holy idiot doth she scorn,
For thou, in vowing chastity, hast sworn
To rob her name and honor, and thereby   305
Commit'st a sin far worse than perjury,
Even sacrilege against her deity,
Through regular and formal purity.
To expiate which sin, kiss and shake hands;
Such sacrifice as this Venus demands.   310
   Thereat she smiled, and did deny him so
As, put thereby, yet might he hope for mo.
Which makes him quickly reinforce his speech,
And her in humble manner thus beseech:
   Though neither gods nor men may thee deserve,   315
Yet for her sake whom you have vowed to serve,
Abandon fruitless cold virginity,
The gentle queen of love's sole enemy.
Then shall you most resemble Venus' nun,
When Venus' sweet rites are performed and done.   320
Flint-breasted Pallas joys in single life,
But Pallas and your mistress are at strife.
Love, Hero, then, and be not tyrannous,
But heal the heart that thou hast wounded thus;
Nor stain thy youthful years with avarice;   325
Fair fools delight to be accounted nice.
The richest corn dies if it be not reaped;
Beauty alone is lost, too warily kept.
These arguments he used, and many more,
Wherewith she yielded, that was won before.   330
Hero's looks yielded, but her words made war;
Women are won when they begin to jar.
Thus having swallowed Cupid's golden hook,

326. *nice:* coy.   332. *jar:* dispute.

The more she strived, the deeper was she strook;
Yet, evilly feigning anger, strove she still,   335
And would be thought to grant against her will.
So having paused a while, at last she said:
Who taught thee rhetoric to deceive a maid?
Ay me! such words as these should I abhor,
And yet I like them for the orator.   340
   With that Leander stooped to have embraced her,
But from his spreading arms away she cast her,
And thus bespake him: Gentle youth, forbear
To touch the sacred garments which I wear.
   Upon a rock, and underneath a hill,   345
Far from the town, where all is whist and still
Save that the sea playing on yellow sand
Sends forth a rattling murmur to the land,
Whose sound allures the golden Morpheus
In silence of the night to visit us,   350
My turret stands; and there, God knows, I play
With Venus' swans and sparrows all the day.
A dwarfish beldame bears me company,
That hops about the chamber where I lie,
And spends the night, that might be better spent,   355
In vain discourse and apish merriment.
Come thither. As she spake this, her tongue tripped,
For unawares, Come thither, from her slipped;
And suddenly her former color changed,
And here and there her eyes through anger ranged.   360
And like a planet moving several ways
At one self instant, she, poor soul, assays,
Loving, not to love at all, and every part
Strove to resist the motions of her heart;
And hands so pure, so innocent, nay such   365
As might have made heaven stoop to have a touch,
Did she uphold to Venus, and again
Vowed spotless chastity, but all in vain.
Cupid beats down her prayers with his wings;
Her vows above the empty air he flings;   370
All deep enraged, his sinewy bow he bent,
And shot a shaft that burning from him went;
Wherewith she, strooken, looked so dolefully,
As made Love sigh to see his tyranny.
And as she wept, her tears to pearl he turned,   375
And wound them on his arm, and for her mourned.

Then towards the palace of the Destinies,
Laden with languishment and grief, he flies,
And to those stern nymphs humbly made request,
Both might enjoy each other, and be blest.   380
But with a ghastly dreadful countenance,
Threat'ning a thousand deaths at every glance,
They answered Love, nor would vouchsafe so much
As one poor word, their hate to him was such.
Hearken awhile, and I will tell you why: 385
Heaven's wingèd herald, Jove-born Mercury,
The self-same day that he asleep had laid
Enchanted Argus, spied a country maid,
Whose careless hair, instead of pearl t' adorn it,
Glistered with dew, as one that seemed to scorn it;   390
Her breath as fragrant as the morning rose,
Her mind pure, and her tongue untaught to gloze;
Yet proud she was, for lofty pride that dwells
In towered courts is oft in shepherds' cells,
And too too well the fair vermilion knew,   395
And silver tincture of her cheeks, that drew
The love of every swain. On her this god
Enamoured was, and with his snaky rod
Did charm her nimble feet, and made her stay,
The while upon a hillock down he lay,   400
And sweetly on his pipe began to play,
And with smooth speech her fancy to assay;
Till in his twining arms he locked her fast,
And then he wooed with kisses, and at last,
As shepherds do, her on the ground he laid,   405
And tumbling in the grass, he often strayed
Beyond the bounds of shame, in being bold
To eye those parts which no eye should behold.
And like an insolent commanding lover,
Boasting his parentage, would needs discover   410
The way to new Elysium; but she,
Whose only dower was her chastity,
Having striv'n in vain, was now about to cry,
And crave the help of shepherds that were nigh.
Herewith he stayed his fury, and began   415
To give her leave to rise; away she ran;
After went Mercury, who used such cunning,

---

392. *gloze:* deceive.

As she, to hear his tale, left off her running;
Maids are not won by brutish force and might,
But speeches full of pleasure and delight;   420
And knowing Hermes courted her, was glad
That she such loveliness and beauty had
As could provoke his liking, yet was mute,
And neither would deny nor grant his suit.
Still vowed he love, she wanting no excuse   425
To feed him with delays, as women use,
Or thirsting after immortality—
All women are ambitious naturally—
Imposed upon her lover such a task
As he ought not perform, nor yet she ask.   430
A draught of flowing nectar she requested,
Wherewith the king of gods and men is feasted.
He, ready to accomplish what she willed,
Stole some from Hebe (Hebe Jove's cup filled)
And gave it to his simple rustic love;   435
Which being known (as what is hid from Jove?)
He inly stormed, and waxed more furious
Than for the fire filched by Prometheus,
And thrusts him down from heaven; he wand'ring here
In mournful terms, with sad and heavy cheer,
Complained to Cupid. Cupid, for his sake,   440
To be revenged on Jove did undertake;
And those on whom heaven, earth, and hell relies,
I mean the adamantine Destinies,
He wounds with love, and forced them equally   445
To dote upon deceitful Mercury.
They offered him the deadly fatal knife
That shears the slender threads of human life;
At his fair-feathered feet the engines laid
Which th' earth from ugly Chaos' den upweighed;   450
These he regarded not, but did entreat
That Jove, usurper of his father's seat,
Might presently be banished into hell,
And aged Saturn in Olympus dwell.
They granted what he craved, and once again   455
Saturn and Ops began their golden reign.
Murder, rape, war, lust, and treachery
Were with Jove closed in Stygian empery.
But long this blessed time continued not;
As soon as he his wishèd purpose got,   460

He, reckless of his promise, did despise
The love of th' everlasting Destinies.
They seeing it, both Love and him abhorred,
And Jupiter unto his place restored.
And but that Learning, in despite of Fate,   465
Will mount aloft, and enter heaven gate,
And to the seat of Jove itself advance,
Hermes had slept in hell with Ignorance;
Yet as a punishment they added this,
That he and Poverty should always kiss.   470
And to this day is every scholar poor;
Gross gold from them runs headlong to the boor.
Likewise, the angry sisters thus deluded,
To avenge themselves on Hermes, have concluded
That Midas' brood shall sit in Honor's chair,   475
To which the Muses' sons are only heir;
And fruitful wits that inaspiring are,
Shall, discontent, run into regions far;
And few great lords in virtuous deeds shall joy,
But be surprised with every garish toy;   480
And still enrich the lofty servile clown,
Who with encroaching guile keeps learning down.
Then muse not Cupid's suit no better sped,
Seeing in their loves the Fates were injurèd.

[Second Sestiad]

By this, sad Hero, with love unacquainted,
Viewing Leander's face, fell down and fainted.
He kissed her and breathed life into her lips,
Wherewith, as one displeased, away she trips.
Yet as she went, full often looked behind,   5
And many poor excuses did she find
To linger by the way, and once she stayed
And would have turned again, but was afraid,
In off'ring parley, to be counted light.
So on she goes, and in her idle flight,   10
Her painted fan of curlèd plumes let fall,
Thinking to train Leander therewithal.
He, being a novice, knew not what she meant,
But stayed, and after her a letter sent,
Which joyful Hero answered in such sort   15

Second Sestiad: 12. *train:* lure.

As he had hope to scale the beauteous fort
Wherein the liberal graces locked their wealth,
And therefore to her tower he got by stealth.
Wide open stood the door, he need not climb;
And she herself, before the 'pointed time,   20
Had spread the board, with roses strewed the room,
And oft looked out, and mused he did not come.
At last he came; oh, who can tell the greeting
These greedy lovers had at their first meeting.
He asked, she gave, and nothing was denied;   25
Both to each other quickly were affied.
Look how their hands, so were their hearts united,
And what he did she willingly requited.
Sweet are the kisses, the embracements sweet,
When like desires and affections meet;   30
For from the earth to heaven is Cupid raised,
Where fancy is in equal balance peised.
Yet she this rashness suddenly repented,
And turned aside, and to herself lamented,
As if her name and honor had been wronged   35
By being possessed of him for whom she longed;
Ay, and she wished, albeit not from her heart,
That he would leave her turret and depart.
The mirthful god of amorous pleasure smiled
To see how he this captive nymph beguiled;   40
For hitherto he did but fan the fire,
And kept it down that it might mount the higher.
Now waxed she jealous lest his love abated,
Fearing her own thoughts made her to be hated.
Therefore unto him hastily she goes,   45
And like light Salmacis, her body throws
Upon his bosom, where with yielding eyes
She offers up herself, a sacrifice
To slake his anger if he were displeased.
Oh, what god would not therewith be appeased?   50
Like Æsop's cock, this jewel he enjoyed,
And as a brother with his sister toyed,
Supposing nothing else was to be done,
Now he her favor and goodwill had won.
But know you not that creatures wanting sense   55

---

26. *affied:* affianced. 32. *peised:* weighted. 51. *Æsop's cock:* who did not
know what to do with a jewel in place of a grain of corn.

By nature have a mutual appetence,
And wanting organs to advance a step,
Moved by love's force, unto each other lep?
Much more in subjects having intellect,
Some hidden influence breeds like effect. 60
Albeit Leander, rude in love and raw,
Long dallying with Hero, nothing saw
That might delight him more, yet he suspected
Some amorous rites or other were neglected.
Therefore unto his body hers he clung; 65
She, fearing on the rushes to be flung,
Strived with redoubled strength; the more she strived,
The more a gentle pleasing heat revived,
Which taught him all that elder lovers know;
And now the same gan so to scorch and glow, 70
As in plain terms, yet cunningly, he craved it;
Love always makes those eloquent that have it.
She, with a kind of granting, put him by it,
And ever as he thought himself most nigh it,
Like to the tree of Tantalus she fled, 75
And, seeming lavish, saved her maidenhead.
Ne'er king more sought to keep his diadem,
Than Hero this inestimable gem.
Above our life we love a steadfast friend,
Yet when a token of great worth we send, 80
We often kiss it, often look thereon,
And stay the messenger that would be gone;
No marvel then though Hero would not yield
So soon to part from that she dearly held;
Jewels being lost are found again, this never; 85
'Tis lost but once, and once lost, lost forever.
  Now had the morn espied her lover's steeds,
Whereat she starts, puts on her purple weeds,
And, red for anger that he stayed so long,
All headlong throws herself the clouds among. 90
And now Leander, fearing to be missed,
Embraced her suddenly, took leave, and kissed.
Long was he taking leave, and loath to go,
And kissed again, as lovers use to do.
Sad Hero wrung him by the hand and wept, 95
Saying, Let your vows and promises be kept.

61. *rude:* ignorant.

Then, standing at the door, she turned about,
As loath to see Leander going out.
And now the sun that through th' horizon peeps,
As pitying these lovers, downward creeps,   100
So that in silence of the cloudy night,
Though it was morning, did he take his flight.
But what the secret trusty night concealed,
Leander's amorous habit soon revealed;
With Cupid's myrtle was his bonnet crowned,   105
About his arms the purple riband wound
Wherewith she wreathed her largely-spreading hair;
Nor could the youth abstain, but he must wear
The sacred ring wherewith she was endowed,
When first religious chastity she vowed;   110
Which made his love through Sestos to be known,
And thence unto Abydos sooner blown
Than he could sail, for incorporeal Fame,
Whose weight consists in nothing but her name,
Is swifter than the wind, whose tardy plumes   115
Are reeking water and dull earthly fumes.
Home, when he came, he seemed not to be there,
But like exilèd air thrust from his sphere,
Set in a foreign place; and straight from thence,
Alcides like, by mighty violence   120
He would have chased away the swelling main
That him from her unjustly did detain.
Like as the sun in a diameter
Fires and inflames objects removèd far,
And heateth kindly, shining lat'rally,   125
So beauty sweetly quickens when 'tis nigh,
But being separated and removed,
Burns where it cherished, murders where it loved.
Therefore even as an index to a book,
So to his mind was young Leander's look.   130
Oh, none but gods have power their love to hide;
Affection by the count'nance is descried.
The light of hidden fire itself discovers,
And love that is concealed betrays poor lovers.
His secret flame apparently was seen;   135
Leander's father knew where he had been,

---

104. *amorous habit:* lover's dress. 113. *Fame:* rumor. 120. *Alcides:* Hercules. 135. *apparently:* clearly.

And for the same mildly rebuked his son,
Thinking to quench the sparkles new begun.
But love, resisted once, grows passionate,
And nothing more than counsel lovers hate;   140
For as a hot proud horse highly disdains
To have his head controlled, but breaks the reins,
Spits forth the ringled bit, and with his hooves
Checks the submissive ground, so he that loves,
The more he is restrained, the worse he fares.   145
What is it now but mad Leander dares?
O Hero, Hero! thus he cried full oft,
And then he got him to a rock aloft,
Where having spied her tower, long stared he on 't,
And prayed the narrow toiling Hellespont   150
To part in twain, that he might come and go;
But still the rising billows answered no.
With that he stripped him to the iv'ry skin,
And crying, Love, I come, leaped lively in.
Whereat the sapphire-visaged god grew proud,   155
And made his cap'ring Triton sound aloud,
Imagining that Ganymede, displeased,
Had left the heavens; therefore on him he seized.
Leander strived; the waves about him wound,
And pulled him to the bottom, where the ground   160
Was strewed with pearl, and in low coral groves
Sweet singing mermaids sported with their loves
On heaps of heavy gold, and took great pleasure
To spurn in careless sort the shipwreck treasure.
For here the stately azure palace stood,   165
Where kingly Neptune and his train abode.
The lusty god embraced him, called him love,
And swore he never should return to Jove.
But when he knew it was not Ganymed,
For under water he was almost dead,   170
He heaved him up, and looking on his face,
Beat down the bold waves with his triple mace,
Which mounted up, intending to have kissed him,
And fell in drops like tears, because they missed him.
Leander, being up, began to swim,   175
And looking back, saw Neptune follow him;
Whereat aghast, the poor soul gan to cry:
Oh, let me visit Hero ere I die!
The god put Helle's bracelet on his arm,

And swore the sea should never do him harm.   180
He clapped his plump cheeks, with his tresses played,
And smiling wantonly, his love bewrayed.
He watched his arms, and as they opened wide,
At every stroke betwixt them would he slide,
And steal a kiss, and then run out and dance,   185
And as he turned, cast many a lustful glance,
And threw him gaudy toys to please his eye,
And dive into the water, and there pry
Upon his breast, his thighs, and every limb,
And up again, and close beside him swim,   190
And talk of love. Leander made reply:
You are deceived, I am no woman, I.
Thereat smiled Neptune, and then told a tale
How that a shepherd, sitting in a vale,
Played with a boy so fair and kind,   195
As for his love both earth and heaven pined;
That of the cooling river durst not drink
Lest water-nymphs should pull him from the brink;
And when he sported in the fragrant lawns,
Goat-footed satyrs and up-staring fauns   200
Would steal him thence. Ere half this tale was done,
Ay me, Leander cried, th' enamoured sun,
That now should shine on Thetis' glassy bower,
Descends upon my radiant Hero's tower.
Oh, that these tardy arms of mine were wings!   205
And as he spake, upon the waves he springs.
Neptune was angry that he gave no ear,
And in his heart revenging malice bear;
He flung at him his mace, but as it went
He called it in, for love made him repent.   210
The mace returning back, his own hand hit,
As meaning to be venged for darting it.
When this fresh bleeding wound Leander viewed,
His color went and came, as if he rued
The grief which Neptune felt. In gentle breasts   215
Relenting thoughts, remorse, and pity rests;
And who have hard hearts and obdurate minds
But vicious, hare-brained, and illit'rate hinds?
The god, seeing him with pity to be moved,
Thereon concluded that he was beloved.   220
(Love is too full of faith, too credulous,
With folly and false hope deluding us.)

Wherefore, Leander's fancy to surprise,
To the rich oceän for gifts he flies.
'Tis wisdom to give much; a gift prevails   225
When deep persuading oratory fails.
By this, Leander being near the land,
Cast down his weary feet, and felt the sand.
Breathless albeit he were, he rested not
Till to the solitary tower he got,   230
And knocked and called, at which celestial noise
The longing heart of Hero much more joys
Than nymphs or shepherds when the timbrel rings,
Or crooked dolphin when the sailor sings;
She stayed not for her robes, but straight arose,   235
And drunk with gladness, to the door she goes;
Where seeing a naked man, she screeched for fear,
(Such sights as this to tender maids are rare)
And ran into the dark herself to hide.
Rich jewels in the dark are soonest spied;   240
Unto her was he led, or rather drawn,
By those white limbs which sparkled through the lawn.
The nearer that he came, the more she fled,
And seeking refuge, slipped into her bed.
Whereon Leander sitting, thus began,   245
Through numbing cold all feeble, faint, and wan:
    If not for love, yet, love, for pity sake,
Me in thy bed and maiden bosom take;
At least vouchsafe these arms some little room,
Who, hoping to embrace thee, cheerly swoom;   250
This head was beat with many a churlish billow,
And therefore let it rest upon thy pillow.
Herewith affrighted Hero shrunk away,
And in her lukewarm place Leander lay,
Whose lively heat like fire from heaven fet,   255
Would animate gross clay, and higher set
The drooping thoughts of base declining souls,
Than dreary Mars carousing nectar bowls.
His hands he cast upon her like a snare;
She, overcome with shame and sallow fear,   260
Like chaste Diana, when Actæon spied her,
Being suddenly betrayed, dived down to hide her;
And as her silver body downward went,
With both her hands she made the bed a tent,
And in her own mind thought herself secure,   265

O'ercast with dim and darksome coverture.
And now she lets him whisper in her ear,
Flatter, entreat, promise, protest, and swear;
Yet ever as he greedily assayed
To touch those dainties, she the harpy played,   270
And every limb did, as a soldier stout,
Defend the fort and keep the foeman out;
For though the rising iv'ry mount he scaled,
Which is with azure circling lines empaled,
Much like a globe (a globe may I term this,   275
By which love sails to regions full of bliss)
Yet there with Sisyphus he toiled in vain,
Till gentle parley did the truce obtain.
Wherein Leander on her quivering breast,
Breathless spoke something, and sighed out the rest;   280
Which so prevailed, as he with small ado
Enclosed her in his arms and kissed her too.
And every kiss to her was as a charm,
And to Leander as a fresh alarm,
So that the truce was broke, and she, alas,   285
Poor silly maiden, at his mercy was.
Love is not full of pity, as men say,
But deaf and cruel where he means to prey.
Even as a bird, which in our hands we wring,
Forth plunges and oft flutters with her wing,   290
She trembling strove; this strife of hers, like that
Which made the world, another world begat
Of unknown joy. Treason was in her thought,
And cunningly to yield herself she sought.
Seeming not won, yet won she was at length;   295
In such wars women use but half their strength.
Leander now, like Theban Hercules,
Entered the orchard of th' Hesperides,
Whose fruit none rightly can describe but he
That pulls or shakes it from the golden tree.   300
And now she wished this night were never done,
And sighed to think upon th' approaching sun;
For much it grieved her that the bright daylight
Should know the pleasure of this blessed night,
And them like Mars and Erycine displayed,   305
Both in each other's arms chained as they laid.

305. *Erycine:* Venus.

Again she knew not how to frame her look,
Or speak to him who in a moment took
That which so long so charily she kept;
And fain by stealth away she would have crept,   310
And to some corner secretly have gone,
Leaving Leander in the bed alone.
But as her naked feet were whipping out,
He on the sudden clinged her so about,
That mermaid-like unto the floor she slid,   315
One half appeared, the other half was hid.
Thus near the bed she blushing stood upright,
And from her countenance behold ye might
A kind of twilight break, which through the hair,
As from an orient cloud, glimpse here and there;   320
And round about the chamber this false morn
Brought forth the day before the day was born.
So Hero's ruddy cheek Hero betrayed,
And her all naked to his sight displayed;
Whence his admiring eyes more pleasure took   325
Than Dis on heaps of gold fixing his look.
By this, Apollo's golden harp began
To sound forth music to the oceän;
Which watchful Hesperus no sooner heard,
But he the day-bright-bearing car prepared,   330
And ran before, as harbinger of light,
And with his flaring beams mocked ugly night
Till she, o'ercome with anguish, shame, and rage,
Danged down to hell her loathsome carriage.
    Desunt nonnulla.   335

❧

THE PASSIONATE SHEPHERD TO HIS LOVE

(1600)

Come live with me and be my love,
And we will all the pleasures prove
That valleys, groves, hills, and fields,
Woods, or steepy mountain yields.

---

326. *Dis:* Pluto, god of wealth. 334. *Danged:* threw. 335. *Desunt nonnulla:* something is missing, *i.e.,* the remaining four Sestiads—later added by George Chapman.

And we will sit upon the rocks,   5
Seeing the shepherds feed their flocks,
By shallow rivers to whose falls
Melodious birds sing madrigals.

And I will make thee beds of roses
And a thousand fragrant posies,   10
A cap of flowers, and a kirtle
Embroidered all with leaves of myrtle;

A gown made of the finest wool
Which from our pretty lambs we pull;
Fair linèd slippers for the cold,   15
With buckles of the purest gold;

A belt of straw and ivy buds,
With coral clasps and amber studs:
And if these pleasures may thee move,
Come live with me, and be my love.   20

The shepherds' swains shall dance and sing
For thy delight each May morning:
If these delights thy mind may move,
Then live with me and be my love.

❧

Sir Walter Ralegh

THE NYMPH'S REPLY TO THE SHEPHERD

(1600)

If all the world and love were young,
And truth in every shepherd's tongue,
These pretty pleasures might me move
To live with thee and be thy love.

Time drives the flocks from field to fold   5
When rivers rage and rocks grow cold,
And Philomel becometh dumb;
The rest complains of cares to come.

The flowers do fade, and wanton fields
To wayward winter reckoning yields;   10

A honey tongue, a heart of gall,
Is fancy's spring, but sorrow's fall.

Thy gowns, thy shoes, thy beds of roses,
Thy cap, thy kirtle, and thy posies
Soon break, soon wither, soon forgotten,—   15
In folly ripe, in reason rotten.

Thy belt of straw and ivy buds,
Thy coral clasps and amber studs,
All these in me no means can move
To come to thee and be thy love.   20

But could youth last and love still breed,
Had joys no date nor age no need,
Then these delights my mind might move
To live with thee and be thy love.

❧

A DESCRIPTION OF LOVE
(1600)

Now what is love? I pray thee, tell.
It is that fountain and that well
Where pleasure and repentance dwell.
It is perhaps that saucing bell
That tolls all into heaven or hell: 5
And this is love, as I hear tell.

Yet what is love? I pray thee say.
It is a work on holy-day;
It is December matched with May;
When lusty bloods, in fresh array,   10
Hear ten months after of the play:
And this is love, as I hear say.

Yet what is love? I pray thee sain.
It is a sunshine mixed with rain;
It is a tooth-ache, or like pain;   15
It is a game where none doth gain;
The lass saith no, and would full fain:
And this is love, as I hear sain.

A DESCRIPTION OF LOVE: 4. *saucing:* sanctus.

Yet what is love? I pray thee say.
It is a yea, it is a nay,   20
A pretty kind of sporting fray;
It is a thing will soon away;
Then take the vantage while you may:
And this is love, as I hear say.

Yet what is love, I pray thee show.   25
A thing that creeps, it cannot go;
A prize that passeth to and fro;
A thing for one, a thing for mo;
And he that proves must find it so:
And this is love, sweet friend, I trow.

&

THE LIE

(1608)

Go, soul, the body's guest,
Upon a thankless arrant.
Fear not to touch the best;
The truth shall be thy warrant.
  Go, since I needs must die,   5
  And give the world the lie.

Say to the court, it glows
And shines like rotten wood;
Say to the church, it shows
What's good, and doth no good: 10
  If church and court reply,
  Then give them both the lie.

Tell potentates, they live
Acting by others' action,
Not loved unless they give,   15
Not strong but by affection:
  If potentates reply,
  Give potentates the lie.

THE LIE: 2. *arrant:* errand.

Tell men of high condition
That manage the estate,   20
Their purpose is ambition,
Their practice only hate:
   And if they once reply,
   Then give them all the lie.

Tell them that brave it most,   25
They beg for more by spending,
Who, in their greatest cost,
Like nothing but commending:
   And if they make reply,
   Then give them all the lie.   30

Tell zeal it wants devotion;
Tell love it is but lust;
Tell time it meets but motion;
Tell flesh it is but dust:
   And wish them not reply,   35
   For thou must give the lie.

Tell age it daily wasteth;
Tell honor how it alters;
Tell beauty how she blasteth;
Tell favor how it falters: 40
   And as they shall reply,
   Give every one the lie.

Tell wit how much it wrangles
In tickle points of niceness;
Tell wisdom she entangles   45
Herself in over-wiseness:
   And when they do reply,
   Straight give them both the lie.

Tell physic of her boldness;
Tell skill it is pretension;   50
Tell charity of coldness;
Tell law it is contention:
   And as they do reply,
   So give them still the lie.

---

25. *brave:* put on a showy front. 44. *tickle . . . niceness:* empty hair-splitting.

Tell fortune of her blindness;　　　　55
Tell nature of decay;
Tell friendship of unkindness;
Tell justice of delay:
　　And if they will reply,
　　Then give them all the lie.　　　　60

Tell arts they have no soundness,
But vary by esteeming;
Tell schools they want profoundness,
And stand too much on seeming:
　　If arts and schools reply,　　　　65
　　Give arts and schools the lie.

Tell faith it's fled the city;
Tell how the country erreth;
Tell manhood shakes off pity,
Tell virtue least preferrèd:　　　　70
　　And if they do reply,
　　Spare not to give the lie.

So when thou hast, as I
Commanded thee, done blabbing,
Because to give the lie　　　　75
Deserves no less than stabbing,
　　Stab at thee he that will—
　　No stab thy soul can kill.

❧

TO HIS SON

Three things there be that prosper all apace
And flourish, while they are asunder far;
But on a day they meet all in a place,
And when they meet, they one another mar.
And they be these: the wood, the weed, the wag.　　　5
The wood is that that makes the gallows tree;
The weed is that that strings the hangman's bag;
The wag, my pretty knave, betokens thee.
Now mark, dear boy: while these assemble not,
Green springs the tree, hemp grows, the wag is wild;　　10
But when they meet, it makes the timber rot,

It frets the halter, and it chokes the child.
God bless the child!

❧

NATURE, THAT WASHED HER HANDS

Nature, that washed her hands in milk,
  And had forgot to dry them,
Instead of earth took snow and silk,
  At love's request to try them,
If she a mistress could compose   5
To please love's fancy out of those.

Her eyes he would should be of light,
  A violet breath, and lips of jelly;
Her hair not black, nor overbright,
  And of the softest down her belly;   10
As for her inside he 'ld have it
Only of wantonness and wit.

At love's entreaty such a one
  Nature made, but with her beauty
She hath framed a heart of stone;   15
  So as love, by ill destiny,
Must die for her whom nature gave him,
Because her darling would not save him.

But time (which nature doth despise
  And rudely gives her love the lie,   20
Makes hope a fool, and sorrow wise)
  His hands do neither wash nor dry;

NATURE, THAT WASHED HER HANDS: *Title:* This poem was not published until 1889. In the year of Ralegh's death the following version of the last stanza was published with the heading "By Sir W. R. which he writ the night before his execution."

Even such is time, which takes in trust
Our youth, our joys, and all we have,
And pays us but with age and dust,
Within the dark and silent grave;
When we have wavered all our ways,
Shuts up the story of our days,
And from which earth, and grave, and dust,
The Lord will raise me up, I trust.

But being made of steel and rust,
Turns snow and silk and milk to dust.

The light, the belly, lips, and breath,   25
   He dims, discolors, and destroys;
With those he feeds but fills not death,
   Which sometimes were the food of joys.
Yea, time doth dull each lively wit,
And dries all wantonness with it.   30

Oh, cruel time! which takes in trust
   Our youth, our joys, and all we have,
And pays us but with age and dust;
   Who in the dark and silent grave
When we have wandered all our ways   35
Shuts up the story of our days.

∼∾

THE PASSIONATE MAN'S PILGRIMAGE
(1604)

Give me my scallop-shell of quiet,
My staff of faith to walk upon,
My scrip of joy, immortal diet,
My bottle of salvation,
My gown of glory, hope's true gage,   5
And thus I'll take my pilgrimage.

Blood must be my body's balmer,
No other balm will there be given,
Whilst my soul like a white palmer
Travels to the land of heaven,   10
Over the silver mountains,
Where spring the nectar fountains;
And there I'll kiss
The bowl of bliss,
And drink my eternal fill   15
On every milken hill.
My soul will be a-dry before,
But after it will ne'er thirst more;

THE PASSIONATE MAN'S PILGRIMAGE: 1. *scallop-shell:* pilgrim's badge. 3.
scrip: small bag

And by the happy blissful way
More peaceful pilgrims I shall see,   20
That have shook off their gowns of clay
And go appareled fresh like me.
I'll bring them first
To slake their thirst,
And then to taste those nectar suckets,   25
At the clear wells
Where sweetness dwells,
Drawn up by saints in crystal buckets.

And when our bottles and all we
Are filled with immortality,   30
Then the holy paths we'll travel,
Strewed with rubies thick as gravel,
Ceilings of diamonds, sapphire floors,
High walls of coral, and pearl bowers.

From thence to heaven's bribeless hall   35
Where no corrupted voices brawl,
No conscience molten into gold,
Nor forged accusers bought and sold,
No cause deferred, nor vain-spent journey,
For there Christ is the king's attorney,   40
Who pleads for all without degrees,
And he hath angels, but no fees.
When the grand twelve million jury
Of our sins and sinful fury,
'Gainst our souls black verdicts give,   45
Christ pleads his death, and then we live.
Be thou my speaker, taintless pleader,
Unblotted lawyer, true proceeder,
Thou movest salvation even for alms,
Not with a bribèd lawyer's palms.   50

And this is my eternal plea
To him that made heaven, earth, and sea,
Seeing my flesh must die so soon,
And want a head to dine next noon,
Just at the stroke when my veins start and spread,   55
Set on my soul an everlasting head.

25. *suckets:* sweets. 41. *without degrees:* regardless of rank. 42. *angels:*
pun on angel, name of coin.

Then am I ready, like a palmer fit,
To tread those blest paths which before I writ.

❧

Fulke Greville

CHORUS SACERDOTUM
(1609)

Oh, wearisome condition of humanity,
Born under one law, to another bound;
Vainly begot, and yet forbidden vanity,
Created sick, commanded to be sound.
What meaneth nature by these diverse laws?　　　　5
Passion and reason self-division cause.
It is the mark or majesty of power
To make offences that it may forgive.
Nature herself doth her own self deflower,
To hate those errors she herself doth give.　　　　10
For how should man think that he may not do,
If nature did not fail and punish too?
Tyrant to others, to herself unjust,
Only commands things difficult and hard,
Forbids us all things which it knows is lust,　　　　15
Makes easy pains, unpossible reward.
If nature did not take delight in blood,
She would have made more easy ways to good.
We that are bound by vows and by promotion,
With pomp of holy sacrifice and rites,　　　　20
To teach belief in God and still devotion,
To preach of heaven's wonders and delights,—
Yet when each of us in his own heart looks
He finds the God there far unlike his books.

❧

CHORUS SACERDOTUM: *Title: Sacerdotum:* priests; the lines are spoken in
the play *Mustapha.* 21. *still:* instil.

SION LIES WASTE
(1609)

Sion lies waste, and thy Jerusalem,
O Lord, is fallen to utter desolation;
Against thy prophets and thy holy men
The sin hath wrought a fatal combination;
    Profaned thy name, thy worship overthrown,   5
    And made thee, living Lord, a God unknown.

Thy powerful laws, thy wonders of creation,
Thy word incarnate, glorious heaven, dark hell,
Lie shadowed under man's degeneration;
Thy Christ still crucified for doing well;   10
    Impiety, O Lord, sits on thy throne,
    Which makes thee, living light, a God unknown.

Man's superstition hath thy truths entombed,
His atheism again her pomps defaceth;
That sensual unsatiable vast womb   15
Of thy seen church thy unseen church disgraceth.
    There lives no truth with them that seem thine own,
    Which makes thee, living Lord, a God unknown.

Yet unto thee, Lord, mirror of transgression,
We who for earthly idols have forsaken   20
Thy heavenly image, sinless, pure impression,
And so in nets of vanity lie taken,
    All desolate implore that to thine own,
    Lord, thou no longer live a God unknown.

Yet, Lord, let Israel's plagues not be eternal,   25
Nor sin forever cloud thy sacred mountains,
Nor with false flames, spiritual but infernal,
Dry up thy mercy's ever springing fountains.
    Rather, sweet Jesus, fill up time and come
    To yield the sin her everlasting doom.   30

CÆLICA, I OVERNIGHT
(1633)

Cælica, I overnight was finely used,
Lodged in the midst of paradise, your heart;
Kind thoughts had charge I might not be refused,
Of every fruit and flower I had part.

But curious knowledge, blown with busy flame, 5
The sweetest fruits had in down shadows hidden,
And for it found mine eyes had seen the same,
I from my paradise was straight forbidden.

Where that cur, rumor, runs in every place,
Barking with care, begotten out of fear; 10
And glassy honor, tender of disgrace,
Stand seraphim to see I come not there;
   While that fine soil which all these joys did yield,
   By broken fence is proved a common field.

AWAY WITH THESE SELF-LOVING LADS
(1600)

Away with these self-loving lads,
Whom Cupid's arrow never glads.
Away, poor souls that sigh and weep,
In love of them that lie and sleep;
   For Cupid is a meadow god, 5
   And forceth none to kiss the rod.

God Cupid's shaft, like destiny,
Doth either good or ill decree.
Desert is born out of his bow,
Reward upon his feet doth go. 10
   What fools are they that have not known
   That Love likes no laws but his own?

My songs they be of Cynthia's praise,
I wear her rings on holy-days,
On every tree I write her name,   15
And every day I read the same.
   Where Honor, Cupid's rival, is,
   There miracles are seen of his.

If Cynthia crave her ring of me,
I blot her name out of the tree.   20
If doubt do darken things held dear,
Then welfare nothing once a year.
   For many run, but one must win;
   Fools only hedge the cuckoo in.

The worth that worthiness should move   25
Is love, which is the due of love.
And love as well the shepherd can
As can the mighty nobleman.
   Sweet nymph, 'tis true you worthy be,
   Yet without love, nought worth to me.   30

❧

Michael Drayton

From *Idea*

(1594, 1599, 1602, 1619)

HOW MANY PALTRY, FOOLISH, PAINTED THINGS

How many paltry, foolish, painted things,
That now in coaches trouble ev'ry street,
Shall be forgotten, whom no poet sings,
Ere they be well wrapped in their winding sheet!
Where I to thee eternity shall give,   5
When nothing else remaineth of these days,
And queens hereafter shall be glad to live
Upon the alms of thy superfluous praise;
Virgins and matrons reading these my rhymes

Shall be so much delighted with thy story   10
That they shall grieve they lived not in these times,
To have seen thee, their sex's only glory.
  So shalt thou fly above the vulgar throng,
  Still to survive in my immortal song.

AS OTHER MEN, SO I MYSELF DO MUSE

As other men, so I myself do muse
Why in this sort I wrest invention so,
And why these giddy metaphors I use,
Leaving the path the greater part do go.
I will resolve you: I am lunatic,   5
And ever this in madmen you shall find—
What they last thought of, when the brain grew sick,
In most distraction they keep that in mind.
Thus talking idly in this bedlam fit,
Reason and I, you must conceive, are twain;   10
'Tis nine years now since first I lost my wit,
Bear with me, then, though troubled be my brain.
  With diet and correction, men distraught
  (Not too far past) may to their wits be brought.

AN EVIL SPIRIT, YOUR BEAUTY, HAUNTS ME STILL

An evil spirit, your beauty, haunts me still,
Wherewith, alas, I have been long possessed,
Which ceaseth not to tempt me to each ill,
Nor gives me once but one poor minute's rest;
In me it speaks, whether I sleep or wake,   5
And when by means to drive it out I try,
With greater torments then it me doth take,

And tortures me in most extremity;
Before my face it lays down my despairs,
And hastes me on unto a sudden death,   10
Now tempting me to drown myself in tears,
And then in sighing to give up my breath.
    Thus am I still provoked to every evil
    By this good wicked spirit, sweet angel devil.

❧

METHINKS I SEE SOME CROOKED MIMIC JEER

Methinks I see some crooked mimic jeer,
And tax my muse with this fantastic grace;
Turning my papers, asks, What have we here?
Making withal some filthy antic face.
I fear no censure, nor what thou canst say,   5
Nor shall my spirit one jot of vigor lose;
Think'st thou my wit shall keep the pack-horse way
That ev'ry dudgeon low invention goes?
Since sonnets thus in bundles are impressed,
And ev'ry drudge doth dull our satiate ear,   10
Think'st thou my love shall in those rags be dressed
That ev'ry dowdy, ev'ry trull doth wear?
    Up to my pitch no common judgment flies,
    I scorn all earthly dung-bred scarabies.

❧

SINCE THERE'S NO HELP,
COME LET US KISS AND PART

Since there's no help, come let us kiss and part;
Nay, I have done, you get no more of me,
And I am glad, yea glad with all my heart
That thus so cleanly I myself can free;
Shake hands forever, cancel all our vows,   5
And when we meet at any time again,
Be it not seen in either of our brows

METHINKS I SEE SOME CROOKED MIMIC JEER: 14. *scarabies:* beetles.

That we one jot of former love retain.
Now at the last gasp of love's latest breath,
When, his pulse failing, passion speechless lies,   10
When faith is kneeling by his bed of death,
And innocence is closing up his eyes,
  Now if thou wouldst, when all have given him over,
  From death to life thou mightst him yet recover.

❧

William Shakespeare

SONNETS

(1609)

I

From fairest creatures we desire increase,
That thereby beauty's rose might never die,
But as the riper should by time decrease,
His tender heir might bear his memory.
But thou, contracted to thine own bright eyes,   5
Feed'st thy light's flame with self-substantial fuel,
Making a famine where abundance lies,
Thyself thy foe, to thy sweet self too cruel.
Thou that art now the world's fresh ornament
And only herald to the gaudy spring,   10
Within thine own bud buriest thy content
And, tender churl, makest waste in niggarding.
  Pity the world, or else this glutton be,
  To eat the world's due, by the grave and thee.

❧

SONNET I: 5. *contracted:* married (compare Narcissus). 6. *self-substantial:* of its own substance. 10. *only:* chief. 11. *content:* happy possibility of parenthood. 12. *churl:* miser.

2

When forty winters shall besiege thy brow
And dig deep trenches in thy beauty's field,
Thy youth's proud livery, so gazed on now,
Will be a tattered weed, of small worth held.
Then being asked where all thy beauty lies,   5
Where all the treasure of thy lusty days,
To say within thine own deep-sunken eyes
Were an all-eating shame and thriftless praise.
How much more praise deserved thy beauty's use
If thou couldst answer, "This fair child of mine   10
Shall sum my count and make my old excuse,"
Proving his beauty by succession thine!
   This were to be new-made when thou art old,
   And see thy blood warm when thou feel'st it cold.

❧

5

Those hours that with gentle work did frame
The lovely gaze where every eye doth dwell
Will play the tyrants to the very same
And that unfair which fairly doth excel.
For never-resting time leads summer on   5
To hideous winter and confounds him there,
Sap checked with frost and lusty leaves quite gone,
Beauty o'ersnowed and bareness everywhere.
Then, were not summer's distillation left,
A liquid prisoner pent in walls of glass,   10
Beauty's effect with beauty were bereft,
Nor it, nor no remembrance what it was.
   But flowers distilled, though they with winter meet,
   Leese but their show. Their substance still lives sweet.

❧

SONNET 2: 4. *weed:* garment. 11. *sum my count:* balance my account; *old excuse:* be an excuse for my being old.

SONNET 5: 2. *gaze:* object gazed at. 4. *that unfair:* destroy the beauty of that. 6. *confounds:* destroys. 14. *Leese:* lose.

12

When I do count the clock that tells the time
And see the brave day sunk in hideous night,
When I behold the violet past prime
And sable curls all silvered o'er with white;
When lofty trees I see barren of leaves   5
Which erst from heat did canopy the herd,
And summer's green all girded up in sheaves,
Borne on the bier with white and bristly beard—
Then of thy beauty do I question make,
That thou among the wastes of time must go,   10
Since sweets and beauties do themselves forsake
And die as fast as they see others grow.
   And nothing 'gainst Time's scythe can make defense
   Save breed, to brave him when he takes thee hence.

14

Not from the stars do I my judgment pluck,
And yet methinks I have astronomy,
But not to tell of good or evil luck,
Of plagues, of dearths, or seasons' quality.
Nor can I fortune to brief minutes tell,   5
Pointing to each his thunder, rain, and wind,
Or say with princes if it shall go well
By oft predict that I in heaven find.
But from thine eyes my knowledge I derive,
And, constant stars, in them I read such art   10
As truth and beauty shall together thrive,
If from thyself to store thou wouldst convert.
   Or else of thee this I prognosticate:
   Thy end is truth's and beauty's doom and date.

SONNET 12: 2. *brave:* splendid. 9. *question make:* reflect about doubtfully.
14. *breed:* children; *brave:* defy.

   SONNET 14: 2. *have astronomy:* have a knowledge of astrology. 8. *oft predict:* repeated signs. 10. *art:* knowledge. 12. *store . . . convert:* breed many children.

15

When I consider everything that grows
Holds in perfection but a little moment,
That this huge stage presenteth naught but shows
Whereon the stars in secret influence comment;
When I perceive that men as plants increase,   5
Cheerèd and checked even by the selfsame sky,
Vaunt in their youthful sap, at height decrease,
And wear their brave state out of memory—
Then the conceit of this inconstant stay
Sets you most rich in youth before my sight,   10
Where wasteful Time debateth with Decay,
To change your day of youth to sullied night.
     And all in war with Time for love of you,
     As he takes from you, I engraft you new.

18

Shall I compare thee to a summer's day?
Thou art more lovely and more temperate.
Rough winds do shake the darling buds of May,
And summer's lease hath all too short a date.
Sometime too hot the eye of heaven shines,   5
And often is his gold complexion dimmed.
And every fair from fair sometime declines,
By chance or nature's changing course untrimmed.
But thy eternal summer shall not fade,
Nor lose possession of that fair thou owest,   10
Nor shall Death brag thou wander'st in his shade
When in eternal lines to time thou grow'st.
     So long as men can breathe, or eyes can see,
     So long lives this, and this gives life to thee.

SONNET 15: 9. *conceit:* idea. 14. *engraft:* restore you in my verse.
SONNET 18: 8. *untrimmed:* shorn of ornament. 10. *owest:* own.

19

Devouring Time, blunt thou the lion's paws,
And make the earth devour her own sweet brood.
Pluck the keen teeth from the fierce tiger's jaws,
And burn the long-lived phoenix in her blood.
Make glad and sorry seasons as thou fleet'st,   5
And do whate'er thou wilt, swift-footed Time,
To the wide world and all her fading sweets,
But I forbid thee one most heinous crime.
Oh, carve not with thy hours my love's fair brow,
Nor draw no lines there with thine antique pen.   10
Him in thy course untainted do allow
For beauty's pattern to succeeding men.
    Yet do thy worst, old Time. Despite thy wrong,
    My love shall in my verse ever live young.

23

As an unperfect actor on the stage,
Who with his fear is put besides his part,
Or some fierce thing replete with too much rage,
Whose strength's abundance weakens his own heart,
So I, for fear of trust, forget to say   5
The perfect ceremony of love's rite,
And in mine own love's strength seem to decay,
O'ercharged with burden of mine own love's might.
Oh, let my books be then the eloquence
And dumb presagers of my speaking breast,   10
Who plead for love, and look for recompense,
More than that tongue that more hath more expressed.
    Oh, learn to read what silent love hath writ.
    To hear with eyes belongs to love's fine wit.

SONNET 19: 4. *phoenix:* a mythical Arabian bird and symbol of resurrection, believed to burn itself after living 500 years and then to be reborn from its ashes.

SONNET 23: 5. *fear of trust:* fearful of my own powers and of the reception I may get. 12. *tongue:* more eloquent person.

25

Let those who are in favor with their stars
Of public honor and proud titles boast,
Whilst I, whom fortune of such triumph bars,
Unlooked for joy in that I honor most.
Great princes' favorites their fair leaves spread   5
But as the marigold at the sun's eye,
And in themselves their pride lies burièd,
For at a frown they in their glory die.
The painful warrior famousèd for fight,
After a thousand victories once foiled,   10
Is from the book of honor razèd quite,
And all the rest forgot for which he toiled.
  Then happy I, that love and am beloved
  Where I may not remove nor be removed.

29

When in disgrace with fortune and men's eyes
I all alone beweep my outcast state,
And trouble deaf Heaven with my bootless cries,
And look upon myself and curse my fate,
Wishing me like to one more rich in hope,   5
Featured like him, like him with friends possessed,
Desiring this man's art and that man's scope,
With what I most enjoy contented least—
Yet in these thoughts myself almost despising,
Haply I think on thee, and then my state,   10
Like to the lark at break of day arising
From sullen earth, sings hymns at Heaven's gate.
  For thy sweet love remembered such wealth brings
  That then I scorn to change my state with kings.

SONNET 25: 4. *Unlooked for joy:* unnoticed take joy. 6. *marigold . . . eye:* which closes when the sun sets or no longer shines on it. 9. *painful:* toiling.
  SONNET 29: 3. *bootless:* fruitless. 7. *art:* skill; *scope:* range of ability and accomplishment.

30

When to the sessions of sweet silent thought
I summon up remembrance of things past,
I sigh the lack of many a thing I sought,
And with old woes new wail my dear time's waste.
Then can I drown an eye, unused to flow,   5
For precious friends hid in death's dateless night,
And weep afresh love's long since canceled woe,
And moan the expense of many a vanished sight.
Then can I grieve at grievances foregone,
And heavily from woe to woe tell o'er   10
The sad account of forebemoanèd moan,
Which I new-pay as if not paid before.
   But if the while I think on thee, dear friend,
   All losses are restored and sorrows end.

33

Full many a glorious morning have I seen
Flatter the mountaintops with sovereign eye,
Kissing with golden face the meadows green,
Gilding pale streams with heavenly alchemy,
Anon permit the basest clouds to ride   5
With ugly rack on his celestial face
And from the forlorn world his visage hide,
Stealing unseen to west with this disgrace.
Even so my sun one early morn did shine
With all-triumphant splendor on my brow.   10
But out, alack! he was but one hour mine,
The region cloud hath masked him from me now.
   Yet him for this my love no whit disdaineth;
   Suns of the world may stain when heaven's sun staineth.

SONNET 30: 4. *dear:* precious. 6. *dateless:* endless. 8. *expense:* loss. 10.
tell: count.

   SONNET 33: 2. *Flatter:* beautify. 6. *rack:* cloud. 12. *region:* the upper air.
14. *stain:* grow dim, be obscured.

34

Why didst thou promise such a beauteous day,
And make me travel forth without my cloak,
To let base clouds o'ertake me in my way,
Hiding thy bravery in their rotten smoke?
'Tis not enough that through the cloud thou break   5
To dry the rain on my storm-beaten face,
For no man well of such a salve can speak
That heals the wound and cures not the disgrace.
Nor can thy shame give physic to my grief.
Though thou repent, yet I have still the loss.   10
The offender's sorrow lends but weak relief
To him that bears the strong offense's cross.
 Ah, but those tears are pearl which thy love sheds,
 And they are rich and ransom all ill deeds.

35

No more be grieved at that which thou hast done.
Roses have thorns, and silver fountains mud,
Clouds and eclipses stain both moon and sun,
And loathsome canker lives in sweetest bud.
All men make faults, and even I in this,   5
Authorizing thy trespass with compare,
Myself corrupting, salving thy amiss,
Excusing thy sins more than thy sins are.
For to thy sensual fault I bring in sense—
Thy adverse party is thy advocate—   10
And 'gainst myself a lawful plea commence.
Such civil war is in my love and hate,
 That I an accessory needs must be
 To that sweet thief which sourly robs from me.

SONNET 34: 4. *bravery:* splendor; *smoke:* mist.
 SONNET 35: 6. *Authorizing . . . compare:* justifying your fault with my
comparisons. 9. *sense:* reason.

36

Let me confess that we two must be twain,
Although our undivided loves are one.
So shall those blots that do with me remain,
Without thy help, by me be borne alone.
In our two loves there is but one respect,   5
Though in our lives a separable spite,
Which though it alter not love's sole effect,
Yet doth it steal sweet hours from love's delight.
I may not evermore acknowledge thee,
Lest my bewailèd guilt should do thee shame,   10
Nor thou with public kindness honor me,
Unless thou take that honor from thy name.
     But do not so; I love thee in such sort,
     As thou being mine, mine is thy good report.

41

Those pretty wrongs that liberty commits,
When I am sometime absent from thy heart,
Thy beauty and thy years full well befits,
For still temptation follows where thou art.
Gentle thou art, and therefore to be won,   5
Beauteous thou art, therefore to be assailed.
And when a woman woos, what woman's son
Will sourly leave her till she have prevailed?
Aye me! but yet thou mightst my seat forbear,
And chide thy beauty and thy straying youth,   10
Who lead thee in their riot even there
Where thou art forced to break a twofold truth--
     Hers, by thy beauty tempting her to thee,
     Thine, by thy beauty being false to me.

SONNET 36: 5. *respect:* essential consideration. 6. *separable:* separating
SONNET 41: 5. *Gentle:* of good family. 9. *seat:* place. 12. *truth:* troth.

49

Against that time, if ever that time come,
When I shall see thee frown on my defects,
When as thy love hath cast his utmost sum,
Called to that audit by advised respects;
Against that time when thou shalt strangely pass,   5
And scarcely greet me with that sun, thine eye,
When love, converted from the thing it was,
Shall reasons find of settled gravity;
Against that time do I ensconce me here
Within the knowledge of mine own desert,   10
And this my hand against myself uprear,
To guard the lawful reasons on thy part.
   To leave poor me thou hast the strength of laws,
   Since why to love I can allege no cause.

52

So am I as the rich, whose blessèd key
Can bring him to his sweet uplockèd treasure,
The which he will not every hour survey,
For blunting the fine point of seldom pleasure.
Therefore are feasts so solemn and so rare,   5
Since, seldom coming, in the long year set
Like stones of worth they thinly placèd are,
Or captain jewels in the carcanet.
So is the time that keeps you as my chest,
Or as the wardrobe which the robe doth hide,   10
To make some special instant special blest
By new-unfolding his imprisoned pride.
   Blessèd are you, whose worthiness gives scope,
   Being had, to triumph—being lacked, to hope.

SONNET 49: 3. *cast his utmost sum:* reckoned the total and closed the account. 4. *advised respects:* careful consideration. 5. *strangely:* like a stranger. 8. *settled gravity:* final and weighty. 9. *ensconce:* fortify.
SONNET 52: 8. *captain:* largest; *carcanet:* necklace.

53

What is your substance, whereof are you made,
That millions of strange shadows on you tend?
Since every one hath, every one, one shade,
And you, but one, can every shadow lend.
Describe Adonis, and the counterfeit   5
Is poorly imitated after you.
On Helen's cheek all art of beauty set,
And you in Grecian tires are painted new.
Speak of the spring and foison of the year,
The one doth shadow of your beauty show,   10
The other as your bounty doth appear,
And you in every blessèd shape we know.
   In all external grace you have some part,
    But you like none, none you, for constant heart.

54

Oh, how much more doth beauty beauteous seem
By that sweet ornament which truth doth give!
The rose looks fair, but fairer we it deem
For that sweet odor which doth in it live.
The canker blooms have full as deep a dye   5
As the perfumèd tincture of the roses,
Hang on such thorns, and play as wantonly
When summer's breath their maskèd buds discloses.
But for their virtue only is their show,
They live unwooed and unrespected fade,   10
Die to themselves. Sweet roses do not so.
Of their sweet deaths are sweetest odors made.
   And so of you, beauteous and lovely youth,
    When that shall fade, my verse distills your truth.

SONNET 53: 2. *strange:* not yours. 8. *tires:* attire. 9. *foison:* harvest.
   SONNET 54: 2. *truth:* faithfulness. 5. *canker blooms:* wild roses, without odor. 9. *for:* since.

55

Not marble, nor the gilded monuments
Of princes, shall outlive this powerful rhyme.
But you shall shine more bright in these contents
Than unswept stone, besmeared with sluttish time.
When wasteful war shall statues overturn, 5
And broils root out the work of masonry,
Nor Mars his sword nor war's quick fire shall burn
The living record of your memory.
'Gainst death and all-oblivious enmity
Shall you pace forth; your praise shall still find room 10
Even in the eyes of all posterity
That wear this world out to the ending doom.
   So, till the judgment that yourself arise,
   You live in this, and dwell in lovers' eyes.

60

Like as the waves make toward the pebbled shore,
So do our minutes hasten to their end,
Each changing place with that which goes before,
In sequent toil all forward do contend.
Nativity, once in the main of light, 5
Crawls to maturity, wherewith being crowned,
Crookèd eclipses 'gainst his glory fight,
And Time that gave doth now his gift confound.
Time doth transfix the flourish set on youth
And delves the parallels in beauty's brow, 10
Feeds on the rarities of nature's truth,
And nothing stands but for his scythe to mow.
   And yet to times in hope my verse shall stand,
   Praising thy worth, despite his cruel hand.

SONNET 55: 4. *stone:* flat grave stone in a church floor. 13. *judgment that:* Judgment Day when.

SONNET 60: 7. *Crookèd:* malignant. 8. *confound:* destroy. 9. *transfix the flourish:* pierce the bloom.

64

When I have seen by Time's fell hand defaced
The rich-proud cost of outworn buried age;
When sometime lofty towers I see down-razed,
And brass eternal slave to mortal rage;
When I have seen the hungry ocean gain   5
Advantage on the kingdom of the shore,
And the firm soil win of the watery main,
Increasing store with loss and loss with store;
When I have seen such interchange of state,
Or state itself confounded to decay—   10
Ruin hath taught me thus to ruminate,
That Time will come and take my love away.
  This thought is as a death, which cannot choose
  But weep to have that which it fears to lose.

65

Since brass, nor stone, nor earth, nor boundless sea
But sad mortality o'ersways their power,
How with this rage shall beauty hold a plea,
Whose action is no stronger than a flower?
Oh, how shall summer's honey breath hold out   5
Against the wreckful siege of battering days,
When rocks impregnable are not so stout,
Nor gates of steel so strong, but Time decays?
O fearful meditation! Where, alack,
Shall Time's best jewel from Time's chest lie hid?   10
Or what strong hand can hold his swift foot back?
Or who his spoil of beauty can forbid?
  Oh, none, unless this miracle have might,
  That in black ink my love may still shine bright.

SONNET 64: 2. *cost:* expensive memorials.

66

Tired with all these, for restful death I cry,
As, to behold desert a beggar born,
And needy nothing trimmed in jollity,
And purest faith unhappily forsworn,
And gilded honor shamefully misplaced,   5
And maiden virtue rudely strumpeted,
And right perfection wrongfully disgraced,
And strength by limping sway disabled,
And art made tongue-tied by authority,
And folly, doctorlike, controlling skill,   10
And simple truth miscalled simplicity,
And captive good attending captain ill.
    Tired with all these, from these would I be gone,
    Save that, to die I leave my love alone.

67

Ah, wherefore with infection should he live
And with his presence grace impiety,
That sin by him advantage should achieve
And lace itself with his society?
Why should false painting imitate his cheek,   5
And steal dead seeing of his living hue?
Why should poor beauty indirectly seek
Roses of shadow, since his rose is true?
Why should he live, now Nature bankrupt is,
Beggared of blood to blush through lively veins?   10
For she hath no exchequer now but his,
And, proud of many, lives upon his gains.
    Oh, him she stores, to show what wealth she had
    In days long since, before these last so bad.

SONNET 66: 3. *trimmed in jollity:* dressed in gay clothes. 8. *limping sway:* misgovernment. 9. *art:* true learning. 10. *doctorlike:* with appearance of learning. 11. *simplicity:* foolishness.

SONNET 67: 1. *infection:* human evil. 4. *lace:* adorn. 6. *seeing:* appearance. 8. *shadow:* paint.

71

No longer mourn for me when I am dead
Than you shall hear the surly sullen bell
Give warning to the world that I am fled
From this vile world, with vilest worms to dwell.
Nay, if you read this line, remember not   5
The hand that writ it, for I love you so
That I in your sweet thoughts would be forgot
If thinking on me then should make you woe.
Oh, if, I say, you look upon this verse
When I perhaps compounded am with clay,   10
Do not so much as my poor name rehearse,
But let your love even with my life decay,
   Lest the wise world should look into your moan,
   And mock you with me after I am gone.

73

That time of year thou mayst in me behold
When yellow leaves, or none, or few, do hang
Upon those boughs which shake against the cold,
Bare ruined choirs where late the sweet birds sang.
In me thou see'st the twilight of such day   5
As after sunset fadeth in the west,
Which by and by black night doth take away,
Death's second self, that seals up all in rest.
In me thou see'st the glowing of such fire,
That on the ashes of his youth doth lie   10
As the deathbed whereon it must expire,
Consumed with that which it was nourished by.
   This thou perceivest, which makes thy love more strong,
   To love that well which thou must leave ere long.

74

But be contented. When that fell arrest
Without all bail shall carry me away,
My life hath in this line some interest,
Which for memorial still with thee shall stay.
When thou reviewest this, thou dost review   5
The very part was consecrate to thee.
The earth can have but earth, which is his due,
My spirit is thine, the better part of me.
So then thou hast but lost the dregs of life,
The prey of worms, my body being dead,   10
The coward conquest of a wretch's knife,
Too base of thee to be rememberèd.
   The worth of that is that which it contains,
   And that is this, and this with thee remains.

76

Why is my verse so barren of new pride,
So far from variation or quick change?
Why with the time do I not glance aside
To new-found methods and to compounds strange?
Why write I still all one, ever the same,   5
And keep invention in a noted weed,
That every word doth almost tell my name,
Showing their birth and where they did proceed?
Oh, know, sweet love, I always write of you,
And you and love are still my argument.   10
So all my best is dressing old words new,
Spending again what is already spent.
   For as the sun is daily new and old,
   So is my love still telling what is told.

SONNET 76: 1. *new pride:* literary novelty. 6. *noted weed:* familiar dress.
10. *argument:* theme.

86

Was it the proud full sail of his great verse,
Bound for the prize of all too precious you,
That did my ripe thoughts in my brain inhearse,
Making their tomb the womb wherein they grew?
Was it his spirit, by spirits taught to write   5
Above a mortal pitch, that struck me dead?
No, neither he, nor his compeers by night
Giving him aid, my verse astonishèd.
He, nor that affable familiar ghost
Which nightly gulls him with intelligence,   10
As victors, of my silence cannot boast.
I was not sick of any fear from thence.
    But when your countenance filled up his line,
    Then lacked I matter; that enfeebled mine.

~❦~

87

Farewell! Thou art too dear for my possessing,
And like enough thou know'st thy estimate.
The charter of thy worth gives thee releasing,
My bonds in thee are all determinate.
For how do I hold thee but by thy granting?   5
And for that riches where is my deserving?
The cause of this fair gift in me is wanting,
And so my patent back again is swerving.
Thyself thou gavest, thy own worth then not knowing,
Or me, to whom thou gavest it, else mistaking.   10
So thy great gift, upon misprision growing,
Comes home again, on better judgment making.
    Thus have I had thee, as a dream doth flatter,
    In sleep a king, but waking no such matter.

~❦~

SONNET 86: 3. *inhearse:* entomb. 8. *astonishèd:* stunned. 10. *gulls:* fools;
intelligence: news reports.
    SONNET 87: 2. *estimate:* value. 4. *determinate:* ended. 8. *patent:* right,
privilege. 11. *misprision:* misunderstanding.

90

Then hate me when thou wilt; if ever, now;
Now while the world is bent my deeds to cross,
Join with the spite of fortune, make me bow,
And do not drop in for an afterloss.
Ah, do not, when my heart hath 'scaped this sorrow,   5
Come in the rearward of a conquered woe.
Give not a windy night a rainy morrow,
To linger out a purposed overthrow.
If thou wilt leave me, do not leave me last,
When other petty griefs have done their spite,   10
But in the onset come. So shall I taste
At first the very worst of fortune's might,
    And other strains of woe, which now seem woe,
    Compared with loss of thee will not seem so.

94

They that have power to hurt and will do none,
That do not do the thing they most do show,
Who, moving others, are themselves as stone,
Unmovèd, cold, and to temptation slow—
They rightly do inherit Heaven's graces   5
And husband nature's riches from expense.
They are the lords and owners of their faces,
Others but stewards of their excellence.
The summer's flower is to the summer sweet,
Though to itself it only live and die,   10
But if that flower with base infection meet,
The basest weed outbraves his dignity.
    For sweetest things turn sourest by their deeds;
    Lilies that fester smell far worse than weeds.

SONNET 94: 6. *expense:* waste. 12. *outbraves his dignity:* surpasses the flower's worth.

97

How like a winter hath my absence been
From thee, the pleasure of the fleeting year!
What freezings have I felt, what dark days seen!
What old December's bareness everywhere!
And yet this time removed was summer's time,   5
The teeming autumn, big with rich increase,
Bearing the wanton burden of the prime,
Like widowed wombs after their lords' decease.
Yet this abundant issue seemed to me
But hope of orphans and unfathered fruit,   10
For summer and his pleasures wait on thee,
And, thou away, the very birds are mute;
    Or if they sing, 'tis with so dull a cheer
    That leaves look pale, dreading the winter's near.

104

To me, fair friend, you never can be old,
For as you were when first your eye I eyed,
Such seems your beauty still. Three winters cold
Have from the forests shook three summers' pride,
Three beauteous springs to yellow autumn turned   5
In process of the seasons have I seen,
Three April perfumes in three hot Junes burned,
Since first I saw you fresh, which yet are green.
Ah, yet doth beauty, like a dial hand,
Steal from his figure, and no pace perceived.   10
So your sweet hue, which methinks still doth stand,
Hath motion, and mine eye may be deceived.
    For fear of which, hear this, thou age unbred—
    Ere you were born was beauty's summer dead.

SONNET 97: 5. *removed:* of absence. 7. *prime:* spring. 10. *orphans and
unfathered fruit:* posthumous children.

106

When in the chronicle of wasted time
I see descriptions of the fairest wights,
And beauty making beautiful old rhyme
In praise of ladies dead and lovely knights,
Then, in the blazon of sweet beauty's best,   5
Of hand, of foot, of lip, of eye, of brow,
I see their antique pen would have expressed
Even such a beauty as you master now.
So all their praises are but prophecies
Of this our time, all you prefiguring,   10
And, for they looked but with divining eyes,
They had not skill enough your worth to sing.
   For we, which now behold these present days,
   Have eyes to wonder, but lack tongues to praise.

107

Not mine own fears, nor the prophetic soul
Of the wide world dreaming on things to come,
Can yet the lease of my true love control,
Supposed as forfeit to a cónfined doom.
The mortal moon hath her eclipse endured,   5
And the sad augurs mock their own presage.
In certainties now crown themselves assured,
And peace proclaims olives of endless age.
Now with the drops of this most balmy time
My love looks fresh, and Death to me subscribes,   10
Since, spite of him, I'll live in this poor rhyme
While he insults o'er dull and speechless tribes.
   And thou in this shalt find thy monument,
   When tyrants' crests and tombs of brass are spent.

SONNET 106: 2. *wights:* persons. 5. *blazon:* chivalric praise; literarily, the description of a coat of arms. 11. *for . . . divining:* if they had not looked with foreseeing.

SONNET 107: 6. *sad augurs:* prophets of disaster. 10. *subscribes:* yields. 12. *insults:* triumphs.

110

Alas, 'tis true I have gone here and there,
And made myself a motley to the view,
Gored mine own thoughts, sold cheap what is most dear,
Made old offenses of affections new.
Most true it is that I have looked on truth   5
Askance and strangely. But, by all above,
These blenches gave my heart another youth,
And worse essays proved thee my best of love.
Now all is done, have what shall have no end.
Mine appetite I never more will grind   10
On newer proof, to try an older friend,
A god in love, to whom I am confined.
  Then give me welcome, next my heaven the best,
  Even to thy pure and most most loving breast.

116

Let me not to the marriage of true minds
Admit impediments. Love is not love
Which alters when it alteration finds,
Or bends with the remover to remove.
Oh no! It is an ever-fixèd mark   5
That looks on tempests and is never shaken.
It is the star to every wandering bark,
Whose worth's unknown, although his height be taken.
Love's not Time's fool, though rosy lips and cheeks
Within his bending sickle's compass come.   10
Love alters not with his brief hours and weeks,
But bears it out even to the edge of doom.
  If this be error and upon me proved,
  I never writ, nor no man ever loved.

SONNET 110: 2. *motley to the view:* a public fool. 7. *blenches:* side glances.
11. *try:* test.

  SONNET 116: 1-2. *Let . . . impediments:* echoes the marriage service in
the Book of Common Prayer—"If any of you know cause or just impedi-
ment," etc. 4. *remover:* the inconstant one. 8. *height be taken:* altitude be
calculated.

118

Like as, to make our appetites more keen,
With eager compounds we our palate urge;
As to prevent our maladies unseen
We sicken to shun sickness when we purge—
Even so, being full of your ne'er-cloying sweetness,   5
To bitter sauces did I frame my feeding,
And sick of welfare found a kind of meetness
To be diseased, ere that there was true needing.
Thus policy in love, to anticipate
The ills that were not, grew to faults assured,   10
And brought to medicine a healthful state,
Which, rank of goodness, would by ill be cured.
  But thence I learn, and find the lesson true,
  Drugs poison him that so fell sick of you.

119

What potions have I drunk of Siren tears,
Distilled from limbecks foul as Hell within,
Applying fears to hopes and hopes to fears,
Still losing when I saw myself to win!
What wretched errors hath my heart committed   5
Whilst it hath thought itself so blessèd never!
How have mine eyes out of their spheres been fitted
In the distraction of this madding fever!
O benefit of ill! Now I find true
That better is by evil still made better,   10
And ruined love, when it is built anew,
Grows fairer than at first, more strong, far greater.
  So I return rebuked to my content,
  And gain by ill thrice more than I have spent.

SONNET 118: 2. *eager:* sharp. 7. *meetness:* fitness. 11. *brought to medicine:* brought about a need for treating. 12. *rank:* overfull.
SONNET 119: 2. *limbecks:* stills. 7. *fitted:* convulsed, as in a fit.

127

In the old age black was not counted fair,
Or if it were, it bore not beauty's name,
But now is black beauty's successive heir,
And beauty slandered with a bastard shame.
For since each hand hath put on Nature's power,   5
Fairing the foul with art's false borrowed face,
Sweet beauty hath no name, no holy bower,
But is profaned, if not lives in disgrace.
Therefore my mistress' eyes are raven-black,
Her eyes so suited, and they mourners seem   10
At such who, not born fair, no beauty lack,
Slandering creation with a false esteem.
   Yet so they mourn, becoming of their woe,
   That every tongue says beauty should look so.

128

How oft, when thou, my music, music play'st
Upon that blessed wood whose motion sounds
With thy sweet fingers, when thou gently sway'st
The wiry concord that mine ear confounds,
Do I envy those jacks that nimble leap   5
To kiss the tender inward of thy hand,
Whilst my poor lips, which should that harvest reap,
At the wood's boldness by thee blushing stand!
To be so tickled, they would change their state
And situation with those dancing chips   10
O'er whom thy fingers walk with gentle gait,
Making dead wood more blest than living lips.
   Since saucy jacks so happy are in this,
   Give them thy fingers, me thy lips to kiss.

SONNET 127: 1. *black:* brunette complexion.   10. *so suited:* matching.
SONNET 128: 2. *wood:* keys, jacks (see l. 5).

129

The expense of spirit in a waste of shame
Is lust in action, and till action, lust
Is perjured, murderous, bloody, full of blame,
Savage, extreme, rude, cruel, not to trust,
Enjoyed no sooner but despisèd straight,   5
Past reason hunted, and no sooner had,
Past reason hated, as a swallowed bait,
On purpose laid to make the taker mad.
Mad in pursuit, and in possession so,
Had, having, and in quest to have, extreme,   10
A bliss in proof, and proved, a very woe.
Before, a joy proposed, behind, a dream.
   All this the world well knows, yet none knows well
   To shun the Heaven that leads men to this Hell.

130

My mistress' eyes are nothing like the sun,
Coral is far more red than her lips' red.
If snow be white, why then her breasts are dun,
If hairs be wires, black wires grow on her head.
I have seen roses damasked, red and white,   5
But no such roses see I in her cheeks.
And in some perfumes is there more delight
Than in the breath that from my mistress reeks.
I love to hear her speak, yet well I know
That music hath a far more pleasing sound.   10
I grant I never saw a goddess go,
My mistress, when she walks, treads on the ground.
   And yet, by Heaven, I think my love as rare
   As any she belied with false compare.

146

Poor soul, the center of my sinful earth,
My sinful earth, these rebel powers that thee array,
Why dost thou pine within and suffer dearth,
Painting thy outward walls so costly gay?
Why so large cost, having so short a lease,   5
Dost thou upon thy fading mansion spend?
Shall worms, inheritors of this excess,
Eat up thy charge? Is this thy body's end?
Then, soul, live thou upon thy servant's loss,
And let that pine to aggravate thy store.   10
Buy terms divine in selling hours of dross,
Within be fed, without be rich no more.
  So shalt thou feed on Death, that feeds on men,
  And Death once dead, there's no more dying then.

❧

Songs from the Plays

WHO IS SYLVIA?

(1591)

Who is Silvia? what is she,
    That all our swains commend her?
Holy, fair, and wise is she;
    The heaven such grace did lend her,
That she might admirèd be.   5

Is she kind as she is fair?
    For beauty lives with kindness.
Love doth to her eyes repair,
    To help him of his blindness,
And, being helped, inhabits there.   10

Then to Silvia let us sing,
    That Silvia is excelling;
She excels each mortal thing
    Upon the dull earth dwelling.
To her let us garlands bring.   15

From *The Two Gentlemen of Verona,* IV, ii, 39

SONNET 146: 2. *My sinful earth:* commonly thought to be a printer's error.
8. *charge:* body on which you have spent so much. 10. *aggravate:* increase.

WHEN DAISIES PIED
(1593)

When daisies pied and violets blue
   And lady smocks all silver-white
And cuckoo buds of yellow hue
   Do paint the meadows with delight,
The cuckoo then, on every tree,   5
Mocks married men; for thus sings he—Cuckoo,
Cuckoo, cuckoo! Oh, word of fear,
Unpleasing to a married ear!

When shepherds pipe on oaten straws,
   And merry larks are plowmen's clocks,   10
When turtles tread, and rooks, and daws,
   And maidens bleach their summer smocks,
The cuckoo then, on every tree,
Mocks married men; for thus sings he—Cuckoo,
Cuckoo, cuckoo! Oh, word of fear,   15
Unpleasing to a married ear!

When icicles hang by the wall,
   And Dick the shepherd blows his nail,
And Tom bears logs into the hall,
   And milk comes frozen home in pail,   20
When blood is nipped and ways be foul,
Then nightly sings the staring owl—Tu-whit,
Tu-who, a merry note,
While greasy Joan doth keel the pot.

When all aloud the wind doth blow,   25
   And coughing drowns the parson's saw,
And birds sit brooding in the snow,
   And Marian's nose looks red and raw,
When roasted crabs hiss in the bowl,
Then nightly sings the staring owl—Tu-whit,   30
Tu-who, a merry note,
While greasy Joan doth keel the pot.

            From *Love's Labour's Lost,* V, ii, 904

WHEN DAISIES PIED: 5. *cuckoo:* lays his eggs in other birds' nests, and hence
a symbol of infidelity. 11. *turtles:* turtle doves. 24. *keel:* cool. 26. *saw:* old
wise saying. 29. *crabs:* crab apples.

YOU SPOTTED SNAKES
(1595)

You spotted snakes with double tongue,
  Thorny hedgehogs, be not seen;
Newts and blindworms, do no wrong,
  Come not near our fairy queen.

  Philomel, with melody   5
  Sing in our sweet lullaby;
Lulla, lulla, lullaby, lulla, lulla, lullaby:
    Never harm,
    Nor spell nor charm,
  Come our lovely lady nigh;   10
  So, good night, with lullaby.

Weaving spiders, come not here;
  Hence, you long-legg'd spinners, hence!
Beetles black, approach not near;
  Worm nor snail, do no offense.   15

    Philomel, with melody, &c.
      From *A Midsummer Night's Dream,* II, ii, 9

TELL ME WHERE IS FANCY BRED
(1596)

  Tell me where is fancy bred,
  Or in the heart or in the head?
  How begot, how nourishèd?
    Reply, reply.
  It is engendered in the eyes,   5
  With gazing fed; and fancy dies
  In the cradle where it lies.
    Let us all ring fancy's knell:
  I'll begin it—Ding, dong, bell.
All. Ding, dong, bell.   10
    From *The Merchant of Venice,* III, ii, 63

TELL ME WHERE: 1 *fancy:* love.

SIGH NO MORE, LADIES
(1599)

Sigh no more, ladies, sigh no more,
   Men were deceivers ever,
One foot in sea and one on shore,
   To one thing constant never.
Then sigh not so, but let them go,   5
   And be you blithe and bonny,
Converting all your sounds of woe
   Into Hey nonny, nonny.

Sing no more ditties, sing no moe
   Of dumps so dull and heavy.   10
The fraud of men was ever so,
   Since summer first was leavy.
Then sigh not so, but let them go,
   And be you blithe and bonny,
Converting all your sounds of woe   15
   Into Hey nonny, nonny.
        From *Much Ado About Nothing,* II, iii, 64.

❦

UNDER THE GREENWOOD TREE
(1600)

Under the greenwood tree
Who loves to lie with me,
And turn his merry note
Unto the sweet bird's throat,
Come hither, come hither, come hither.   5
   Here shall he see
   No enemy
But winter and rough weather.

Who doth ambition shun,
And loves to live i' the sun,   10

UNDER THE GREENWOOD TREE: 3. *turn:* time.

Seeking the food he eats,
And pleased with what he gets,
Come hither, come hither, come hither.
Here shall he see
No enemy   15
But winter and rough weather.

From *As You Like It,* II, v, 1

❧

BLOW, BLOW, THOU WINTER WIND
(1600)

Blow, blow, thou winter wind.
Thou are not so unkind
As man's ingratitude.
Thy tooth is not so keen,
Because thou art not seen,   5
Although thy breath be rude.
Heigh-ho! Sing, heigh-ho! unto the green holly.
Most friendship is feigning, most loving mere folly.
Then, heigh-ho, the holly!
This life is most jolly.   10

Freeze, freeze, thou bitter sky,
That dost not bite so nigh
As benefits forgot.
Though thou the waters warp,
Thy sting is not so sharp   15
As friend remembered not.
Heigh-ho! Sing, &c.

From *As You Like It,* II, vii, 174

❧

IT WAS A LOVER AND HIS LASS
(1600)

It was a lover and his lass,
With a hey, and a ho, and a hey nonino,

_____

BLOW, BLOW: 14. *warp:* freeze.

That o'er the green corn field did pass
In spring time, the only pretty ring time,
When birds do sing, hey ding a ding, ding: 5
Sweet lovers love the spring.

Between the acres of the rye,
With a hey, and a ho, and a hey nonino,
These pretty country folks would lie,
In spring time, &c.   10

This carol they began that hour,
With a hey, and a ho, and a hey nonino,
How that a life was but a flower
In spring time, &c.

And therefore take the present time,   15
With a hey, and a ho, and a hey nonino;
For love is crownèd with the prime
In spring time, &c.

From *As You Like It,* V, iii, 17

O MISTRESS MINE

(1601)

O mistress mine, where are you roaming?
Oh, stay and hear, your truelove's coming,
That can sing both high and low.
Trip no further, pretty sweeting,
Journeys end in lovers meeting,   5
Every wise man's son doth know.

What is love? 'Tis not hereafter,
Present mirth hath present laughter,
What's to come is still unsure.
In delay there lies no plenty,   10
Then come kiss me, sweet and twenty,
Youth's a stuff will not endure.

From *Twelfth Night,* II, iii, 40

COME AWAY, COME AWAY, DEATH
(1601)

Come away, come away, death,
  And in sad cypress let me be laid.
Fly away, fly away, breath,
  I am slain by a fair cruel maid.
My shroud of white, stuck all with yew,   5
    Oh, prepare it!
My part of death, no one so true
    Did share it!

Not a flower, not a flower sweet,
  On my black coffin let there be strown.   10
Not a friend, not a friend greet
  My poor corpse, where my bones shall be thrown.
A thousand thousand sighs to save,
    Lay me, oh, where
Sad truelover never find my grave,   15
    To weep there!

From Twelfth Night, II. iv, 52

WHEN THAT I WAS
(1601)

When that I was and a little tiny boy,
  With hey, ho, the wind and the rain,
A foolish thing was but a toy,
  For the rain it raineth every day.

But when I came to man's estate,   5
  With hey, ho, the wind and the rain,
'Gainst knaves and thieves men shut their gate,
  For the rain it raineth every day.

But when I came, alas! to wive,
  With hey, ho, the wind and the rain,   10
By swaggering could I never thrive,
  For the rain it raineth every day.

But when I came unto my beds,
  With hey, ho, the wind and the rain,
With tosspots still had drunken heads,   15
  For the rain it raineth every day.

A great while ago the world begun,
  With hey, ho, the wind and the rain,
But that's all one, our play is done,
  And we'll strive to please you every day.   20

From *Twelfth Night*, V, i, 398

TAKE, OH, TAKE THOSE LIPS AWAY
(1604)

Take, O, take those lips away
  That so sweetly were forsworn,
And those eyes, the break of day,
  Lights that do mislead the morn.
But my kisses bring again, bring again,   5
Seals of love, but sealed in vain, sealed in vain.

From *Measure for Measure,* IV, i, 1

THE POOR SOUL SAT SIGHING
(1604)

The poor soul sat sighing by a sycamore tree,
  Sing all a green willow.
Her hand on her bosom, her head on her knee,
  Sing willow, willow, willow.

The fresh streams ran by her, and murmured her moans,   5
  Sing willow, willow, willow.
Her salt tears fell from her, and softened the stones—
  Sing willow, willow, willow.

Let nobody blame him; his scorn I approve—
I called my love false love, but what said he then?   10

Sing willow, willow, willow.
If I court moe women, you'll couch with moe men.

From *Othello,* IV, iii, 41

HARK, HARK! THE LARK
(1609)

Hark, hark! the lark at heaven's gate sings,
  And Phoebus 'gins arise,
His steeds to water at those springs
  On chaliced flowers that lies;
And winking Mary-buds begin   5
  To ope their golden eyes:
With every thing that pretty is,
  My lady sweet, arise:
  Arise, arise!

From *Cymbeline,* II, iii, 22

FEAR NO MORE THE HEAT O' THE SUN
(1609)

Guiderius
Fear no more the heat o' the sun,
  Nor the furious winter's rages;
Thou thy worldly task hast done,
  Home art gone, and ta'en thy wages:
Golden lads and girls all must,   5
As chimney-sweepers, come to dust.

Arviragus
Fear no more the frown o' the great;
  Thou art past the tyrant's stroke;
Care no more to clothe and eat;
  To thee the reed is as the oak: 10
The scepter, learning, physic, must
All follow this, and come to dust.

Guiderius
Fear no more the lightning-flash,

Arviragus
Nor the all-dreaded thunder-stone;

Guiderius
Fear not slander, censure rash;   15

Arviragus
Thou hast finished joy and moan:

Both
All lovers young, all lovers must
Consign to thee, and come to dust.

Guiderius
No exorciser harm thee!

Arviragus
Nor no witchcraft charm thee!   20

Guiderius
Ghost unlaid forbear thee!

Arviragus
Nothing ill come near thee!

Both
Quiet consummation have;
And renownèd be thy grave!
From *Cymbeline*, IV, ii, 258

&

FULL FATHOM FIVE

(1611)

Full fathom five thy father lies;
Of his bones are coral made;
Those are pearls that were his eyes:
Nothing of him that doth fa'
But doth suffer a sea change

FEAR NO MORE: 18. *consign:* submit.

Into something rich and strange.
Sea nymphs hourly ring his knell:
                    Burthen. Ding-dong.
Hark! now I hear them,—Ding-dong, bell.
From The Tempest, I, ii, 394

WHERE THE BEE SUCKS

(1611)

Where the bee sucks, there suck I:
In a cowslip's bell I lie;
There I couch when owls do cry.
On the bat's back I do fly
After summer merrily.   5
Merrily, merrily shall I live now
Under the blossom that hangs on the bough.
From The Tempest, V, i, 88

John Donne

From *Songs and Sonnets*

(1633)

THE GOOD-MORROW

I wonder, by my troth, what thou and I
   Did till we lov'd? Were we not wean'd till then,
But suck'd on country pleasures childishly?
   Or snorted we in the Seven Sleepers' den?
'Twas so; but this, all pleasures fancies be.   5
If ever any beauty I did see
Which I desir'd, and got, 'twas but a dream of thee.

And now good morrow to our waking souls,
   Which watch not one another out of fear;
For love all love of other sights controls,   10

And makes one little room an everywhere.
Let sea-discoverers to new worlds have gone,
Let maps to other, worlds on worlds have shown,
Let us possess one world: each hath one, and is one.

My face in thine eye, thine in mine appears,   15
    And true plain hearts do in the faces rest.
Where can we find two better hemispheres,
    Without sharp North, without declining West?
Whatever dies was not mix'd equally;
    If our two loves be one, or thou and I   20
Love so alike that none do slacken, none can die.

GO AND CATCH A FALLING STAR

Go and catch a falling star,
    Get with child a mandrake root,
Tell me where all past years are,
    Or who cleft the devil's foot,
Teach me to hear mermaids singing,   5
Or to keep off envy's stinging,
            And find
            What wind
Serves t' advance an honest mind.

If thou be'st born to strange sights,   10
    Things invisible to see,
Ride ten thousand days and nights
    Till age snow white hairs on thee;
Thou, when thou return'st, wilt tell me
All strange wonders that befell thee,   15
            And swear
            Nowhere
Lives a woman true, and fair.

If thou find'st one, let me know;
    Such a pilgrimage were sweet;   20
Yet do not, I would not go
    Though at next door we might meet.

GO AND CATCH A FALLING STAR: 2. *mandrake root*: its v-shaped root was
thought to make it resemble a person.

Though she were true when you met her,
And last till you write your letter,
            Yet she   25
            Will be
False ere I come, to two or three.

                    ❧

WOMAN'S CONSTANCY

Now thou hast lov'd me one whole day,
Tomorrow when thou leav'st, what wilt thou say?
Wilt thou then antedate some new-made vow?
            Or say that now
We are not just those persons which we were?   5
Or that oaths made in reverential fear
Of Love and his wrath, any may forswear?
Or, as true deaths true marriages untie,
So lovers' contracts, images of those,
Bind but till sleep, death's image, them unloose?   10
            Or, your own end to justify,
For having purpos'd change and falsehood, you
Can have no way but falsehood to be true?
Vain lunatic, against these 'scapes I could
            Dispute and conquer, if I would,   15
            Which I abstain to do,
For by tomorrow I may think so too.

                    ❧

THE UNDERTAKING: PLATONIC LOVE

            I have done one braver thing
               Than all the Worthies did,
            And yet a braver thence doth spring,
               Which is, to keep that hid.

            It were but madness now t' impart   5
               The skill of specular stone,

THE UNDERTAKING: 6. *specular stone:* crystal gazing.

When he which can have learn'd the art
    To cut it can find none.

So, if I now should utter this,
    Others (because no more   10
Such stuff to work upon there is)
    Would love but as before.

But he who loveliness within
    Hath found, all outward loathes,
For he who color loves, and skin,   15
    Loves but their oldest clothes.

If as I have, you also do
    Virtue'attir'd in woman see,
And dare love that, and say so too,
    And forget the He and She,   20

And if this love, though placèd so,
    From profane men you hide,
Which will no faith on this bestow,
    Or if they do, deride,

Then you have done a braver thing   25
    Than all the Worthies did;
And a braver thence will spring,
    Which is, to keep that hid.

*   *   *

THE SUN RISING

Busy old fool, unruly sun,
    Why dost thou thus
Through windows and through curtains call on us?
Must to thy motions lovers' seasons run?
    Saucy, pedantic wretch, go chide   5
    Late schoolboys and sour prentices,
  Go tell court huntsmen that the king will ride,
  Call country ants to harvest offices.
Love, all alike, no season knows nor clime,
Nor hours, days, months, which are the rags of time.   10

    Thy beams, so reverend and strong
        Why shouldst thou think?

I could eclipse and cloud them with a wink,
But that I would not lose her sight so long.
    If her eyes have not blinded thine,   15
    Look, and tomorrow late tell me
  Whether both th' Indias of spice and mine
  Be where thou left'st them, or lie here with me;
Ask for those kings whom thou saw'st yesterday,
And thou shalt hear: All here in one bed lay.   20

    She's all states, and all princes I;
      Nothing else is.
Princes do but play us; compar'd to this,
All honor's mimic, all wealth alchemy.
    Thou, sun, art half as happy's we,   25
    In that the world's contracted thus;
  Thine age asks ease, and since thy duties be
  To warm the world, that's done in warming us.
Shine here to us, and thou art everywhere;
This bed thy center is, these walls thy sphere.   30

❧

BREAK OF DAY

    'Tis true, 'tis day. What though it be?
    O, wilt thou therefore rise from me?
      Why should we rise because 'tis light?
      Did we lie down because 'twas night?
Love, which in spite of darkness brought us hither,   5
Should in despite of light keep us together.

    Light hath no tongue, but is all eye;
    If it could speak as well as spy,
      This were the worst that it could say:
      That being well I fain would stay,   10
And that I lov'd my heart and honor so,
That I would not from him that had them go.

    Must business thee from hence remove?
    O, that's the worst disease of love;
      The poor, the foul, the false, love can   15

THE SUN RISING: 24. *alchemy:* false gold.

    Admit, but not the busied man.
He which hath business and makes love, doth do
Such wrong as when a married man doth woo.

❧

THE INDIFFERENT

    I can love both fair and brown,
Her whom abundance melts, and her whom want betrays,
Her who loves loneness best, and her who masks and plays,
    Her whom the country form'd, and whom the town,
      Her who believes, and her who tries,   5
      Her who still weeps with spongy eyes,
        And her who is dry cork and never cries;
    I can love her, and her, and you, and you;
    I can love any, so she be not true.

    Will no other vice content you?   10
Will it not serve your turn to do as did your mothers?
Or have you all old vices spent, and now would find out others?
    Or doth a fear that men are true torment you?
      O we are not; be not you so.
      Let me, and do you, twenty know.   15
      Rob me, but bind me not, and let me go.
    Must I, who came to travail through you,
    Grow your fix'd subject because you are true?

    Venus heard me sigh this song,
And by love's sweetest part, variety, she swore   20
She heard not this till now, and that it should be so no more.
    She went, examin'd, and return'd ere long,
      And said, "Alas, some two or three
      Poor heretics in love there be,
      Which think to 'stablish dangerous constancy,   25
    But I have told them, 'Since you will be true,
    You shall be true to them who're false to you.'"

❧

THE INDIFFERENT: 5. *tries:* tests sceptically.

THE CANONIZATION

For God's sake hold your tongue and let me love!
   Or chide my palsy or my gout,
My five grey hairs or ruin'd fortune flout;
With wealth your state, your mind with arts improve,
    Take you a course, get you a place,   5
    Observe his Honor or his Grace,
Or the king's real or his stampèd face
    Contemplate, what you will approve,
       So you will let me love.

Alas, alas, who's injur'd by my love?   10
    What merchant's ships have my sighs drown'd?
Who says my tears have overflow'd his ground?
When did my colds a forward spring remove?
    When did the heats which my veins fill
    Add one man to the plaguy bill?   15
Soldiers find wars, and lawyers find out still
    Litigious men which quarrels move,
       Though she and I do love.

Call us what you will, we are made such by love.
    Call her one, me another fly,   20
We're tapers too, and at our own cost die;
And we in us find th' eagle and the dove.
    The phoenix riddle hath more wit
    By us; we two being one, are it.
So to one neutral thing both sexes fit,   25
    We die and rise the same, and prove
       Mysterious by this love.

We can die by it, if not live by love;
    And if unfit for tombs and hearse
Our legend be, it will be fit for verse;   30
And if no piece of chronicle we prove,
    We'll build in sonnets pretty rooms
    (As well a well-wrought urn becomes
The greatest ashes, as half-acre tombs),

THE CANONIZATION: *7. stampèd face:* money.

And by these hymns all shall approve   35
  Us canoniz'd for love,

And thus invoke us: "You whom reverent love
  Made one another's hermitage,
You to whom love was peace, that now is rage,
Who did the whole world's soul extract, and drove   40
  Into the glasses of your eyes
  (So made such mirrors and such spies
That they did all to you epitomize)
  Countries, towns, courts; beg from above
  A pattern of your love!"   45

∾

LOVE'S INFINITENESS

If yet I have not all thy love,
  Dear, I shall never have it all;
I cannot breathe one other sigh to move,
  Nor can entreat one other tear to fall,
And all my treasure which should purchase thee,   5
  Sighs, tears, and oaths, and letters I have spent.
Yet no more can be due to me
  Than at the bargain made was meant.
If then thy gift of love were partial,
That some to me, some should to others fall,   10
Dear, I shall never have thee all.

Or if then thou gavest me all,
  All was but all which thou hadst then;
But if in thy heart since there be, or shall
  New love created be by other men   15
Which have their stocks entire, and can in tears,
  In sighs, in oaths, and letters outbid me,
This new love may beget new fears,
  For this love was not vow'd by thee—
And yet it was: thy gift being general,   20
The ground, thy heart, is mine; whatever shall
Grow there, dear, I should have it all.

Yet I would not have all yet.
  He that hath all can have no more,
And since my love doth every day admit   25

New growth, thou shouldst have new rewards in store.
Thou canst not every day give me thy heart;
   If thou canst give it, then thou never gavest it.
Love's riddles are that though thy heart depart,
   It stays at home, and thou with losing savest it.   30
But we will have a way more liberal
Than changing hearts—to join them, so we shall
Be one, and one another's all.

❧

SWEETEST LOVE

Sweetest love, I do not go
   For weariness of thee,
Nor in hope the world can show
   A fitter love for me;
     But since that I   5
Must die at last, 'tis best
To use myself in jest
   Thus by feign'd deaths to die.

Yesternight the sun went hence,
   And yet is here today;   10
He hath no desire nor sense,
   Nor half so short a way.
     Then fear not me,
But believe that I shall make
Speedier journeys, since I take   15
   More wings and spurs than he.

O how feeble is man's power,
   That if good fortune fall,
Cannot add another hour,
   Nor a lost hour recall!   20
     But come bad chance,
And we join to it our strength,
And we teach it art and length,
   Itself o'er us t' advance.

When thou sigh'st, thou sigh'st not wind,   25
   But sigh'st my soul away;
When thou weep'st, unkindly kind,
   My life's blood doth decay.

It cannot be
That thou lov'st me as thou say'st,   30
If in thine my life thou waste,
 Thou art the best of me.

Let not thy divining heart
 Forethink me any ill;
Destiny may take thy part,   35
 And may thy fears fulfill;
  But think that we
Are but turn'd aside to sleep.
They who one another keep
 Alive, ne'er parted be.   40

❥

AIR AND ANGELS

Twice or thrice had I lov'd thee
 Before I knew thy face or name;
 So in a voice, so in a shapeless flame
Angels affect us oft, and worshipp'd be;
 Still when to where thou wert I came,   5
Some lovely glorious nothing I did see.
 But since my soul, whose child love is,
Takes limbs of flesh (and else could nothing do),
 More subtile than the parent is,
Love must not be, but take a body too;   10
 And therefore what thou wert, and who,
  I bid love ask, and now
That it assume thy body I allow,
And fix itself in thy lip, eye, and brow.

Whilst thus to ballast love I thought   15
 (And so more steadily to have gone),
 With wares which would sink admiration,
I saw I had love's pinnace overfraught.
 Ev'ry thy hair for love to work upon
Is much too much; some fitter must be sought.   20
 For nor in nothing, nor in things
Extreme and scatt'ring bright can love inhere.
 Then, as an angel, face and wings
Of air not pure as it, yet pure, doth wear,

    So thy love may be my love's sphere.   25
      Just such disparity
   As is 'twixt air and angels' purity,
  'Twixt women's love and men's will ever be.

⚜⚜

THE ANNIVERSARY

    All kings and all their favorites,
    All glory of honors, beauties, wits,
  The sun itself, which makes times as they pass,
  Is elder by a year now than it was
  When thou and I first one another saw.   5
  All other things to their destruction draw;
    Only our love hath no decay;
  This, no tomorrow hath nor yesterday;
  Running, it never runs from us away,
But truly keeps his first, last, everlasting day.   10

    Two graves must hide thine and my corse.
    If one might, death were no divorce.
  Alas, as well as other princes, we
  (Who prince enough in one another be)
  Must leave at last in death these eyes and ears,   15
  Oft fed with true oaths and with sweet salt tears;
    But souls where nothing dwells but love
  (All other thoughts being inmates) then shall prove
  This, or a love increasèd there above,
When bodies to their graves, souls from their graves, remove.   20

    And then we shall be throughly blest,
    But we no more than all the rest.
  Here upon earth we're kings, and none but we
  Can be such kings, nor of such, subjects be.
  Who is so safe as we, where none can do   25
  Treason to us, except one of us two?
    True and false fears let us refrain,
  Let us love nobly, and live, and add again
  Years and years unto years till we attain
To write threescore.—This is the second of our reign.   30

THE ANNIVERSARY: 3. *makes times:* marks the seasons and years.

LOVE'S GROWTH

I scarce believe my love to be so pure
    As I had thought it was,
    Because it doth endure
Vicissitude and season as the grass.
Methinks I lied all winter when I swore   5
My love was infinite, if spring mak't more.

But it this med'cine, love, which cures all sorrow
    With more, not only be no quintessence,
    But mix'd of all stuffs paining soul or sense,
And of the sun his working vigor borrow,   10
Love's not so pure and abstract as they use
To say, which have no mistress but their muse;
But as all else, being elemented too,
Love sometimes would contemplate, sometimes do.

And yet no greater, but more eminent,   15
    Love by the spring is grown,
    As in the firmament
Stars by the sun are not enlarg'd, but shown.
Gentle love-deeds, as blossoms on a bough,
From love's awaken'd root do bud out now.   20

If, as in water stirr'd more circles be
    Produc'd by one, love such additions take,
    Those like so many spheres but one heaven make,
For they are all concentric unto thee.
And though each spring do add to love new heat,   25
As princes do in times of action get
New taxes and remit them not in peace,
No winter shall abate the spring's increase.

❧

LOVE'S EXCHANGE

    Love, any devil else but you
Would for a given soul give something too.
    At court your fellows every day

Give th' art of rhyming, huntsmanship, or play
   For them which were their own before.   5
   Only I have nothing, which gave more,
But am, alas, by being lowly, lower.

   I ask no dispensation now
To falsify a tear or sigh or vow;
   I do not sue from thee to draw   10
A *non obstante* on nature's law.
   These are prerogatives; they inhere
   In thee and thine; none should forswear
Except that he Love's minion were.

   Give me thy weakness, make me blind   15
Both ways, as thou and thine, in eyes and mind;
   Love, let me never know that this
Is love, or that love childish is.
   Let me not know that others know
   That she knows my pain, lest that so   20
A tender shame make me mine own new woe.

   If thou give nothing, yet thou'rt just,
Because I would not thy first motions trust;
   Small towns which stand stiff till great shot
Enforce them, by war's law condition not.   25
   Such in love's warfare is my case:
   I may not article for grace,
Having put Love at last to show this face.

   This face, by which he could command
And change th' idolatry of any land,   30
   This face, which wheresoe'er it comes,
Can call vow'd men from cloisters, dead from tombs,
   And melt both poles at once, and store
   Deserts with cities, and make more
Mines in the earth than quarries were before.   35

   For this, Love is enrag'd with me,
Yet kills not. If I must example be
   To future rebels, if th' unborn
Must learn by my being cut up and torn,
   Kill and dissect me, Love; for this   40
   Torture against thine own end is—
Rack'd carcases make ill anatomies.

LOVE'S EXCHANGE: 11. *non obstante:* waiver. 14. *minion:* favorite.

THE DREAM

Dear love, for nothing less than thee
Would I have broke this happy dream;
   It was a theme
For reason, much too strong for fantasy;
 Therefore thou wak'dst me wisely. Yet   5
My dream thou brok'st not, but continuedst it;
Thou art so Truth that thoughts of thee suffice
To make dreams truths, and fables histories.
Enter these arms, for since thou thought'st it best
Not to dream all my dream, let's act the rest.   10

 As lightning or a taper's light,
 Thine eyes and not thy noise wak'd me.
   Yet I thought thee
(For thou lov'st truth) an angel at first sight;
 But when I saw thou saw'st my heart,   15
And knew'st my thoughts (beyond an angel's art),
When thou knew'st what I dreamt, when thou knew'st when
Excess of joy would wake me, and cam'st then,
I do confess it could not choose but be
Profane to think thee anything but thee.   20

 Coming and staying show'd thee, thee,
 But rising makes me doubt that now
   Thou art not thou.
That love is weak where fear's as strong as he.
 'Tis not all spirit, pure and brave,   25
If mixture it of fear, shame, honor, have.
Perchance as torches which must ready be,
Men light and put out, so thou deal'st with me:
Thou cam'st to kindle, go'st to come; then I
Will dream that hope again, but else would die.   30

A VALEDICTION: OF WEEPING

Let me pour forth
My tears before thy face whilst I stay here,
For thy face coins them, and thy stamp they bear,
And by this mintage they are something worth,
　　　For thus they be　　　　　　　　　　　　　5
　　　Pregnant of thee;
Fruits of much grief they are, emblems of more:
When a tear falls, that *thou* falls which it bore;
So thou and I are nothing then, when on a divers shore.

On a round ball　　　　　　　　　　　　　10
A workman that hath copies by, can lay
An Europe, Afric, and an Asia,
And quickly make that which was nothing, all;
　　　So doth each tear
　　　Which *thee* doth wear,　　　　　　　　15
A globe, yea world, by that impression grow,
Till thy tears mix'd with mine do overflow
This world: by waters sent from tnee, my heaven dissolvèd so.

O more than moon,
Draw not up seas to drown me in thy sphere,　　20
Weep me not dead in thine arms, but forbear
To teach the sea what it may do too soon;
　　　Let not the wind
　　　Example find
To do me more harm than it purposeth;　　　25
Since thou and I sigh one another's breath,
Whoe'er sighs most is cruelest, and hastes the other's death.

❧

LOVE'S ALCHEMY: MUMMY

Some that have deeper digg'd love's mine than I,
Say where his centric happiness doth lie.
　　　I have lov'd, and got, and told,
But should I love, get, tell, till I were old,
I should not find that hidden mystery.　　　　5

O, 'tis imposture all!
And as no chemic yet th' elixir got,
    But glorifies his pregnant pot
    If by the way to him befall
Some odorif'rous thing, or med'cinal,   10
    So lovers dream a rich and long delight,
    But get a winter-seeming summer's night.

Our ease, our thrift, our honor, and our day,
Shall we for this vain bubble's shadow pay?
        Ends love in this, that my man   15
Can be as happy's I can, if he can
Endure the short scorn of a bridegroom's play?
        That loving wretch that swears
'Tis not the bodies marry, but the minds
    (Which he in her angelic finds),   20
    Would swear as justly that he hears,
In that day's rude, hoarse minstrelsy, the spheres.
    Hope not for mind in women. At their best
    Sweetness and wit, they're but mummy possess'd.

&

THE FLEA

    Mark but this flea, and mark in this
How little that which thou deny'st me is;
    It suck'd me first, and now sucks thee,
And in this flea our two bloods mingled be.
    Thou know'st that this cannot be said   5
A sin, nor shame, nor loss of maidenhead;
    Yet this enjoys before it woo,
And pamper'd, swells with one blood made of two,
And this, alas, is more than we would do.

    O stay, three lives in one flea spare,   10
Where we almost, yea more than married are.
    This flea is you and I, and this
Our marriage bed and marriage temple is;
    Though parents grudge, and you, we're met
And cloister'd in these living walls of jet.   15

LOVE'S ALCHEMY: 7. *chemic:* alchemist.
THE FLEA: 8. *pamper'd:* fed full.

Though use make you apt to kill me,
Let not to that, self-murder added be,
And sacrilege: three sins in killing three.

Cruel and sudden, hast thou since
Purpled thy nail in blood of innocence?   20
    Wherein could this flea guilty be,
Except in that drop which it suck'd from thee?
    Yet thou triumph'st, and say'st that thou
Find'st not thyself nor me the weaker now.
    'Tis true. Then learn how false fears be: 25
Just so much honor, when thou yield'st to me,
Will waste, as this flea's death took life from thee.

⤙⤚

THE BAIT

Come live with me and be my love,
And we will some new pleasures prove
Of golden sands and crystal brooks,
With silken lines and silver hooks.

There will the river whispering run,   5
Warm'd by thine eyes more than the sun,
And there th' enamor'd fish will stay,
Begging themselves they may betray.

When thou wilt swim in that live bath,
Each fish which every channel hath   10
Will amorously to thee swim,
Gladder to catch thee than thou him.

If thou to be so seen be'st loath,
By sun or moon, thou dark'nest both,
And if myself have leave to see,   15
I need not their light, having thee.

Let others freeze with angling reeds,
And cut their legs with shells and weeds,
Or treacherously poor fish beset
With strangling snare or windowy net;   20

Let coarse bold hands from slimy nest
The bedded fish in banks outwrest,
Or curious traitors, sleave-silk flies,
Bewitch poor fishes' wand'ring eyes,

For thee, thou need'st no such deceit,   25
For thou thyself art thine own bait;
That fish that is not catch'd thereby,
Alas, is wiser far than I.

THE APPARITION

When by thy scorn, O murd'ress, I am dead,
 And that thou think'st thee free
 From all solicitation from me,
Then shall my ghost come to thy bed,
 And thee, feign'd vestal, in worse arms shall see.   5

Then thy sick taper will begin to wink,
 And he whose thou art then, being tir'd before,
Will, if thou stir or pinch to wake him, think
        Thou call'st for more,
And in false sleep will from thee shrink,   10

And then, poor aspen wretch, neglected, thou
 Bath'd in a cold, quicksilver sweat wilt lie
        A verier ghost than I.
What I will say, I will not tell thee now,
Lest that preserve thee; and since my love is spent, 15
I'd rather thou shouldst painfully repent
Than by my threat'nings rest still innocent.

THE BROKEN HEART

 He is stark mad, whoever says
That he hath been in love an hour,
 Yet not that love so soon decays,
But that it can ten in less space devour.
 Who will believe me if I swear   5

That I have had the plague a year?
Who would not laugh at me if I should say
I saw a fiask of powder burn a day?

    Ah, what a trifle is a heart
If once into Love's hands it come!   10
    All other griefs allow a part
To other griefs, and ask themselves but some;
    They come to us, but us Love draws;
    He swallows us and never chaws;
By him, as by chain'd shot, whole ranks do die;   15
He is the tyrant pike, our hearts the fry.

    If 'twere not so, what did become
Of my heart when I first saw thee?
    I brought a heart into the room,
But from the room I carried none with me.   20
    If it had gone to thee, I know
    Mine would have taught thine heart to show
More pity unto me; but Love, alas,
At one first blow did shiver it as glass.

    Yet nothing can to nothing fall,   25
Nor any place be empty quite;
    Therefore I think my breast hath all
Those pieces still, though they be not unite;
    And now as broken glasses show
    A hundred lesser faces, so   30
My rags of heart can like, wish, and adore,
But after one such love can love no more.

             ❧

A VALEDICTION: FORBIDDING MOURNING

As virtuous men pass mildly away,
    And whisper to their souls to go,
Whilst some of their sad friends do say,
    "The breath goes now," and some say, "No,"

So let us melt and make no noise,   5
    No tear-floods nor sigh-tempests move;
'Twere profanation of our joys
    To tell the laity our love.

Moving of th' earth brings harms and fears;
   Men reckon what it did and meant;   10
But trepidation of the spheres,
   Though greater far, is innocent.

Dull sublunary lovers' love,
   Whose soul is sense, cannot admit
Absence, because it doth remove   15
   Those things which elemented it.

But we by a love so much refin'd
   That ourselves know not what it is,
Interassurèd of the mind,
   Care less eyes, lips, and hands to miss.   20

Our two souls, therefore, which are one,
   Though I must go, endure not yet
A breach, but an expansion,
   Like gold to airy thinness beat.

If they be two, they are two so   25
   As stiff twin compasses are two;
Thy soul, the fix'd foot, makes no show
   To move, but doth if th' other do.

And though it in the center sit,
   Yet when the other far doth roam,   30
It leans and hearkens after it,
   And grows erect as that comes home.

Such wilt thou be to me, who must,
   Like th' other foot, obliquely run;
Thy firmness makes my circle just,   35
   And makes me end where I begun.

❧

THE ECSTASY

Where, like a pillow on a bed,
   A pregnant bank swell'd up to rest

A VALEDICTION: 11. *trepidation of the spheres:* the precession of the equinoxes caused, according to Ptolemaic astronomy, by the movements of the ninth or crystalline sphere. 12. *innocent:* harmless. 16. *elemented:* composed.

The violet's reclining head,
  Sat we two, one another's best.

Our hands were firmly cemented   5
  With a fast balm which thence did spring,
Our eye-beams twisted, and did thread
  Our eyes upon one double string;

So t' intergraft our hands, as yet
  Was all the means to make us one,   10
And pictures on our eyes to get
  Was all our propagation.

As 'twixt two equal armies, fate
  Suspends uncertain victory,
Our souls, which to advance their state   15
  Were gone out, hung 'twixt her and me.

And whilst our souls negotiate there,
  We like sepulchral statues lay;
All day the same our postures were,
  And we said nothing all the day.   20

If any (so by love refin'd
  That he soul's language understood,
And by good love were grown all mind)
  Within convenient distance stood,

He (though he knew not which soul spake,   25
  Because both meant, both spake the same)
Might thence a new concoction take,
  And part far purer than he came.

This ecstasy doth unperplex,
  We said, and tell us what we love;   30
We see by this it was not sex,
  We see we saw not what did move;

But as all several souls contain
  Mixture of things, they know not what,
Love these mix'd souls doth mix again,   35
  And makes both one, each this and that.

A single violet transplant,
  The strength, the color, and the size
(All which before was poor and scant)
  Redoubles still and multiplies.   40

When love with one another so
  Interinanimates two souls,
That abler soul which thence doth flow
  Defects of loneliness controls.

We then, who are this new soul, know   45
  Of what we are compos'd and made,
For th' atomies of which we grow
  Are souls, whom no change can invade.

But O, alas, so long, so far
  Our bodies why do we forbear?   50
They're ours, though they're not we; we are
  Th' intelligences, they the spheres;

We owe them thanks because they thus
  Did us to us at first convey,
Yielded their forces, sense, to us,   55
  Nor are dross to us, but allay.

On man heaven's influence works not so,
  But that it first imprints the air;
So soul into the soul may flow
  Though it to body first repair.   60

As our blood labors to beget
  Spirits as like souls as it can,
Because such fingers need to knit
  That subtile knot which makes us man,

So must pure lovers' souls descend   65
  T' affections and to faculties
Which sense may reach and apprehend;
  Else a great prince in prison lies.

T' our bodies turn we then, that so
  Weak men on love reveal'd may look;   70
Love's mysteries in souls do grow,
  But yet the body is his book.

And if some lover, such as we,
  Have heard this dialogue of one,
Let him still mark us; he shall see   75
  Small change when we're to bodies gone.

LOVE'S DEITY

I long to talk with some old lover's ghost
    Who died before the god of love was born.
I cannot think that he who then lov'd most
    Sunk so low as to love one which did scorn.
But since this god produc'd a destiny,   5
And that vice-nature, custom, lets it be,
        I must love her that loves not me.

Sure they which made him god meant not so much,
    Nor he in his young godhead practic'd it;
But when an even flame two hearts did touch,   10
    His office was indulgently to fit
Actives to passives. Correspondency
Only, his subject was. It cannot be
        Love till I love her that loves me.

But every modern god will now extend   15
    His vast prerogative as far as Jove.
To rage, to lust, to write to, to commend,
    All is the purlieu of the god of love.
O were we waken'd by this tyranny
T' ungod this child again, it could not be   20
        I should love her who loves not me.

Rebel and atheist too, why murmur I,
    As though I felt the worst that Love could do?
Love might make me leave loving, or might try
    A deeper plague, to make her love me too,   25
Which, since she loves before, I'm loath to see.
Falsehood is worse than hate, and that must be
        If she whom I love should love me.

THE WILL

Before I sigh my last gasp, let me breathe,
Great Love, some legacies: Here I bequeath
Mine eyes to Argus, if mine eyes can see;

If they be blind, then, Love, I give them thee;
My tongue to Fame, t' ambassadors mine ears,   5
    To women or the sea my tears.
    Thou, Love, hast taught me heretofore,
By making me serve her who'd twenty more,
That I should give to none but such as had too much before.

My constancy I to the planets give,   10
My truth to them who at the court do live,
Mine ingenuity and openness
To Jesuits, to buffoons my pensiveness,
My silence t' any who abroad hath been,
    My money to a Capuchin.   15
    Thou, Love, taught'st me, by appointing me
To love there where no love receiv'd can be,
Only to give to such as have an incapacity.

My faith I give to Roman Catholics,
All my good works unto the schismatics   20
Of Amsterdam, my best civility
And courtship to an university;
My modesty I give to soldiers bare;
    My patience let gamesters share.
    Thou, Love, taught'st me, by making me   25
Love her that holds my love disparity,
Only to give to those that count my gifts indignity.

I give my reputation to those
Which were my friends, mine industry to foes;
To schoolmen I bequeath my doubtfulness,   30
My sickness to physicians or excess,
To nature all that I in rhyme have writ,
    And to my company my wit.
    Thou, Love, by making me adore
Her who begot this love in me before,   35
Taught'st me to make as though I gave, when I did but restore.

To him for whom the passing-bell next tolls
I give my physic books; my written rolls
Of moral counsels I to Bedlam give,

THE WILL: 15. *Capuchin:* Franciscan monk of an austere branch. 20.
schismatics of Amsterdam: extreme Puritans, who believed in justification
by faith only, as opposed to the Catholic belief in good works as well. 38.
physic: medical. 39. *Bedlam:* Bethlehem insane asylum.

My brazen medals unto them which live   40
    In want of bread, to them which pass among
      All foreigners, mine English tongue.
      Thou, Love, by making me love one
    Who thinks her friendship a fit portion
For younger lovers, dost my gifts thus disproportion.   45

Therefore I'll give no more; but I'll undo
    The world by dying, because love dies too.
    Then all your beauties will be no more worth
    Than gold in mines where none doth draw it forth,
And all your graces no more use shall have   50
      Than a sundial in a grave.
      Thou, Love, taught'st me, by making me
    Love her who doth neglect both me and thee,
T' invent and practice this one way t' annihilate all three.

THE FUNERAL

Whoever comes to shroud me, do not harm
      Nor question much
    That subtile wreath of hair which crowns mine arm;
    The mystery, the sign, you must not touch,
      For 'tis my outward soul,   5
    Viceroy to that, which then to heav'n being gone,
      Will leave this to control
And keep these limbs, her provinces, from dissolution.

For if the sinewy thread my brain lets fall
      Through every part   10
    Can tie those parts and make me one of all,
    These hairs, which upward grew, and strength and art
      Have, from a better brain,
    Can better do't; except she meant that I
      By this should know my pain,   15
As prisoners then are manacled, when they're condemn'd to die.

Whate'er she meant by't, bury it with me,
      For since I am
    Love's martyr, it might breed idolatry
    If into others' hands these relics came.   20
      As 'twas humility

T' afford to it all which a soul can do,
    So 'tis some bravery
That since you would save none of me, I bury some of you.

THE RELIC

When my grave is broke up again
    Some second guest to entertain
    (For graves have learn'd that womanhead
    To be to more than one a bed)
      And he that digs it spies   5
A bracelet of bright hair about the bone,
      Will he not let'us alone,
And think that there a loving couple lies,
Who thought that this device might be some way
To make their souls at the last busy day   10
Meet at this grave, and make a little stay?

If this fall in a time or land
    Where mis-devotion doth command,
    Then he that digs us up will bring
    Us to the bishop and the king   15
      To make us relics; then
Thou shalt be'a Mary Magdalen, and I
      A something else thereby.
All women shall adore us, and some men;
And since at such time miracles are sought,   20
I would have that age by this paper taught
What miracles we harmless lovers wrought.

First, we lov'd well and faithfully,
    Yet knew not what we lov'd, nor why;
    Difference of sex no more we knew   25
    Than our guardian angels do;
      Coming and going, we
Perchance might kiss, but not between those meals;
      Our hands ne'er touch'd the seals
Which nature, injur'd by late law, sets free.   30
These miracles we did; but now, alas,
All measure and all language I should pass,
Should I tell what a miracle she was.

THE PROHIBITION

Take heed of loving me,
At least remember I forbid it thee;
　　Not that I shall repair my'unthrifty waste
Of breath and blood upon thy sighs and tears,
　　By being to thee then what to me thou wast;　　　　5
But so great joy our life at once outwears.
　　Then, lest thy love by my death frustrate be,
　　If thou love me, take heed of loving me.

Take heed of hating me,
Or too much triumph in the victory;　　　　　　　　10
　　Not that I shall be mine own officer,
And hate with hate again retaliate,
　　But thou wilt lose the style of conqueror
If I, thy conquest, perish by thy hate.
　　Then, lest my being nothing lessen thee,　　　　15
　　If thou hate me, take heed of hating me.

Yet love and hate me too,
So these extremes shall neither office do;
　　Love me, that I may die the gentler way;
Hate me, because thy love's too great for me;　　　20
　　Or let these two, themselves, not me, decay;
So shall I live thy stage, not triumph be.
　　Then, lest thy love, hate, and me thou undo,
　　O let me live; yet love and hate me too.

❧

THE COMPUTATION

For the first twenty years since yesterday,
I scarce believ'd thou couldst be gone away;
For forty more I fed on favors past,
And forty'n hopes that thou wouldst they might last.
　　Tears drown'd one hundred, and sighs blew out two,　　5

THE PROHIBITION: 22. *triumph:* final conquest, as opposed to a stage where
she can be continually acclaimed.

A thousand, I did neither think nor do,
Or not divide, all being one thought of you,
Or in a thousand more forgot that too.
ᵉt call not this long life, but think that I
ᵢm, by being dead, immortal. Can ghosts die?   10

A LECTURE UPON THE SHADOW

Stand still, and I will read to thee
A lecture, Love, in love's philosophy.
These three hours that we have spent
Walking here, two shadows went
Along with us, which we ourselves produc'd;   5
But, now the sun is just above our head,
We do those shadows tread,
And to brave clearness all things are reduc'd.
So whilst our infant loves did grow,
Disguises did, and shadows, flow   10
From us and our cares; but now 'tis not so.

'That love hath not attain'd the high'st degree
Which is still diligent lest others see.

Except our loves at this noon stay,
We shall new shadows make the other way.   15
As the first were made to blind
Others, these which come behind
Will work upon ourselves and blind our eyes.
If our loves faint and westwardly decline,
To me thou falsely thine,   20
And I to thee mine actions shall disguise.
The morning shadows wear away,
But these grow longer all the day,
But O, love's day is short if love decay!

Love is a growing, or full constant light,   25
And his first minute after noon is night.

TWICKENHAM GARDEN

Blasted with sighs and surrounded with tears,
    Hither I come to seek the spring,
    And at mine eyes, and at mine ears,
Receive such balms as else cure everything;
    But O, self-traitor, I do bring   5
The spider love, which transubstantiates all,
    And can convert manna to gall;
And that this place may thoroughly be thought
True Paradise, I have the serpent brought.

'Twere wholesomer for me that winter did   10
    Benight the glory of this place,
    And that a grave frost did forbid
These trees to laugh and mock me to my face;
    But that I may not this disgrace
Endure, nor leave this garden, Love, let me   15
    Some senseless piece of this place be:
Make me a mandrake so I may grow here,
Or a stone fountain weeping out my year.

Hither with crystal vials, lovers, come,
    And take my tears, which are love's wine,   20
    And try your mistress' tears at home,
For all are false that taste not just like mine.
    Alas! hearts do not in eyes shine,
Nor can you more judge woman's thoughts by tears,
    Than by her shadow what she wears.   25
O perverse sex, where none is true but she,
Who's therefore true because her truth kills me.

❧

A NOCTURNAL UPON ST. LUCY'S DAY
BEING THE SHORTEST DAY

'Tis the year's midnight, and it is the day's,
Lucy's, who scarce seven hours herself unmasks.

TWICKENHAM GARDEN: I. *surrounded:* overflowing.

    The sun is spent, and now his flasks
    Send forth light squibs, no constant rays;
      The world's whole sap is sunk;   5
The general balm th' hydroptic earth hath drunk,
Whither, as to the bed's feet, life is shrunk,
Dead and interr'd; yet all these seem to laugh
Compar'd with me, who am their epitaph.

Study me then, you who shall lovers be   10
At the next world (that is, at the next spring),
    For I am every dead thing,
    In whom Love wrought new alchemy;
      For his art did express
A quintessence even from nothingness,   15
From dull privations and lean emptiness.
He ruin'd me, and I am re-begot
Of absence, darkness, death: things which are not.

All others from all things draw all that's good:
Life, soul, form, spirit, whence they being have;   20
    I, by love's limbec, am the grave
    Of all that's nothing. Oft a flood
      Have we two wept, and so
Drown'd the whole world—us two. Oft did we grow
To be two Chaoses when we did show   25
Care to aught else; and often absences
Withdrew our souls and made us carcases.

But I am by her death (which word wrongs her)
Of the first nothing the elixir grown;
    Were I a man, that I were one   30
    I needs must know; I should prefer,
      If I were any beast,
Some ends, some means; yea plants, yea stones detest
And love; all, all some properties invest;
If I an ordinary nothing were,   35
As shadow, a light and body must be here.

But I am none; nor will my Sun renew.
You lovers, for whose sake the lesser sun
    At this time to the Goat is run
    To fetch new lust and give it you,   40
      Enjoy your summer all.
Since she enjoys her long night's festival,
Let me prepare towards her, and let me call

This hour her vigil and her eve, since this
Both the year's and the day's deep midnight is.   45

❧

ELEGY XVI

ON HIS MISTRESS

(1635)

By our first strange and fatal interview,
By all desires which thereof did ensue,
By our long starving hopes, by that remorse
Which my words' masculine, persuasive force
Begot in thee, and by the memory   5
Of hurts which spies and rivals threaten'd me.
I calmly beg; but by thy parents' wrath,
By all pains which want and divorcement hath,
I conjure thee; and all those oaths which I
And thou have sworn to seal joint constancy,   10
Here I unswear, and overswear them thus:
Thou shalt not love by means so dangerous.
Temper, O fair love, love's impetuous rage;
Be my true mistress still, not my feign'd page.
I'll go, and by thy kind leave, leave behind   15
Thee, only worthy to nurse in my mind
Thirst to come back. O, if thou die before,
From other lands my soul towards thee shall soar.
Thy (else almighty) beauty cannot move
Rage from the seas, nor thy love teach them love,   20
Nor tame wild Boreas' harshness. Thou hast read
How roughly he in pieces shivered
Fair Orithyia, whom he swore he lov'd.
Fall ill or good, 'tis madness to have prov'd
Dangers unurg'd. Feed on this flattery: 25
That absent lovers one in th' other be.
Dissemble nothing, not a boy, nor change
Thy body's habit, nor mind's; be not strange
To thyself only; all will spy in thy face
A blushing womanly discovering grace.   30
Richly cloth'd apes are call'd apes, and as soon
Eclips'd as bright, we call the moon the moon.

Men of France, changeable chameleons,
Spitals of diseases, shops of fashions,
Love's fuelers, and the rightest company   35
Of players which upon the world's stage be,
Will quickly know thee, and know thee, and alas!
Th' indifferent Italian, as we pass
His warm land, well content to think thee page,
Will haunt thee with such lust and hideous rage   40
As Lot's fair guests were vex'd. But none of these,
Nor spongy, hydroptic Dutch shall thee displease
If thou stay here. O stay here! for, for thee
England is only a worthy gallery
To walk in expectation, till from thence   45
Our great King call thee into his presence.
When I am gone, dream me some happiness,
Nor let thy looks our long-hid love confess,
Nor praise nor dispraise me, bless nor curse
Openly love's force, nor in bed fright thy nurse   50
With midnight's startings, crying out, "O! O!
Nurse! O! my love is slain! I saw him go
O'er the white Alps alone; I saw him, I,
Assail'd, fight, taken, stabb'd, bleed, fall, and die."
Augur me better chance, except dread Jove   55
Think it enough for me t' have had thy love.

❧

SATIRE III

OF RELIGION

(1633)

Though Truth and Falsehood be
Near twins, yet Truth a little elder is;
Be busy to seek her; believe me this,
He's not of none, nor worst, which seeks the best.
T' adore, or scorn an image, or protest,   5
May all be bad. Doubt wisely; in strange way

ELEGY XVI: 34. *Spitals:* hospitals, receptacles.

To stand inquiring right is not to stray;
To sleep or run wrong is. On a high hill,
Ragged and steep, Truth dwells, and he that will
Reach her, about must, and about must go;   10
And what th' hill's suddenness resists, win so.
Yet strive so, that before age, death's twilight,
Thy mind rest, for none can work in that night.

·   ·   ·   ·   ·   ·   ·   ·   ·

∽

SATIRE IV

THE COURT

(1633)

Well, I may now receive and die. My sin,
Indeed, is great, but I've been in
A purgatory, such as fear'd hell is
A re-creation and scant map of this.
My mind, nor with pride's itch, nor yet hath been   5
Poison'd with love to see or to be seen.
I had no suit there, nor new suit to show;
Yet went to court. But as Glare, which did go
T' a mass in jest, catch'd, was fain to disburse
The hundred marks which is the statute's curse,   10
Before he 'scap'd, so't pleas'd my destiny
(Guilty of my sin of going) to think me
As prone to all ill and of good as forget-
ful, as proud, lustful, and as much in debt,
As vain, as witless, and as false as they   15
Which dwell at court, for once going that way.
Therefore I suffer'd this:—Towards me did run
A thing more strange than on Nile's slime the sun
E'er bred, or all which into Noah's Ark came,
A thing which would have pos'd Adam to name,   20
Stranger than seven antiquaries' studies,
Than Afric's monsters, Guiana's rarities,
Stranger than strangers, one who for a Dane
In the Danes' massacre had sure been slain
If he had liv'd then, and without help dies   25
When next the prentices 'gainst strangers rise,
One whom the watch at noon lets scarce go by,

One t' whom th' examining justice sure would cry,
"Sir, by your priesthood, tell me what you are!"
His clothes were strange, though coarse; and black, though bare;   30
Sleeveless his jerkin was, and it had been
Velvet, but 'twas now (so much ground was seen)
Become tufftaffaty; and our children shall
See it plain rash awhile, then nought at all.
This thing hath travel'd, and (saith) speaks all tongues,   35
And only knows what to all states belongs.
Made of th' accents and best phrase of all these,
He speaks one language. If strange meats displease,
Art can deceive, or hunger force my taste,
But pedant's motley tongue, soldier's bombast,   40
Mountebank's drug-tongue, nor the terms of law
Are strong enough preparatives to draw
Me to bear this. Yet I must be content
With his tongue—in his tongue call'd compliment—
In which he can win widows and pay scores,   45
Make men speak treason, cozen subtlest whores,
Outflatter favorites, and outlie either
Jovius or Surius, or both together.
He names me'nd comes to me. I whisper, "God!
How have I sinn'd that thy wrath's furious rod,   50
This fellow, chooseth me?" He saith, "Sir,
I love your judgment. Whom do you prefer
For the best linguist?" And I sillily
Said that I thought Calepine's *Dictionary*—
"Nay, but of men, most sweet Sir?" Beza then,   55
Some Jesuits, and two reverend men
Of our two academies I nam'd. There
He stopp'd me'nd said, "Nay, your apostles were
Good pretty linguists, and so Panurge was;
Yet a poor gentleman all these may pass   60
By travel." Then, as if he would have sold
His tongue, he prais'd it, and such wonders told
That I was fain to say, "If you'd liv'd, Sir,
Time enough to have been interpreter
To Babel's bricklayers, sure that tower had stood."   65
He adds, "If of court life you knew the good,
You would leave loneness." I said, "Not alone

SATIRE IV: 48. *Jovius or Surius:* Catholic historians. 54. *Calepine's* Dictionary: a polyglot dictionary which grew by 1590 to include eleven lan-
guages.

My loneness is, but Spartans' fashion.
To teach by painting drunkards doth not last
Now; Aretine's pictures have made few chaste;   70
No more can princes' courts, though there be few
Better pictures of vice, teach me virtue."
He, like a too high-stretch'd lute string, squeak'd, "O Sir,
'Tis sweet to talk of kings." "At Westminster,"
Said I, "the man that keeps the Abbey tombs,   75
And for his price doth with whoever comes
Of all our Harrys and our Edwards talk,
From king to king and all their kin can walk.
Your ears shall hear nought but "king," your eyes meet
Kings only. The way to it is King's Street."   80
He smack'd and cried, "He's base, mechanic, coarse;
So're all your Englishmen in their discourse.
Are not your Frenchmen neat?" "Mine? As you see,
I have but one Frenchman. Look, he follows me."
"Certes they are neatly cloth'd. I of this mind am,   85
Your only wearing is your grogaram."
"Not so, Sir; I have more." Under this pitch
He would not fly; I chaf'd him, but as itch
Scratch'd into smart, and as blunt iron ground
Into an edge hurts worse, so I, fool, found   90
Crossing hurt me. To fit my sullenness,
He to another key his style doth 'dress,
And asks, "What news?" I tell him of new plays.
He takes my hand, and as a still, which stays
A sem'breve 'twixt each drop, he niggardly,   95
As loath t' enrich me so, tells many a lie.
More than ten Holinsheds or Halls or Stows,
Of trivial household trash he knows; he knows
When the Queen smil'd or frown'd, and he knows what
A subtile statesman may gather of that;   100
He knows who loves whom, and who by poison
Hastes t' an office's reversion;
He knows who'th sold his land and now doth beg
A license, old iron, shoes, boots, or egg-
shells to transport. Shortly boys shall not play   105
At blow-point or span-counter but they pay

---

70. *Aretine's pictures:* sonnets by Pietro Aretino for Giulio Romano's lascivious pictures. 95. *sem'breve:* semibreve: whole note. 97. *Holinsheds or Halls
or Stows:* Elizabethan chroniclers.

Toll to some courtier; and wiser than all us,
He knows which lady is not painted. Thus
He with home-meats tries me. I belch, spew, spit,
Look pale and sickly like a patient; yet   110
He thrusts more, and as if he'd undertook
To say Gallo-Belgicus without book,
Speaks of all states and deeds which have been since
The Spaniards came, t' the loss of Amiens.
Like a big wife, at sight of loathèd meat,   115
Ready to travail, so I sigh and sweat
To hear his Macaron talk—in vain! for yet,
Either my humor or his own to fit,
He, like a privileg'd spy whom nothing can
Discredit, libels now 'gainst each great man.   120
He names a price for every office paid;
He says our wars thrive ill because delay'd,
That offices are entail'd, and that there are
Perpetuities of them lasting as far
As the Last Day, and that great officers   125
Do with the pirates share, and Dunkirkers.
Who wastes in meat, in clothes, in horse, he notes;
Who loves whores, who boys, and who goats.
I, more amaz'd than Circe's prisoners when
They felt themselves turn beasts, felt myself then   130
Becoming traitor, and methought I saw
One of our giant statutes ope his jaw
To suck me in for hearing him. I found
That as burnt venom'd lechers do grow sound
By giving others their sores, I might grow   135
Guilty, and he free. Therefore I did show
All signs of loathing; but since I am in,
I must pay mine and my forefathers' sin
To the last farthing. Therefore to my power,
Toughly and stubbornly, I bear this cross; but th' hour   140
Of mercy now was come. He tries to bring
Me to pay a fine to 'scape his torturing,
And says, "Sir, can you spare me—" I said, "Willingly!"
"Nay, Sir, can you spare me a crown?" Thankfully I
Gave it as ransom, but as fiddlers still,   145

112. *Gallo-Belgicus: Mercurius Gallo-Belgicus,* a news journal started at
Cologne in 1598. 114. *Spaniards came:* 1588; *loss of Amiens:* 1597. 117.
Macaron: stupid fop. 124. *Perpetuities:* inalienable rights.

Though they be paid to be gone, yet needs will
Thrust one more jig upon you, so did he
With his long complimental thanks vex me.
But he is gone, thanks to his needy want,
And the prerogative of my crown. Scant   150
His thanks were ended, when I, which did see
All the court fill'd with more strange things than he,
Run from thence with such or more haste than one
Who fears more actions doth make from prison.
At home in wholesome solitariness   155
My piteous soul began the wretchedness
Of suitors at court to mourn, and a trance
Like his who dreamt he saw hell, did advance
Itself o'er me. And such men as he saw there,
I saw at court, and worse, and more. Low fear   160
Becomes the guilty, not th' accuser. Then,
Shall I, none's slave, of highborn or rais'd men
Fear frowns? and, my mistress Truth, betray thee
To th' huffing braggart, puff'd Nobility?
No, no, thou which since yesterday hast been   165
Almost about the whole world, hast thou seen,
O sun, in all thy journey, vanity
Such as swells the bladder of our court? I
Think he which made yon waxen garden and
Transplanted it from Italy to stand   170
With us at London, flouts our court here, for
Just such gay painted things which no sap nor
Taste have in them, ours are; and natural
Some of the stocks are, their fruits bastard all.
'Tis ten o'clock and past; all whom the mews,   175
Ballone, tennis, diet, or the stews
Had all the morning held, now the second
Time made ready that day, in flocks are found
In the Presence—and I, God pardon me!
As fresh and sweet th' apparels be as be   180
The fields they sold to buy them. "For a king
Those hose are," cries his flatterers, and bring
Them next week to the theater to sell.
Wants reach all states; meseems they do as well
At stage as court. All are players; whoe'er looks 185
(For themselves dare not go) o'er Cheapside books

175. *mews:* hawking. 176. *Ballone:* a ball game, something like soccer;
stews: brothels. 186. *Cheapside:* secondhand store.

Shall find their wardrobe's inventory. Now
The ladies come. As pirates which did know
That there came weak ships fraught with cutchannel,
The men board them and praise, as they think, well   190
Their beauties; they the men's wits. Both are bought.
Why good wits ne'er wear scarlet gowns, I thought
This cause: these men men's wits for speeches buy,
And women buy all reds which scarlet dye.
He call'd her beauty lime twigs, her hair net;   195
She fears her drugs ill laid, her hair loose set.
Would not Heraclitus laugh to see Macrine
From hat to shoe himself at door refine
As the Presence were a meschite, and lift
His skirts and hose and call his clothes to shrift,   200
Making them confess not only mortal
Great stains and holes in them, but venial
Feathers or dust, with which they fornicate,
And then by Dürer's rules surveys the state
Of his each limb, and with strings th' odds tries   205
Of his neck to his leg and waist to thighs?
So in immaculate clothes, and symmetry
Perfect as circles, with such nicety
As a young preacher at his first time goes
To preach, he enters, and a lady which owes   210
Him not so much as good will, straight arrests,
And unto her protests, protests, protests,
So much as at Rome would serve to have thrown
Ten cardinals into th' Inquisition,
And whisper'd "By Jesu!" so often that a   215
Pursuivant would have ravish'd him away
For saying of Our Lady's psalter; but 'tis fit
That they each other plague; they merit it.
But here comes Glorius, that will plague them both,
Who, in the other extreme, only doth   220
Call a rough carelessness good fashion.
Whose cloak his spurs tear, whom he spits on
He cares not; his ill words do no harm

---

189. *cutchannel:* cochineal, a dye made from the dried bodies of female
scale insects, and perhaps suggested by the ladies' rouge. There is a record
of cochineal being seized by English pirates from a Venetian ship about
1603. 195. *lime twigs:* a snare. 196. *drugs:* cosmetics. 199. *meschite:* (mes-
quita) mosque. 216. *Pursuivant:* government agent to ferret out Catholics.

To him! He rusheth in as if "Arm, arm!"
He came to cry. And though his face be's ill   225
As theirs which in old hangings whip Christ, still
He strives to look worse; he keeps all in awe,
Jests like a licens'd fool, commands like law.
Tir'd, now I'll leave this place, and, but pleas'd so
As men which from jails t' execution go,   230
Go through the great chamber (Why is it hung
With the Seven Deadly Sins?). Being among
Those Ascaparts (men big enough to throw
Charing Cross for a bar, men which do know
No token of worth but "Queen's man," and fine   235
Living, barrels of beef, flagons of wine),
I shook like a spied spy. Preachers, which are
Seas of wit and arts, you can, then dare
Drown the sins of this place, for, for me,
Which am but a scarce brook, it enough shall be   240
To wash their stains away. Though I yet
With Maccabee's modesty the merit
Of my work lessen, yet some wise men shall,
I hope, esteem my writs canonical.

❧

THE FIRST ANNIVERSARY

AN ANATOMY OF THE WORLD

Wherein, by Occasion of the untimely death of Mistress
Elizabeth Drury, the Frailty and the Decay of This Whole
World is Represented

(1611)

The entry into   When that rich soul which to her heaven is gone,
the work.   Whom all they celebrate who know they have one
                          (For who is sure he hath a soul, unless
                          It see and judge and follow worthiness,

233. *Ascaparts:* a thirty-foot giant in the story of Sir Bevis of Southampton.
242. *Maccabee's modesty:* 2 Maccabees xv, 38: "And if I have done well,
and as is fitting the story, it is that which I have desired; but if slenderly
and meanly, it is that which I could attain unto."

THE FIRST ANNIVERSARY: *Title: Elizabeth Drury:* daughter of Donne's
wealthy patron, Sir Robert Drury; she died in 1610 at the age of fifteen.

And by deeds praise it? He who doth not this   5
May lodge an inmate soul, but 'tis not his),
When that queen ended here her progress time,
And as t' her standing house, to heaven did climb,
Where, loath to make the saints attend her long,
She's now a part both of the choir and song,   10
This world in that great earthquake languishèd;
For in a common bath of tears it bled,
Which drew the strongest vital spirits out;
But succor'd then with a perplexèd doubt,
Whether the world did lose or gain in this   15
(Because, since now no other way there is
But goodness, to see her whom all would see,
All must endeavor to be good as she),
This great consumption to a fever turn'd,
And so the world had fits; it joy'd, it mourn'd. 20
And as men think that agues physic are,
And th' ague being spent give over care,
So thou, sick world, mistak'st thyself to be
Well, when alas, thou'rt in a lethargy.
Her death did wound and tame thee then, and
    then   25
Thou mightst have better spar'd the sun, or man.
That wound was deep, but 'tis more misery
That thou hast lost thy sense and memory.
'Twas heavy then to hear thy voice of moan,
But this is worse, that thou art speechless
    grown.   30
Thou hast forgot thy name thou hadst. Thou wast
Nothing but she, and her thou hast o'erpass'd.
For, as a child kept from the font until
A prince, expected long, come to fulfill
The ceremonies, thou unnam'd hadst laid,   35
Had not her coming, thee her palace made.
Her name defin'd thee, gave thee form and frame,
And thou forget'st to celebrate thy name.
Some months she hath been dead (but being dead,
Measures of times are all determinèd)   40
But long she'ath been away, long, long; yet none
Offers to tell us who it is that's gone.
But as in states doubtful of future heirs,

---

40. *determinèd:* ended.

When sickness without remedy impairs
The present prince, they're loath it should be
    said,   45
"The Prince doth languish," or "The Prince is
    dead,"
So mankind, feeling now a general thaw,
A strong example gone, equal to law,
The cement which did faithfully compact
And glue all virtues, now resolv'd and slack'd,   50
Thought it some blasphemy to say sh' was dead,
Or that our weakness was discoverèd
In that confession; therefore spoke no more
Than tongues, the soul being gone, the loss deplore.
But though it be too late to succor thee,   55
Sick world, yea dead, yea putrefied, since she,
Thy'ntrinsic balm and thy preservative,
Can never be renew'd, thou never live,
I, since no man can make thee live, will try
What we may gain by thy anatomy.   60
Her death hath taught us dearly that thou art
Corrupt and mortal in thy purest part.
Let no man say, the world itself being dead,
'Tis labor lost to have discoverèd
The world's infirmities since there is none   65
What life the
world hath still.
Alive to study this dissection,
For there's a kind of world remaining still;
Though she which did inanimate and fill
The world be gone, yet in this last, long night
Her ghost doth walk; that is, a glimmering
    light,   70
A faint, weak love of virtue and of good
Reflects from her on them which understood
Her worth; and though she have shut in all day,
The twilight of her memory doth stay,
Which, from the carcase of the old world free,   75
Creates a new world, and new creatures be
Produc'd. The matter and the stuff of this,
Her virtue, and the form our practice is.
And though to be thus elemented arm
These creatures from home-born, intrinsic
    harm   80
(For all assum'd unto this dignity
So many weedless paradises be,

Which of themselves produce no venomous sin,
Except some foreign serpent bring it in),
Yet, because outward storms the strongest
    break,   85
And strength itself by confidence grows weak,

*The sicknesses
of the world.*

This new world may be safer, being told
The dangers and diseases of the old;
For with due temper men do then forego,
Or covet things, when they their true worth
    know.   90

*Impossibility
of health.*

There is no health; physicians say that we
At best enjoy but a neutrality.
And can there be worse sickness than to know
That we are never well, nor can be so?
We are born ruinous: poor mothers cry   95
That children come not right nor orderly
Except they headlong come and fall upon
An ominous precipitation.
How witty's ruin! how importunate
Upon mankind! It labor'd to frustrate   100
Even God's purpose, and made woman, sent
For man's relief, cause of his languishment.
They were to good ends, and they are so still,
But accessory, and principal in ill.
For that first marriage was our funeral;   105
One woman at one blow then kill'd us all,
And singly, one by one, they kill us now.
We do delightfully ourselves allow
To that consumption, and, profusely blind,
We kill ourselves to propagate our kind.   110
And yet we do not that; we are not men:
There is not now that mankind which was then

*Shortness
of life.*

Whenas the sun and man did seem to strive,
Joint tenants of the world, who should survive;
When stag and raven and the long-liv'd tree,   115
Compar'd with man, died in minority;
When, if a slow-pac'd star had stol'n away
From the observer's marking, he might stay
Two or three hundred years to see't again,
And then make up his observation plain;   120
When, as the age was long, the size was great
(Man's growth confess'd and recompens'd the
    meat),

So spacious and large that every soul
Did a fair kingdom and large realm control;
And when the very stature thus erect   125
Did that soul a good way towards heaven direct.
Where is this mankind now? Who lives to age
Fit to be made Methusalem his page?
Alas, we scarce live long enough to try
Whether a new-made clock run right or lie.   130
Old grandsires talk of yesterday with sorrow,
And for our children we reserve tomorrow.
So short is life that every peasant strives
In a torn house or field to have three lives.
And as in lasting, so in length is man,   135
Smallness of
stature. Contracted to an inch, who was a span;
For had a man at first in forests stray'd,
Or shipwrack'd in the sea, one would have laid
A wager that an elephant or whale
That met him would not hastily assail   140
A thing so equal to him. Now alas,
The fairies and the pigmies well may pass
As credible. Mankind decays so soon,
We're scarce our fathers' shadows cast at noon.
Only death adds t' our length; nor are we grown   145
In stature to be men till we are none.
But this were light, did our less volume hold
All the old text, or had we chang'd to gold
Their silver, or dispos'd into less glass
Spirits of virtue which then scatt'red was;   150
But 'tis not so. W' are not retir'd, but damp'd,
And as our bodies, so our minds are cramp'd.
'Tis shrinking, not close weaving, that hath thus
In mind and body both, bedwarfed us.
We seem ambitious God's whole work t' undo.   155
Of nothing he made us, and we strive too,
To bring ourselves to nothing back; and we
Do what we can to do't so soon as he.
With new diseases on ourselves we war,
And with new physic—a worse engine far!   160
Thus man, this world's vice-emperor, in whom
All faculties, all graces are at home

---

151. *retir'd, but damp'd:* contracted and concentrated, but deadened.

(And if in other creatures they appear,
They're but man's ministers and legates there
To work on their rebellions and reduce   165
Them to civility and to man's use),
This man, whom God did woo, and, loath t' attend
Till man came up, did down to man descend,
This man, so great that all that is is his,
O what a trifle and poor thing he is!   170
If man were anything, he's nothing now.
Help, or at least some time to waste, allow
T' his other wants; yet when he did depart
With her whom we lament, he lost his heart.
She, of whom th' ancients seem'd to prophesy   175
When they call'd virtues by the name of *she,*
She, in whom virtue was so much refin'd
That for alloy unto so pure a mind
She took the weaker sex; she that could drive
The poisonous tincture and the stain of Eve   180
Out of her thoughts and deeds, and purify
All by a true religious alchemy;
She, she is dead. She's dead. When thou know'st
          this,
Thou know'st how poor a trifling thing man is,
And learn'st thus much by our anatomy,   185
The heart being perish'd, no part can be free;
And that, except thou feed (not banquet) on
The supernatural food, religion,
Thy better growth grows withered and scant.
Be more than man, or thou'rt less than an ant.   190
Then as mankind, so is the world's whole frame
Quite out of joint, almost created lame;
For before God had made up all the rest,
Corruption ent'red and deprav'd the best.
It seiz'd the angels, and then first of all   195
The world did in her cradle take a fall
And turn'd her brains and took a general maim,
Wringing each joint of th' universal frame.
The noblest part, man, felt it first, and then

Decay of nature in other parts. Both beasts and plants, curs'd in the curse of
          man.   200
So did the world from the first hour decay;
That evening was beginning of the day,
And now the springs and summers which we see,

Like sons of women after fifty be.
And new philosophy calls all in doubt;   205
The element of fire is quite put out;
The sun is lost, and th' earth, and no man's wit
Can well direct him where to look for it.
And freely men confess that this world's spent,
When in the planets and the firmament   210
They seek so many new; they see that this
Is crumbled out again to his atomies.
'Tis all in pieces, all coherence gone,
All just supply, and all relation:
Prince, subject, father, son are things forgot,   215
For every man alone thinks he hath got
To be a phoenix, and that then can be
None of that kind of which he is, but he.
This is the world's condition now, and now
She that should all parts to reunion bow,   220
She that had all magnetic force alone
To draw and fasten sund'red parts in one,
She whom wise Nature had invented then
When she observ'd that every sort of men
Did in their voyage in this world's sea stray   225
And needed a new compass for their way,
She that was best and first original
Of all fair copies, and the general
Steward to fate, she whose rich eyes and breast
Gilt the West Indies and perfum'd the East,   230
Whose having breath'd in this world did bestow
Spice on those Isles, and bade them still smell so—
And that rich Indy which doth gold inter
Is but as single money coin'd from her—
She to whom this world must itself refer,   235
As suburbs or the microcosm of her,
She, she is dead. She's dead. When thou know'st
      this,
Thou know'st how lame a cripple this world is,
And learn'st thus much by our anatomy,
That this world's general sickness doth not lie   240
In any humor or one certain part,
But, as thou saw'st it rotten at the heart,
Thou seest a hectic fever hath got hold
Of the whole substance, not to be controll'd,
And that thou hast but one way not t' admit   245

The world's infection, to be none of it.
For the world's subtil'st immaterial parts
Feel this consuming wound, and age's darts,
For the world's beauty is decay'd or gone—
Beauty, that's color and proportion.   250

Disformity
of parts.

We think the heavens enjoy their spherical,
Their round proportion, embracing all;
But yet their various and perplexèd course,
Observ'd in divers ages, doth enforce
Men to find out so many eccentric parts,   255
Such divers downright lines, such overthwarts,
As disproportion that pure form. It tears
The firmament in eight and forty shires,
And in those constellations then arise
New stars, and old do vanish from our eyes,   260
As though heav'n suff'red earthquakes, peace or
          war,
When new towers rise and old demolish'd are.
They have impal'd within a zodiac
The free-born sun, and keep twelve signs awake
To watch his steps: the Goat and Crab control   265
And fright him back, who else to either pole
(Did not these tropics fetter him) might run,
For his course is not round; nor can the sun
Perfit a circle, or maintain his way
One inch direct, but where he rose today   270
He comes no more, but with a cozening line
Steals by that point and so is serpentine;
And seeming weary with his reeling thus,
He means to sleep, being now fall'n nearer us.
So, of the stars, which boast that they do run   275
In circle still, none ends where he begun.
All their proportion's lame, it sinks, it swells;
For of meridians and parallels
Man hath weav'd out a net, and this net thrown
Upon the heavens, and now they are his own.   280
Loath to go up the hill, or labor thus
To go to heaven, we make heaven come to us.
We spur, we rein the stars, and in their race
They're diversly content t' obey our pace.
But keeps the earth her round proportion
          still?   285

_____ _____

269. *Perfit:* complete.

Doth not a Tenerife or higher hill
Rise so high like a rock that one might think
The floating moon would shipwrack there and
          sink?
Seas are so deep that whales, being struck today,
Perchance tomorrow, scarce at middle way   290
Of their wish'd journey's end, the bottom, die;
And men, to sound depths, so much line untie,
As one might justly think that there would rise
At end thereof one of th' antipodies.
If under all a vault infernal be   295
(Which sure is spacious, except that we
Invent another torment, that there must
Millions into a strait, hot room be thrust)
Then solidness and roundness have no place.
Are these but warts and pockholes in the face   300
Of th' earth? Think so; but yet confess, in this
The world's proportion disfigured is,

Disorder in
the world.

That those two legs whereon it doth rely,
Reward and punishment, are bent awry.
And, O, it can no more be questionèd   305
That beauty's best, proportion, is dead,
Since even grief itself, which now alone
Is left us, is without proportion.
She by whose lines proportion should be
Examin'd, measure of all symmetry,   310
Whom had that ancient seen, who thought souls
          made
Of harmony, he would at next have said
That harmony was she, and thence infer
That souls were but resultances from her
And did from her into our bodies go   315
As to our eyes the forms from objects flow—
She, who if those great doctors truly said
That th' Ark to man's proportions was made,
Had been a type for that, as that might be
A type of her in this: that contrary   320
Both elements and passions liv'd at peace
In her, who caus'd all civil war to cease,
She, after whom, what form soe'er we see
Is discord and rude incongruity,
She, she is dead. She's dead. When thou know'st
          this,
                    325

Thou know'st how ugly a monster this world is,
And learn'st thus much by our anatomy,
That here is nothing to enamor thee,
And that not only faults in inward parts,
Corruptions in our brains or in our hearts,   330
Poisoning the fountains whence our actions spring,
Endanger us, but that if everything
Be not done fitly'nd in proportion,
To satisfy wise and good lookers-on
(Since most men be such as most think they
    be),   335
They're loathsome too by this deformity;
For good and well must in our actions meet;
Wicked is not much worse than indiscreet.
But beauty's other, second element,
Color and luster, now is as near spent.   340
And had the world his just proportion,
Were it a ring still, yet the stone is gone.
As a compassionate turquoise which doth tell,
By looking pale, the wearer is not well,
As gold falls sick, being stung with mercury,   345
All the world's parts of such complexion be.
When Nature was most busy, the first week,
Swaddling the new-born earth, God seem'd to like
That she should sport herself sometimes and play,
To mingle and vary colors every day;   350
And then, as though she could not make enow,
Himself his various rainbow did allow.
Sight is the noblest sense of any one;
Yet sight hath only color to feed on,
And color is decay'd: summer's robe grows   355
Dusky, and like an oft-dyed garment shows;
Our blushing red, which us'd in cheeks to spread,
Is inward sunk, and only our souls are red.
Perchance the world might have recoverèd
If she whom we lament had not been dead,   360
But she, in whom all white and red and blue
(Beauty's ingredients) voluntary grew
As in an unvex'd paradise, from whom
Did all things' verdure and their luster come,
Whose composition was miraculous,   365
Being all color, all diaphanous—
For air and fire but thick gross bodies were,

And liveliest stones but drowsy and pale to her—
She, she is dead. She's dead. When thou know'st
   this,
Thou know'st how wan a ghost this our world
   is,   370
And learn'st thus much by our anatomy,
That it should more affright than pleasure thee,
And that, since all fair color then did sink,
'Tis now but wicked vanity to think
To color vicious deeds with good pretense,   375
Or with bought colors to illude men's sense.

Weakness in
the want of
correspondence
of heaven
and earth.

Nor in aught more this world's decay appears
Than that her influence the heav'n forbears,
Or that the elements do not feel this;
The father or the mother barren is.   380
The clouds conceive not rain, or do not pour,
In the due birth time, down the balmy shower;
Th' air doth not motherly sit on the earth
To hatch her seasons and give all things birth.
Springtimes were common cradles, but are
   tombs,   385
And false conceptions fill the general wombs.
Th' air shows such meteors as none can see,
Not only what they mean, but what they be;
Earth such new worms as would have troubled
   much
Th' Egyptian mages to have made more such.   390
What artist now dares boast that he can bring
Heaven hither, or constellate anything
So as the influence of those stars may be
Imprison'd in an herb or charm or tree,
And do by touch all which those stars could
   do?   395
The art is lost, and correspondence too,
For heaven gives little, and the earth takes less,
And man least knows their trade and purposes.
If this commerce 'twixt heaven and earth were not
Embarr'd, and all this traffic quite forgot,   400
She for whose loss we have lamented thus,
Would work more fully'and pow'rfully on us.
Since herbs and roots by dying lose not all,
But they, yea ashes too, are med'cinal,
Death could not quench her virtue so but that 405

It would be (if not follow'd) wond'red at,
And all the world would be one dying swan
To sing her funeral praise, and vanish then.
But as some serpents' poison hurteth not
Except it be from the live serpent shot,   410
So doth her virtue need her here to fit
That unto us, she working more than it.
But she in whom to such maturity
Virtue was grown, past growth, that it must die,
She from whose influence all impressions came   415
(But by receivers' impotencies lame),
Who, though she could not transubstantiate
All states to gold, yet gilded every state,
So that some princes have some temperance,
Some councilors some purpose to advance   420
The common profit, and some people have
Some stay, no more than kings should give, to crave,
Some women have some taciturnity,
Some nunneries some grains of chastity;
She that did thus much, and much more could
    do   425
But that our age was iron, and rusty too,
She, she is dead. She's dead. When thou know'st
    this,
Thou know'st how dry a cinder this world is,
And learn'st thus much by our anatomy,
That 'tis in vain to dew or mollify   430
It with thy tears, or sweat, or blood. No thing
Is worth our travail, grief, or perishing
But those rich joys which did possess her heart,
Of which she's now partaker, and a part.
Conclusion. But as in cutting up a man that's dead,   435
The body will not last out to have read
On every part, and therefore men direct
Their speech to parts that are of most effect,
So the world's carcase would not last if I
Were punctual in this anatomy.   440
Nor smells it well to hearers if one tell
Them their disease, who fain would think they're
    well.
Here, therefore, be the end. And, blessèd maid,
Of whom is meant whatever hath been said
Or shall be spoken well by any tongue,   445

Whose name refines coarse lines and makes prose
    song,
Accept this tribute, and his first year's rent,
Who till his dark, short taper's end be spent,
As oft as thy feast sees this widow'd earth,
Will yearly celebrate thy second birth—   450
That is, thy death; for though the soul of man
Be got when man is made, 'tis born but then
When man doth die. Our body's as the womb,
And as a midwife death directs it home.
And you her creatures, whom she works
    upon,   455
And have your last and best concoction
From her example and her virtue, if you
In reverence to her do think it due
That no one should her praises thus rehearse,
As matter fit for chronicle, not verse,   460
Vouchsafe to call to mind that God did make
A last and lasting'st piece, a song. He spake
To Moses to deliver unto all
That song, because he knew they would let fall
The law, the prophets, and the history,   465
But keep the song still in their memory.
Such an opinion (in due measure) made
Me this great office boldly to invade.
Nor could incomprehensibleness deter
Me from thus trying to imprison her,   470
Which when I saw that a strict grave could do,
I saw not why verse might not do so too.
Verse hath a middle nature: heaven keeps souls,
The grave keeps bodies, verse the fame enrolls.

THE SECOND ANNIVERSARY
OF THE PROGRESS OF THE SOUL

Wherein, by Occasion of the Religious Death of Mistress
Elizabeth Drury, the Incommodities of the Soul in This
Life and Her Exaltation in the Next are Contemplated

(1612)

The entrance.

Nothing could make me sooner to confess
That this world had an everlastingness,
Than to consider that a year is run
Since both this lower world's and the sun's Sun,
The luster and the vigor of this All,   5
Did set; 'twere blasphemy to say, "did fall."
But as a ship which hath struck sail doth run
By force of that force which before it won,
Or as sometimes in a beheaded man,
Though at those two Red Seas which freely
          ran,   10
One from the trunk, another from the head,
His soul be sail'd to her eternal bed,
His eyes will twinkle, and his tongue will roll
As though he beckon'd and call'd back his soul,
He grasps his hands, and he pulls up his feet,   15
And seems to reach, and to step forth to meet
His soul (when all these motions which we saw
Are but as ice which crackles at a thaw),
Or as a lute which in moist weather rings
Her knell alone by cracking of her strings—   20
So struggles this dead world now she is gone,
For there is motion in corruption.
As some days are at the Creation nam'd
Before the sun, the which fram'd days, was fram'd,
So after this Sun's set some show appears,   25
And orderly vicissitude of years.
Yet a new Deluge, and of Lethe flood,
Hath drown'd us all: all have forgot all good,
Forgetting her, the main reserve of all.
Yet in this deluge, gross and general,   30
Thou seest me strive for life. My life shall be

To be hereafter prais'd for praising thee,
Immortal maid, who, though thou wouldst refuse
The name of mother, be unto my Muse
A father, since her chaste ambition is   35
Yearly to bring forth such a child as this.
These hymns may work on future wits, and so
May great-grandchildren of thy praises grow,
And so, though not revive, embalm and spice
The world, which else would putrefy with vice; 40
For thus man may extend thy progeny
Until man do but vanish, and not die.
These hymns thy issue may increase so long
As till God's great *Venite* change the song.

A just dis-
estimation of
this world

Thirst for that time, O my insatiate soul,   45
And serve thy thirst with God's safe-sealing bowl.
Be thirsty still and drink still till thou go
To th' only health, to be hydroptic so.
Forget this rotten world, and unto thee
Let thine own times as an old story be.   50
Be not concern'd. Study not why nor when;
Do not so much as not believe a man,
For though to err be worst, to try truths forth
Is far more business than this world is worth.
The world is but a carcase; thou art fed   55
By it but as a worm that carcase bred.
And why shouldst thou, poor worm, consider more
When this world will grow better than before,
Than those thy fellow-worms do think upon
That carcase's last resurrection!   60
Forget this world, and scarce think of it so
As of old clothes cast off a year ago.
To be thus stupid is alacrity;
Men thus lethargic have best memory.
Look upward; that's towards her whose happy
          state   65
We now lament not, but congratulate.
She to whom all this world was but a stage
Where all sat heark'ning how her youthful age
Should be employ'd, because in all she did
Some figure of the golden times was hid,   70
Who could not lack whate'er this world could give,
Because she was the form that made it live,
Nor could complain that this world was unfit

To be stay'd in then when she was in it,
She that first tried indifferent desires   75
By virtue, and virtue by religious fires,
She to whose person paradise adher'd
As courts to princes, she whose eyes enspher'd
Star-light enough t' have made the South control
(Had she been there) the star-full northern
      pole,   80
She, she is gone. She's gone. When thou know'st
      this,
What fragmentary rubbish this world is
Thou know'st, and that it is not worth a thought;
He honors it too much that thinks it nought.
Think then, my soul, that Death is but a groom   85
Which brings a taper to the outward room,
Whence thou spiest first a little, glimmering light,
And after brings it nearer to thy sight;
For such approaches doth heaven make in death.
Think thyself laboring now with broken breath,   90
And think those broken and soft notes to be
Division and thy happiest harmony.
Think thee laid on thy deathbed, loose and slack,
And think that, but unbinding of a pack
To take one precious thing, thy soul, from
      thence.   95
Think thyself parch'd with fever's violence;
Anger thine ague more by calling it
Thy physic; chide the slackness of the fit.
Think that thou hear'st thy knell, and think no
      more
But that as bells call'd thee to church before,   100
So this to the Triumphant Church calls thee.
Think Satan's sergeants round about thee be,
And think that but for legacies they thrust;
Give one thy pride, t' another give thy lust;
Give them those sins which they gave thee be-
      fore,   105
And trust th' immaculate blood to wash thy score,
Think thy friends weeping round, and think
      that they
Weep but because they go not yet thy way.

*Contemplation
of our state
in our deathbed.*

THE SECOND ANNIVERSARY: 92. *Division:* music.

Think that they close thine eyes, and think in this,
That they confess much in the world amiss,   110
Who dare not trust a dead man's eye with that
Which they from God and angels cover not.
Think that they shroud thee up, and think
     from thence
They reinvest thee in white innocence.
Think that thy body rots, and (if so low,   115
Thy soul exalted so, thy thoughts can go)
Think thee a prince, who of themselves create
Worms which insensibly devour their state.
Think that they bury thee, and think that rite
Lays thee to sleep but a Saint Lucy's night.   120
Think these things cheerfully, and if thou be
Drowsy or slack, remember then that she,
She whose complexion was so even made
That which of her ingredients should invade
The other three no fear, no art could guess   125
So far were all remov'd from more or less;
But as in mithridate or just perfumes
Where, all good things being met, no one presumes
To govern or to triumph on the rest,
Only because all were, no part was best,   130
And as, though all do know that quantities
Are made of lines, and lines from points arise,
None can these lines or quantities unjoint
And say this is a line, or this a point,
So, though the elements and humors were   135
In her, one could not say, "This governs there";
Whose even constitution might have won
Any disease to venture on the sun
Rather than her, and make a spirit fear
That he to disuniting subject were;   140
To whose proportions if we would compare
Cubes, they're unstable, circles angular;
She who was such a chain as Fate employs
To bring mankind all fortunes it enjoys,
So fast, so even wrought, as one would think   145
No accident could threaten any link;
She, she embrac'd a sickness, gave it meat,
The purest blood and breath that e'er it eat,

---

123. *complexion:* composition of four elements or humors.

And hath taught us that though a good man hath
Title to heaven, and plead it by his faith,   150
And though he may pretend a conquest (since
Heaven was content to suffer violence),
Yea, though he plead a long possession too
(For they're in heaven on earth, who heaven's
          works do),
Though he had right and power and place
          before,   155
Yet death must usher, and unlock the door.

Incommodities Think further on thyself, my soul, and think
of the soul How thou at first wast made but in a sink;
in the body. Think that it argued some infirmity
That those two souls which then thou found'st
          in me   160
Thou fed'st upon and drew'st into thee, both
My second soul of sense and first of growth.
Think but how poor thou wast, how obnoxious,
Whom a small lump of flesh could poison thus.
This curded milk, this poor unlitter'd whelp,   165
My body, could, beyond escape or help,
Infect thee with original sin, and thou
Couldst neither then refuse, nor leave it now.
Think that no stubborn, sullen anchorit
Which, fix'd t' a pillar or a grave, doth sit   170
Bedded and bath'd in all his ordures, dwells
So foully as our souls in their first-built cells.
Think in how poor a prison thou didst lie
After, enabled but to suck and cry.
Think, when 'twas grown to most, 'twas a
          poor inn,   175
A province pack'd up in two yards of skin,
And that usurp'd or threaten'd with the rage
Of sicknesses or their true mother, age.
But think that death hath now enfranchis'd thee;
Thou hast thy expansion now, and liberty.   180
Her liberty Think that a rusty piece, discharg'd, is flown
by death. In pieces, and the bullet is his own
And freely flies. This to thy soul allow:
Think thy shell broke, think thy soul hatch'd
          but now,
And think this slow-pac'd soul, which late did
          cleave   185

T' a body, and went but by the body's leave,
Twenty, perchance, or thirty mile a day,
Dispatches in a minute all the way
'Twixt heaven and earth. She stays not in the air
To look what meteors there themselves
                    prepare;   190
She carries no desire to know, nor sense,
Whether th' air's middle region be intense;
For th' element of fire, she doth not know
Whether she pass'd by such a place or no;
She baits not at the moon, nor cares to try   195
Whether in that new world men live and die.
Venus retards her not t' inquire how she
Can, being one star, Hesper and Vesper be.
He that charm'd Argus' eyes, sweet Mercury,
Works not on her, who now is grown all eye,   200
Who, if she meet the body of the sun,
Goes through, not staying till his course be run,
Who finds in Mars his camp no corps of guard,
Nor is by Jove nor by his father barr'd,
But ere she can consider how she went,   205
At once is at, and through the firmament.
And as these stars were but so many beads
Strung on one string, speed undistinguish'd leads
Her through those spheres as through the beads a
                    string
Whose quick succession makes it still one
                    thing.   210
As doth the pith, which, lest our bodies slack,
Strings fast the little bones of neck and back,
So by the soul doth death string heaven and earth,
For when our soul enjoys this her third birth
(Creation gave her one, a second, grace),   215
Heaven is as near and present to her face
As colors are, and objects, in a room
Where darkness was before, when tapers come.
This must, my soul, thy long-short progress be.
T' advance these thoughts remember then
                    that she,   220
She, whose fair body no such prison was
But that a soul might well be pleas'd to pass

----

95. baits: rests. 208. *undistinguish'd:* instantaneous.

An age in her, she whose rich beauty lent
Mintage to others' beauties, for they went
But for so much as they were like to her,   225
She, in whose body (if we dare prefer
This low world to so high a mark as she)
The Western treasure, Eastern spicery,
Europe and Afric and the unknown rest
Were easily found, or what in them was best   230
(And when we've made this large discovery
Of all in her some one part then will be
Twenty such parts, whose plenty and riches is
Enough to make twenty such worlds as this),
She, whom had they known, who did first
          betroth   235
The tutelar angels, and assign'd one both
To nations, cities, and to companies,
To functions, offices, and dignities,
And to each several man, to him, and him,
They would have given her one for every
          limb,   240
She, of whose soul, if we may say 'twas gold,
Her body was th' electrum, and did hold
Many degrees of that; we understood
Her by her sight; her pure and eloquent blood
Spoke in her cheeks, and so distinctly
          wrought   245
That one might almost say her body thought;
She, she, thus richly and largely hous'd, is gone,
And chides us slow-pac'd snails who crawl upon
Our prison's prison, earth, nor think us well
Longer than whilst we bear our brittle shell.   250

Her ignorance in this life and knowledge in the next.

But 'twere but little to have chang'd our room
If, as we were in this our living tomb
Oppress'd with ignorance, we still were so.
Poor soul, in this thy flesh what dost thou know?
Thou know'st thyself so little, as thou know'st
          not   255
How thou didst die nor how thou wast begot.
Thou neither know'st how thou at first cam'st in
Nor how thou took'st the poison of man's sin.
Nor dost thou (though thou know'st that thou art
          so)

---

242. *electrum:* natural alloy of gold and silver.

By what way thou art made immortal, know.   260
Thou art too narrow, wretch, to comprehend
Even thyself, yea, though thou wouldst but bend
To know thy body. Have not all souls thought
For many ages that our body's wrought
Of air and fire and other elements?   265
And now they think of new ingredients,
And one soul thinks one, and another way
Another thinks, and 'tis an even lay.
Know'st thou but how the stone doth enter in
The bladder's cave and never break the skin?   270
Know'st thou how blood which to the heart doth
    flow
Doth from one ventricle to th' other go?
And for the putrid stuff which thou dost spit,
Know'st thou how thy lungs have attracted it?
There are no passages; so that there is   275
(For ought thou know'st) piercing of substances.
And of those many opinions which men raise
Of nails and hairs, dost thou know which to praise?
What hope have we to know ourselves, when we
Know not the least things which for our use
    be?   280
We see in authors, too stiff to recant,
A hundred controversies of an ant,
And yet one watches, starves, freezes, and sweats
To know but catechisms and alphabets
Of unconcerning things, matters of fact: 285
How others on our stage their parts did act,
What Caesar did, yea, and what Cicero said.
Why grass is green, or why our blood is red
Are mysteries which none have reach'd unto.
In this low form, poor soul, what wilt thou
    do?   290
When wilt thou shake off this pedantery
Of being taught by sense and fantasy?
Thou look'st through spectacles; small things seem
    great
Below; but up unto the watch-tower get,
And see all things despoil'd of fallacies.   295
Thou shalt not peep through lattices of eyes,
Nor hear through labyrinths of ears, nor learn
By circuit or collections to discern.

In heaven thou straight know'st all concerning it,
And what concerns it not, shalt straight for-
    get. 300
There thou (but in no other school) mayst be,
Perchance, as learnèd and as full as she,
She who all libraries had throughly read
At home in her own thoughts, and practicèd
So much good as would make as many more, 305
She whose example they must all implore
Who would or do or think well, and confess
That all the virtuous actions they express
Are but a new and worse edition
Of her some one thought or one action, 310
She who in th' art of knowing heaven was grown
Here upon earth to such perfection
That she hath, ever since to heaven she came
(In a far fairer print) but read the same,
She, she, not satisfied with all this weight 315
(For so much knowledge as would overfreight
Another did but ballast her) is gone
As well t' enjoy as get perfection,
And calls us after her in that she took
(Taking herself) our best and worthiest book. 320

Of our company
in this life
and in the next.

Return not, my soul, from this ecstasy
And meditation of what thou shalt be,
To earthly thoughts till it to thee appear,
With whom thy conversation must be there.
With whom wilt thou converse? what station 325
Canst thou choose out, free from infection,
That will nor give thee theirs nor drink in thine?
Shalt thou not find a spongy, slack divine
Drink and suck in th' instructions of great men,
And for the word of God vent them again? 330
Are there not some courts (and then, no things be
So 'like as courts) which in this let us see
That wits and tongues of libelers are weak,
Because they do more ill than these can speak?
The poison's gone through all; poisons affect 335
Chiefly the chiefest parts, but some effect
In nails and hairs, yea excrements, will show;
So lies the poison of sin in the most low.
Up, up, my drowsy soul, where thy new ear
Shall in the angels' songs no discord hear, 340

Where thou shalt see the blessed Mother-maid
Joy in not being that which men have said,
Where she's exalted more for being good
Than for her interest of motherhood.
Up to those patriarchs, which did longer sit   345
Expecting Christ than they've enjoy'd him yet.
Up to those prophets, which now gladly see
Their prophecies grown to be history.
Up to th' apostles, who did bravely run
All the sun's course with more light than the
    sun.   350
Up to those martyrs, who did calmly bleed
Oil to th' apostles' lamps, dew to their seed.
Up to those virgins, who thought that almost
They made joint-tenants with the Holy Ghost
If they to any should His temple give.   355
Up, up! for in that squadron there doth live
She who hath carried thither new degrees
(As to their number) to their dignities,
She who, being to herself a state, enjoy'd
All royalties which any state employ'd,   360
For she made wars and triumph'd—reason still
Did not o'erthrow, but rectify her will—
And she made peace, for no peace is like this,
That beauty and chastity together kiss;
She did high justice, for she crucified   365
Every first motion of rebellious pride;
And she gave pardons and was liberal,
For, only herself except, she pardon'd all;
She coin'd, in this, that her impressions gave
To all our actions all the worth they have;   370
She gave protections: the thoughts of her breast
Satan's rude officers could ne'er arrest.
As these prerogatives, being met in one,
Made her a sovereign state, religion
Made her a church, and these two made her
    all.   375
She who was all this All, and could not fall
To worse by company, for she was still
More antidote than all the world was ill,
She, she doth leave it, and by death survive
All this in heaven, whither who doth not
    strive   380

The more because she's there, he doth not know
That accidental joys in heaven do grow.
But pause, my soul, and study, ere thou fall

Of essential joy
in this life
and in the next

On accidental joys, th' essential.
Still before accessories do abide   385
A trial, must the principal be tried.
And what essential joy canst thou expect
Here upon earth? what permanent effect
Of transitory causes? Dost thou love
Beauty? (And beauty worthiest is to move.)   390
Poor cozen'd coz'ner, that she and that thou
Which did begin to love are neither now.
You are both fluid, chang'd since yesterday;
Next day repairs (but ill) last day's decay.
Nor are, although the river keep the name,   395
Yesterday's waters and today's the same.
So flows her face and thine eyes; neither now
That saint nor pilgrim which your loving vow
Concern'd remains, but whilst you think you be
Constant, you're hourly in inconstancy.   400
Honor may have pretense unto our love,
Because that God did live so long above
Without this honor and then lov'd it so
That he at last made creatures to bestow
Honor on him, not that he needed it,   405
But that to his hands man might grow more fit.
But since all honors from inferiors flow
(For they do give it; princes do but show
Whom they would have so honor'd) and that this
On such opinions and capacities   410
Is built as rise and fall to more and less,
Alas, 'tis but a casual happiness.
Hath ever any man t' himself assign'd
This or that happiness t' arrest his mind
But that another man which takes a worse   415
Think him a fool for having ta'en that course?
They who did labor Babel's tower to'rect
Might have consider'd that for that effect
All this whole solid earth could not allow
Nor furnish forth materials enow,   420
And that this center, to raise such a place,

---

391. *cozen'd coz'ner:* deceived deceiver.

Was far too little to have been the base.
No more affords this world foundation
To erect true joy, were all the means in one.
But as the heathen made them several gods   425
Of all God's benefits and all his rods
(For as the wine and corn and onions are
Gods unto them, so agues be, and war),
And as, by changing that whole precious gold
To such small copper coins, they lost the old,   430
And lost their only God, who ever must
Be sought alone, and not in such a thrust,
So much mankind true happiness mistakes:
No joy enjoys that man that many makes.
Then, soul, to thy first pitch work up again;   435
Know that all lines which circles do contain,
For once that they the center touch, do touch
Twice the circumference; and be thou such:
Double on heaven thy thoughts on earth employ'd.
All will not serve. Only who have enjoy'd   440
The sight of God in fullness, can think it,
For it is both the object and the wit.
This is essential joy, where neither He
Can suffer diminution, nor we.
'Tis such a full and such a filling good,   445
Had th' angels once look'd on him, they had stood.
To fill the place of one of them, or more,
She whom we celebrate is gone before,
She, who had here so much essential joy
As no chance could distract, much less de-
          stroy,   450
Who with God's presence was acquainted so
(Hearing and speaking to him) as to know
His face in any natural stone or tree
Better than when in images they be,
Who kept by diligent devotion   455
God's image in such reparation
Within her heart that what decay was grown
Was her first parents' fault, and not her own,
Who, being solicited to any act,
Still heard God pleading his safe precontract,   460
Who by a faithful confidence was here
Bethroth'd to God, and now is married there,
Whose twilights were more clear than our midday,

Who dreamt devoutlier than most use to pray,
Who, being here fill'd with grace, yet strove
    to be   465
Both where more grace and more capacity
At once is given—she to heaven is gone,
Who made this world in some proportion
A heaven, and here became unto us all,
Joy (as our joys admit) essential.   470

*Of accidental
joys in both
places.*

But could this low world joys essential touch,
Heaven's accidental joys would pass them much.
How poor and lame must then our casual be?
If thy prince will his subjects to call thee
"My Lord," and this do swell thee, thou art
    then,   475
By being a greater, grown to be less man.
When no physician of redress can speak,
A joyful, casual violence may break
A dangerous aposteme in thy breast,
And whilst thou joyest in this, the dangerous
    rest,   480
The bag, may rise up, and so strangle thee.
Whate'er was casual, may ever be.
What should the nature change? or make the same
Certain, which was but casual when it came?
All casual joy doth loud and plainly say,   485
Only by coming, that it can away.
Only in heaven joy's strength is never spent,
And accidental things are permanent.
Joy of a soul's arrival ne'er decays,
For that soul ever joys and ever stays;   490
Joy that their last great consummation
Approaches in the resurrection,
When earthly bodies more celestial
Shall be than angels were (for they could fall)—
This kind of joy doth every day admit   495
Degrees of growth, but none of losing it.
In this fresh joy 'tis no small part that she,
She, in whose goodness he that names degree
Doth injure her ('tis loss to be call'd best
There where the stuff is not such as the rest),   500
She, who left such a body as even she

479. *aposteme:* abscess.

Only in heaven could learn how it can be
Made better (for she rather was two souls,
Or like to full, on-both-sides-written rolls,
Where eyes might read upon the outward
   skin   505
As strong records for God, as minds within),
She, who by making full perfection grow,
Pieces a circle and still keeps it so—
Long'd for, and longing for it, to heaven is gone,
Where she receives and gives addition. 510

Conclusion.

Here in a place where misdevotion frames
A thousand prayers to saints whose very names
The ancient church knew not—heaven knows not
   yet—
And where what laws of poetry admit,
Laws of religion have at least the same, 515
Immortal maid, I might invoke thy name.
Could any saint provoke that appetite,
Thou here shouldst make me a French convertite,
But thou wouldst not, nor wouldst thou be content
To take this for my second year's true rent, 520
Did this coin bear any other stamp than his
That gave thee power to do, me to say this.
Since his will is that to posterity
Thou shouldst for life and death a pattern be,
And that the world should notice have of this, 525
The purpose and th' authority is his.
Thou art the proclamation, and I am
The trumpet at whose voice the people came.

❧

From *Divine Poems*

(1633, 1635)

HOLY SONNETS

7

At the round earth's imagin'd corners, blow
Your trumpets, angels, and arise, arise
From death, you numberless infinities

Of souls, and to your scatter'd bodies go,
All whom the flood did, and fire shall o'erthrow,   5
All whom war, dearth, age, agues, tyrannies,
Despair, law, chance hath slain, and you whose eyes
Shall behold God and never taste death's woe.
But let them sleep, Lord, and me mourn a space,
For if above all these my sins abound,   10
'Tis late to ask abundance of thy grace
When we are there. Here on this lowly ground
Teach me how to repent, for that's as good
As if thou'dst seal'd my pardon with thy blood.

9

If poisonous minerals, and if that tree
Whose fruit threw death on else immortal us,
If lecherous goats, if serpents envious
Cannot be damn'd, alas, why should I be?
Why should intent or reason, born in me,   5
Make sins, else equal, in me more heinous?
And mercy being easy and glorious
To God, in his stern wrath why threatens he?
But who am I that dare dispute with thee
O God? O! of thine only worthy blood   10
And my tears make a heavenly Lethean flood,
And drown in it my sins' black memory.
That thou remember them, some claim as debt;
I think it mercy if thou wilt forget.

10

Death, be not proud, though some have called thee
Mighty and dreadful, for thou art not so;
For those whom thou think'st thou dost overthrow
Die not, poor Death, nor yet canst thou kill me.
From rest and sleep, which but thy pictures be,   5
Much pleasure, then from thee much more must flow;
And soonest our best men with thee do go,
Rest of their bones and soul's delivery.
Thou'rt slave to fate, chance, kings, and desperate men,

And dost with poison, war, and sickness dwell; 10
And poppy or charms can make us sleep as well,
And better than thy stroke. Why swell'st thou then?
One short sleep pass'd, we wake eternally,
And death shall be no more. Death, thou shalt die.

14

Batter my heart, three-person'd God, for you
As yet but knock, breathe, shine, and seek to mend;
That I may rise and stand, o'erthrow me 'nd bend
Your force to break, blow, burn, and make me new.
I, like an usurp'd town t' another due, 5
Labor t' admit you, but O, to no end!
Reason, your viceroy in me, me should defend,
But is captiv'd, and proves weak or untrue.
Yet dearly' I love you 'nd would be loved fain,
But am betroth'd unto your enemy. 10
Divorce me, untie, or break that knot again,
Take me to you, imprison me, for I,
Except y' enthrall me, never shall be free,
Nor ever chaste except you ravish me.

18

Show me, dear Christ, thy spouse so bright and clear.
What! is it she which on the other shore
Goes richly painted? or which, robb'd and tore,
Laments and mourns in Germany and here?
Sleeps she a thousand, then peeps up one year? 5
Is she self-truth and errs? now new, now outwore?
Doth she, and did she, and shall she evermore
On one, on seven, or on no hill appear?
Dwells she with us, or, like adventuring knights,
First travel we to seek, and then make love? 10
Betray, kind husband, thy spouse to our sights,
And let mine amorous soul court thy mild dove,
Who is most true and pleasing to thee then,
When she's embrac'd and open to most men.

HYMN TO GOD MY GOD, IN MY SICKNESS

Since I am coming to that holy room
  Where with thy choir of saints for evermore
I shall be made thy music, as I come
    I tune the instrument here at the door,
    And what I must do then, think here before.   5

Whilst my physicians by their love are grown
  Cosmographers, and I their map, who lie
Flat on this bed, that by them may be shown
    That this is my Southwest discovery
    Per fretum febris, by these straits to die,   10

I joy that in these straits I see my West;
  For though their currents yield return to none,
What shall my West hurt me? As West and East
    In all flat maps (and I am one) are one,
    So death doth touch the resurrection.   15

Is the Pacific Sea my home? Or are
  The Eastern riches? Is Jerusalem?
Anian and Magellan and Gibraltar,
    All straits, and none but straits, are ways to them,
    Whether where Japhet dwelt, or Cham or Shem.   20

We think that Paradise and Calvary,
  Christ's Cross and Adam's tree, stood in one place.
Look, Lord, and find both Adams met in me;
    As the first Adam's sweat surrounds my face,
    May the last Adam's blood my soul embrace.   25

So, in his purple wrapp'd, receive me, Lord,
  By these his thorns give me his other crown;
And as to others' souls I preach'd thy word,
    Be this my text, my sermon to mine own:
    Therefore that he may raise, the Lord throws down.   30

HYMN TO GOD MY GOD: 10. *Per fretum febris:* through the raging of fever.
14. *flat maps . . . are one: i.e.,* when pasted on a globe, as Donne explained
in a sermon. 18. *Anian:* Behring Strait.

Ben Jonson

COME, MY CELIA
(1607)

Come, my Celia, let us prove
While we may the sports of love;
Time will not be ours forever,
He at length our good will sever.
Spend not then his gifts in vain;   5
Suns that set may rise again,
But if once we lose this light,
'Tis with us perpetual night.
Why should we defer our joys?
Fame and rumor are but toys.   10
Cannot we delude the eyes
Of a few poor household spies?
Or his easier ears beguile,
So removèd by our wile?
'Tis no sin love's fruit to steal;   15
But the sweet theft to reveal,
To be taken, to be seen,
These have crimes accounted been.

                              From *Volpone,* III, vii, 165

❧

SONG, TO CELIA

Drink to me only with thine eyes,
   And I will pledge with mine;
Or leave a kiss but in the cup,
   And I'll not look for wine.
The thirst that from the soul doth rise   5
   Doth ask a drink divine;
But might I of Jove's nectar sup,
   I would not change for thine.

COME, MY CELIA: 1. *prove:* experience.

I sent thee late a rosy wreath,
　　Not so much honoring thee,   10
As giving it a hope that there
　　It could not withered be.
But thou thereon didst only breathe,
　　And sent'st it back to me,
Since when it grows and smells, I swear,   15
　　Not of itself, but thee.

❧

HER TRIUMPH

(1616)

See the chariot at hand here of love,
　　Wherein my lady rideth!
Each that draws is a swan or a dove,
　　And well the car love guideth.
As she goes all hearts do duty   5
　　　Unto her beauty,
An enamoured do wish so they might
　　　But enjoy such a sight,
That they still were to run by her side,
Through swords, through seas, whither she would ride.   10

Do but look on her eyes; they do light
　　All that love's world compriseth!
Do but look on her hair; it is bright
　　As love's star when it riseth!
Do but mark, her forehead's smoother   15
　　　Than words that soothe her;
And from her arched brows, such a grace
　　　Sheds itself through the face,
As alone there triumphs to the life
All the gain, all the good of the elements' strife.   20

Have you seen but a bright lily grow
　　Before rude hands have touched it?
Ha' you marked but the fall o' the snow
　　Before the soil hath smutched it?
Ha' you felt the wool of beaver,   25
　　　Or swan's down ever?

Or have smelt o' the bud o' the briar?
Or the nard in the fire?
Or have tasted the bag of the bee?
O so white! O so soft! O so sweet is she!   30

❧

QUEEN AND HUNTRESS
(1601)

Queen and huntress, chaste and fair,
Now the sun is laid to sleep,
Seated in thy silver chair
State in wonted manner keep;
    Hesperus entreats thy light,   5
    Goddess excellently bright.

Earth, let not thy envious shade
Dare itself to interpose;
Cynthia's shining orb was made
Heaven to clear, when day did close;   10
    Bless us then with wishèd sight,
    Goddess excellently bright.

Lay thy bow of pearl apart,
And thy crystal shining quiver;
Give unto the flying hart   15
Space to breathe, how short soever,
    Thou that mak'st a day of night,
    Goddess excellently bright.

From *Cynthia's Revels*

❧

STILL TO BE NEAT
(1609)

Still to be neat, still to be dressed
As you were going to a feast;
Still to be powdered, still perfumed:

HER TRIUMPH: 28. *nard:* spikenard: aromatic herb.

Lady, it is to be presumed,
Though art's hid causes are not found,   5
All is not sweet, all is not sound.

Give me a look, give me a face
That makes simplicity a grace;
Robes loosely flowing, hair as free:
Such sweet neglect more taketh me   10
Than all th' adulteries of art;
They strike mine eyes, but not my heart.

From *Epicœne, or the Silent Woman*

❧

SLOW, SLOW, FRESH FOUNT
(1601)

Slow, slow, fresh fount, keep time with my salt tears;
  Yet slower yet, oh faintly, gentle springs;
List to the heavy part the music bears,
  Woe weeps out her division when she sings.
    Droop herbs and flowers,   5
    Fall grief in showers;
    Our beauties are not ours;
      Oh, I could still,
Like melting snow upon some craggy hill,
  Drop, drop, drop, drop,   10
Since nature's pride is now a withered daffodil.

From *Cynthia's Revels*

❧

OH, THAT JOY SO SOON SHOULD WASTE
(1601)

Oh, that joy so soon should waste!
  Or so sweet a bliss
  As a kiss
  Might not forever last!

SLOW, SLOW, FRESH FOUNT: 4. *division:* a musical run.

So sugared, so melting, so soft, so delicious!   5
    The dew that lies on roses
When morn herself discloses,
    Is not so precious.
Oh, rather than I would it smother,
Were I to taste such another,   10
    It should be my wishing
    That I might die kissing.

From *Cynthia's Revels*

TO MY MERE ENGLISH CENSURER

(1616)

To thee my way in epigrams seems new,
    When both it is the old way and the true.
Thou sayst that cannot be, for thou hast seen
    Davies and Weever, and the best have been,
And mine come nothing like. I hope so; yet   5
    As theirs did with thee, mine might credit get,
If thou'dst but use thy faith, as thou didst then
    When thou wert wont t' admire, not censure men.
Prithee believe still, and not judge so fast,
    Thy faith is all the knowledge that thou hast.   10

ON SOMETHING THAT WALKS SOMEWHERE

(1616)

At court I met it, in clothes brave enough
    To be a courtier, and looks grave enough
To seem a statesman; as I near it came,
    It made me a great face; I asked the name.
A Lord, it cried, buried in flesh and blood,   5
    And such from whom let no man hope least good,

TO MY MERE ENGLISH CENSURER: *Title: Mere:* unqualified. 4. *Davies and Weever·* Sir John Davies (1569-1626) and John Weever (1576-1632) wrote epigrams and satires.

For I will do none; and as little ill,
   For I will dare none. Good Lord, walk dead still.

INVITING A FRIEND TO SUPPER
(1616)

To-night, grave sir, both my poor house and I
   Do equally desire your company;
Not that we think us worthy such a guest,
   But that your worth will dignify our feast
With those that come, whose grace may make that seem   5
   Something, which else could hope for no esteem.
It is the fair acceptance, sir, creates
   The entertainment perfect, not the cates.
Yet shall you have, to rectify your palate,
   An olive, capers, or some better salad   10
Ush'ring the mutton; with a short-legged hen,
   If we can get her, full of eggs, and then
Lemons and wine for sauce; to these, a coney
   Is not to be despaired of, for our money;
And though fowl now be scarce, yet there are clerks,   15
   The sky not falling, think we may have larks.
I'll tell you of more, and lie, so you will come,
   Of partridge, pheasant, woodcock, of which some
May yet be there; and godwit, if we can,
   Gnat, rail, and ruff too. Howsoe'er, my man   20
Shall read a piece of Virgil, Tacitus,
   Livy, or of some better book to us,
Of which we'll speak our minds amidst our meat;
   And I'll profess no verses to repeat;
To this, if aught appear which I know not of,   25
   That will the pastry, not my paper, show of.
Digestive cheese, and fruit there sure will be;
   But that which most doth take my muse, and me,
Is a pure cup of rich Canary wine,
   Which is the Mermaid's now, but shall be mine;   30
Of which had Horace or Anacreon tasted,
   Their lives, as do their lines, till now had lasted.

INVITING A FRIEND TO SUPPER: 15. *clerks:* scholars. 20. *godwit, Gnat, rail, ruff:* three birds and a fish.

Tobacco, nectar, or the Thespian springs
 Are all but Luther's beer to this I sing.
Of this we will sup free, but moderately,   35
 And we will have no polly, or parrot by;
Nor shall our cups make any guilty men,
 But at our parting we will be as when
We innocently met. No simple word
 That shall be uttered at our mirthful board   40
Shall make us sad next morning, or affright
 The liberty that we'll enjoy to-night.

       ❧

TO PENSHURST

(1616)

Thou art not, Penshurst, built to envious show
 Of touch or marble, nor canst boast a row
Of polished pillars, or a roof of gold;
 Thou hast no lantern whereof tales are told,
Or stairs or courts; but stand'st an ancient pile,   5
 And these, grudged at, art reverenced the while.
Thou joy'st in better marks, of soil, of air,
 Of wood, of water; therein thou art fair.
Thou hast thy walks for health as well as sport;
 Thy mount, to which the Dryads do resort,   10
Where Pan and Bacchus their high feasts have made
 Beneath the broad beech, and the chestnut shade,
That taller tree, which of a nut was set
 At his great birth, where all the Muses met.
There in the writhèd bark are cut the names   15
 Of many a sylvan, taken with his flames;
And thence the ruddy satyrs oft provoke
 The lighter fauns to reach thy Lady's oak.
Thy copse too, named of Gamage, thou hast there,
 That never fails to serve thee seasoned deer   20
When thou wouldst feast, or exercise thy friends.
 The lower land, that to the river bends,

TO PENSHURST: 1. *Penshurst:* the Sidney country place in Kent. 2. *touch:*
touchstone. 4. *lantern:* light tower. 14. *his:* Sir Philip Sidney. 19. *Gamage:*
Barbara Gamage, wife of the owner of Penshurst, Sir Robert Sidney,
younger brother of Sir Philip.

Thy sheep, thy bullocks, kine, and calves do feed;
   The middle grounds thy mares and horses breed.
Each bank doth yield thee conies; and the tops,   25
   Fertile of wood, Ashore and Sidney's copse,
To crown thy open table, doth provide
   The purpled pheasant with the speckled side;
The painted partridge lies in every field,
   And, for thy mess, is willing to be killed.   30
And if the high-swollen Medway fail thy dish,
   Thou hast thy ponds that pay thee tribute fish,
Fat agèd carps that run into thy net,
   And pikes, now weary their own kind to eat,
As loath the second draught or cast to stay,   35
   Officiously at first themselves betray;
Bright eels that emulate them, and leap on land
   Before the fisher, or into his hand.
Then hath thy orchard fruit, thy garden flowers
   Fresh as the air, and new as are the hours.   40
The early cherry, with the later plum,
   Fig, grape, and quince, each in his time doth come;
The blushing apricot and woolly peach
   Hang on thy walls, that every child may reach.
And though thy walls be of the country stone,   45
   They'are reared with no man's ruin, no man's groan;
There's none that dwell about them wish them down,
   But all come in, the farmer and the clown,
And no one empty handed, to salute
   Thy lord and lady, though they have no suit.   50
Some bring a capon, some a rural cake,
   Some nuts, some apples; some that think they make
The better cheeses bring 'em, or else send
   By their ripe daughters whom they would commend
This way to husbands, and whose baskets bear   55
   An emblem of themselves in plum or pear.
But what can this, more than express their love,
   Add to thy free provisions, far above
The need of such, whose liberal board doth flow
   With all that hospitality doth know?   60
Where comes no guest but is ailowed to eat
   Without his fear, and of thy lord's own meat;
Where the same beer and bread, and self-same wine

---

48. *clown:* rustic.

That is his lordship's shall be also mine.
And I not fain to sit, as some this day   65
   At great men's tables, and yet dine away.
Here no man tells my cups, nor, standing by,
   A waiter doth my gluttony envý,
But gives me what I call and lets me eat;
   He knows below he shall find plenty of meat.   70
Thy tables hoard not up for the next day,
   Nor when I take my lodging need I pray
For fire or lights or livery; all is there
   As if thou then wert mine, or I reigned here;
There's nothing I can wish, for which I stay.   75
   That found King James, when hunting late this way
With his brave son, the prince, they saw thy fires
   Shine bright on every hearth as the desires
Of thy Penates had been set on flame
   To entertain them, or the country came   80
With all their zeal to warm their welcome here.
   What great I will not say, but sudden cheer
Didst thou then make 'em! and what praise was heaped
   On thy good lady then! who therein reaped
The just reward of her high huswifery;   85
   To have her linen, plate, and all things nigh
When she was far, and not a room but dressed
   As if it had expected such a guest!
These, Penshurst, are thy praise, and yet not all.
   Thy lady's noble, fruitful, chaste withal;   90
His children thy great lord may call his own,
   A fortune in this age but rarely known.
They are and have been taught religion; thence
   Their gentler spirits have sucked innocence.
Each morn and even they are taught to pray   95
   With the whole household, and may every day
Read, in their virtuous parents' noble parts,
   The mysteries of manners, arms, and arts.
Now, Penshurst, they that will proportion thee
   With other edifices when they see   100
Those proud, ambitious heaps and nothing else,
   May say, their lords have built, but thy lord dwells.

❧

---

67. *tells:* counts.

AN EPITAPH ON S. P., A CHILD OF Q[UEEN]
EL[IZABETH'S] CHAPEL
(1616)

Weep with me, all you that read
   This little story;
And know, for whom a tear you shed
   Death's self is sorry.
'Twas a child that so did thrive   5
   In grace and feature,
As heaven and nature seemed to strive
   Which owned the creature.
Years he numbered scarce thirteen
   When fates turned cruel,   10
Yet three filled zodiacs had he been
   The stage's jewel;
And did act, what now we moan,
   Old men so duly,
As, sooth, the Parcæ thought him one,   15
   He played so truly.
So by error, to his fate
   They all consented;
But viewing him since, alas too late,
   They have repented,   20
And have sought, to give new birth,
   In baths to steep him;
But being so much too good for earth,
   Heaven vows to keep him.

AN EPITAPH ON S. P.: *Title: S. P.:* Solomon Pavy, a child actor, who appeared in two of Jonson's plays, and died in 1603, aged 13. 15. *Parcæ:* the three Fates. 22. *baths:* as Æson was rejuvenated by baths prepared by his son Jason's wife, Medea.

EPITAPH ON ELIZABETH, L. H.
(1616)

Wouldst thou hear what man can say
  In a little? Reader, stay.
Underneath this stone doth lie
  As much beauty as could die;
Which in life did harbor give   5
  To more virtue than doth live.
If at all she had a fault,
  Leave it buried in this vault.
One name was Elizabeth,
  Th' other let it sleep with death;   10
Fitter, where it died to tell,
  Than that it lived at all. Farewell.

TO THE MEMORY OF MY BELOVED THE AUTHOR, MR. WILLIAM SHAKESPEARE, AND WHAT HE HATH LEFT US
(1623)

To draw no envy, Shakespeare, on thy name,
  Am I thus ample to thy book and fame,
While I confess thy writings to be such
  As neither man nor Muse can praise too much;
'Tis true, and all men's suffrage. But these ways   5
  Were not the paths I meant unto thy praise,
For seeliest ignorance on these may light,
  Which when it sounds at best but echoes right;
Or blind affection which doth ne'er advance
  The truth, but gropes and urgeth all by chance;   10
Or crafty malice might pretend this praise,
  And think to ruin where it seemed to raise.
These are as some infamous bawd or whore

TO SHAKESPEARE: 5. *suffrage:* vote. 7. *seeliest:* most foolish. 9. *affection:* emotion.

Should praise a matron; what could hurt her more?
But thou art proof against them, and indeed   15
   Above th' ill fortune of them, or the need.
I, therefore, will begin. Soul of the age!
   The applause, delight, the wonder of our stage!
My Shakespeare, rise; I will not lodge thee by
   Chaucer, or Spenser, or bid Beaumont lie   20
A little further to make thee a room;
   Thou art a monument, without a tomb,
And art alive still, while thy book doth live
   And we have wits to read and praise to give.
That I not mix thee so, my brain excuses—   25
   I mean with great but disproportioned muses,—
For if I thought my judgment were of years
   I should commit thee surely with thy peers,
And tell how far thou didst our Lyly outshine,
   Or sporting Kyd, or Marlowe's mighty line.   30
And though thou hadst small Latin and less Greek,
   From thence to honor thee I would not seek
For names, but call forth thund'ring Æschylus,
   Euripides, and Sophocles to us,
Pacuvius, Accius, him of Cordova dead,   35
   To life again, to hear thy buskin tread
And shake a stage; or, when thy socks were on,
   Leave thee alone for the comparison
Of all that insolent Greece or haughty Rome
   Sent forth, or since did from their ashes come.   40
Triumph, my Britain, thou hast one to show
   To whom all scenes of Europe homage owe.
He was not of an age, but for all time!
   And all the Muses still were in their prime,
When like Apollo he came forth to warm   45
   Our ears, or like a Mercury to charm!
Nature herself was proud of his designs,
   And joyed to wear the dressing of his lines
Which were so richly spun, and woven so fit,
   As since, she will vouchsafe no other wit;   50
The merry Greek, tart Aristophanes,
   Neat Terence, witty Plautus, now not please,
But antiquated and deserted lie
   As they were not of nature's family.

---

35. *Pacuvius, Accius:* early Roman writers of tragedies; *him of Cordova:* Seneca. 36. *buskin:* tragedy. 37. *socks:* comedy.

Yet must I not give nature all; thy art,   55
   My gentle Shakespeare, must enjoy a part;
For though the poet's matter nature be,
   His art doth give the fashion; and that he
Who casts to write a living line, must sweat,
   Such as thine are, and strike the second heat   60
Upon the Muses' anvil, turn the same,
   And himself with it, that he thinks to frame;
Or for the laurel he may gain a scorn,
   For a good poet's made, as well as born;
And such wert thou. Look how the father's face   65
   Lives in his issue; even so the race
Of Shakespeare's mind and manners brightly shines
   In his well-turnèd and true-filèd lines,
In each of which he seems to shake a lance,
   As brandished at the eyes of ignorance.   70
Sweet swan of Avon! what a sight it were
   To see thee in our waters yet appear,
And makes those flights upon the banks of Thames
   That so did take Eliza, and our James!
But stay, I see thee in the hemisphere   75
   Advanced, and made a constellation there!
Shine forth, thou star of poets, and with rage
   Or influence chide or cheer the drooping stage;
Which since thy flight from hence, hath mourned like night,
   And despairs day, but for thy volume's light.   80

                From *Mr. William Shakespeare's Comedies,*
                          Histories, and Tragedies

TO HEAVEN

(1641)

Good, and great God, can I not think of thee,
   But it must, straight, my melancholy be?
Is it interpreted in me disease,
   That, laden with my sins, I seek for ease?
O, be thou witness, that the reins dost know,   5
   And hearts of all, if I be sad for show,

TO HEAVEN: 5. *reins:* kidneys.

And judge me after: if I dare pretend
  To ought but grace, or aim at other end.
As thou art all, so be thou all to me,
  First, midst, and last, converted one, and three;   10
My faith, my hope, my love: and in this state,
  My judge, my witness, and my advocate.
Where have I been this while exil'd from thee?
  And whither rap'd, now thou but stoop'st to me?
Dwell, dwell here still: O, being everywhere,   15
  How can I doubt to find thee ever, here?
I know my state, both full of shame, and scorn,
  Conceiv'd in sin, and unto labour born,
Standing with fear, and must with horror fall,
  And destin'd unto judgement, after all.   20
I feel my griefs too, and there scarce is ground
  Upon my flesh t'inflict another wound.
Yet dare I not complain, or wish for death
  With holy Paul, lest it be thought the breath
Of discontent; or that these prayers be   25
  For weariness of life, not love of thee.

❧

Robert Herrick

From *Hesperides*
(1648)

THE ARGUMENT OF HIS BOOK

I sing of brooks, of blossoms, birds, and bowers,
Of April, May, of June, and July flowers;
I sing of may-poles, hock-carts, wassails, wakes,
Of bridegrooms, brides, and of their bridal cakes;
I write of youth, of love, and have access   5
By these to sing of cleanly wantonness;
I sing of dews, of rains, and piece by piece
Of balm, of oil, of spice, and ambergris;
I sing of times trans-shifting, and I write

THE ARGUMENT OF HIS BOOK: 3. *hock-carts:* last harvest wagons, followed
by the celebration of "harvest home."

How roses first came red, and lilies white;　　　10
I write of groves, of twilights, and I sing
The court of Mab, and of the Fairy King;
I write of hell; I sing, and ever shall,
Of heaven, and hope to have it after all.

❦

WHEN HE WOULD HAVE HIS VERSES READ

In sober mornings do not thou rehearse
The holy incantation of a verse;
But when that men have both well drunk and fed,
Let my enchantments then be sung, or read.
When laurel spirts i' th' fire, and when the hearth　　　5
Smiles to itself and gilds the roof with mirth;
When up the thyrse is raised, and when the sound
Of sacred orgies flies—A round, a round!
When the rose reigns, and locks with ointments shine,
Let rigid Cato read these lines of mine.　　　10

❦

AN ODE FOR HIM

Ah Ben!
Say how, or when
Shall we thy guests
Meet at those lyric feasts
Made at the Sun,　　　5
The Dog, the Triple Tun,
Where we such clusters had
As made us nobly wild, not mad;
And yet each verse of thine
Outdid the meat, outdid the frolic wine.　　　10

My Ben!
Or come again,

WHEN HE WOULD HAVE HIS VERSES READ: 7. *thyrse:* a javelin twined with ivy.

AN ODE FOR HIM: 5-6. *Sun . . . Tun:* London taverns where Ben Jonson and his followers gathered. 7. *clusters:* grapes, wine.

Or send to us
Thy wit's great overplus;
    But teach us yet   15
Wisely to husband it.
Lest we that talent spend,
And having once brought to an end
    That precious stock, the store
Of such a wit the world should have no more.   20

❧

TO THE VIRGINS, TO MAKE MUCH OF TIME

Gather ye rosebuds while ye may,
    Old time is still a-flying,
And this same flower that smiles to-day,
    To-morrow will be dying.

The glorious lamp of heaven, the sun,   5
    The higher he's a-getting,
The sooner will his race be run,
    And nearer he's to setting.

That age is best which is the first,
    When youth and blood are warmer;   10
But being spent, the worse, and worst
    Times still succeed the former.

Then be not coy, but use your time,
    And while ye may, go marry;
For having lost but once your prime,   15
    You may for ever tarry.

❧

DELIGHT IN DISORDER

A sweet disorder in the dress
Kindles in clothes a wantonness;
A lawn about the shoulders thrown
Into a fine distraction,
An erring lace, which here and there   5
Enthralls the crimson stomacher,

A cuff neglectful, and thereby
Ribands to flow confusedly,
A winning wave, deserving note,
In the tempestuous petticoat,   10
A careless shoe-string, in whose tie
I see a wild civility,
Do more bewitch me than when art
Is too precise in every part.

THE NIGHT PIECE, TO JULIA

Her eyes the glow-worm lend thee,
The shooting stars attend thee;
   And the elves also,
   Whose little eyes glow
Like the sparks of fire, befriend thee.   5

No will-o'-th'-wisp mis-light thee,
Nor snake, or slow-worm bite thee;
   But on, on thy way
   Not making a stay,
Since ghost there's none to affright thee.   10

Let not the dark thee cumber;
What though the moon does slumber?
   The stars of the night
   Will lend thee their light,
Like tapers clear without number.   15

Then, Julia, let me woo thee,
Thus, thus to come unto me;
   And when I shall meet
   Thy silv'ry feet,
My soul I'll pour into thee.   20

UPON JULIA'S CLOTHES

Whenas in silks my Julia goes,
Then, then, methinks, how sweetly flows

That liquefaction of her clothes.
Next, when I cast mine eyes and see
That brave vibration each way free,   5
Oh, how that glittering taketh me!

∾

CHERRY-RIPE

Cherry-ripe, ripe, ripe, I cry,
Full and fair ones; come and buy.
If so be you ask me where
They do grow, I answer: There,
Where my Julia's lips do smile;   5
There's the land, or cherry-isle,
Whose plantations fully show
All the year where cherries grow.

∾

TO ANTHEA, WHO MAY COMMAND
HIM ANYTHING

Bid me live, and I will live
    Thy protestant to be;
Or bid me love, and I will give
    A loving heart to thee.

A heart as soft, a heart as kind,   5
    A heart as sound and free
As in the whole world thou canst find,
    That heart I'll give to thee.

Bid that heart stay, and it will stay
    To honor thy decree;   10
Or bid it languish quite away,
    And 't shall do so for thee.

Bid me to weep, and I will weep
    While I have eyes to see;

And having none, yet I will keep   15
  A heart to weep for thee.

Bid me despair, and I'll despair
  Under that cypress tree;
Or bid me die, and I will dare
  E'en death, to die for thee.   20

Thou art my life, my love, my heart,
  The very eyes of me;
And hast command of every part,
  To live and die for thee.

❧

CORINNA'S GOING A-MAYING

Get up, get up for shame, the blooming morn
Upon her wings presents the god unshorn.
  See how Aurora throws her fair
  Fresh-quilted colors through the air;
  Get up, sweet slug-a-bed, and see   5
  The dew bespangling herb and tree.
Each flower has wept and bowed toward the east
Above an hour since, yet you not dressed;
  Nay, not so much as out of bed.
  When all the birds have matins said,   10
  And sung their thankful hymns, 'tis sin,
  Nay, profanation to keep in,
Whenas a thousand virgins on this day
Spring, sooner than the lark, to fetch in May.

Rise and put on your foliage, and be seen   15
To come forth like the springtime, fresh and green,
  And sweet as Flora. Take no care
  For jewels for your gown or hair;
  Fear not, the leaves will strew
  Gems in abundance upon you;   20
Besides, the childhood of the day has kept,
Against you come, some orient pearls unwept;
  Come and receive them while the light
  Hangs on the dew-locks of the night,

CORINNA'S GOING A-MAYING: 2. *god:* Apollo.

And Titan on the eastern hill   25
Retires himself, or else stands still
Till you come forth. Wash, dress, be brief in praying:
Few beads are best when once we go a-maying.

Come, my Corinna, come; and coming, mark
How each field turns a street, each street a park   30
    Made green and trimmed with trees; see how
    Devotion gives each house a bough
    Or branch; each porch, each door, ere this,
    An ark, a tabernacle is,
Made up of white-thorn neatly interwove,   35
As if here were those cooler shades of love.
    Can such delights be in the street
    And open fields, and we not see't?
    Come, we'll abroad, and let's obey
    The proclamation made for May,   40
And sin no more, as we have done, by staying;
But, my Corinna, come, let's go a-maying.

There's not a budding boy or girl this day
But is got up, and gone to bring in May.
    A deal of youth, ere this, is come   45
    Back, and with white-thorn laden, home.
    Some have despatched their cakes and cream
    Before that we have left to dream;
And some have wept, and wooed, and plighted troth,
And chose their priest, ere we can cast off sloth;   50
    Many a green-gown has been given,
    Many a kiss, both odd and even,
    Many a glance too has been sent
    From out the eye, love's firmament,
Many a jest told of the keys betraying   55
This night, and locks picked, yet we're not a-maying.

Come, let us go while we are in our prime,
And take the harmless folly of the time.
    We shall grow old apace, and die
    Before we know our liberty.   60
    Our life is short, and our days run
    As fast away as does the sun;
And as a vapor, or a drop of rain

---

34. *ark:* basket.

Once lost, can ne'er be found again,
  So when or you or I are made   65
  A fable, song, or fleeting shade,
  All love, all liking, all delight
  Lies drowned with us in endless night.
Then while time serves, and we are but decaying,
Come, my Corinna, come, let's go a-maying.   70

OBERON'S FEAST

Shapcot, to thee the fairy state
I with discretion, dedicate,
Because thou prizest things that are
Curious and unfamiliar.
Take first the feast; these dishes gone,   5
We'll see the fairy court anon.

A little mushroom table spread,
After short prayers, they set on bread;
A moon-parched grain of purest wheat,
With some small glitt'ring grit to eat   10
His choice bits with; then in a trice
They make a feast less great than nice.
But all this while his eye is served,
We must not think his ear was starved,
But that there was in place to stir   15
His spleen, the chirring grasshopper,
The merry cricket, puling fly,
The piping gnat, for minstrelsy.
And now we must imagine first,
The elves present to quench his thirst   20
A pure seed-pearl of infant dew,
Brought and besweetened in a blue
And pregnant violet; which done,
His kitling eyes begin to run
Quite through the table, where he spies   25
The horns of papery butterflies,
Of which he eats, and tastes a little

OBERON'S FEAST: 1. *Shapcot:* Thomas Shapcot, lawyer, and friend of Herrick's. 17. *puling:* whining. 24. *kitling:* tiny.

Of that we call the cuckoo's spittle.
A little fuzz-ball pudding stands
By, yet not blessed by his hands;   30
That was too coarse, but then forthwith
He ventures boldly on the pith
Of sugared rush, and eats the sag
And well-bestrutted bee's sweet bag,
Gladding his palate with some store   35
Of emmets' eggs, what would he more?
But beards of mice, a newt's stewed thigh,
A bloated earwig, and a fly,
With the red-capped worm that's shut
Within the conclave of a nut,   40
Brown as his tooth. A little moth,
Late fattened in a piece of cloth;
With withered cherries, mandrakes' ears,
Moles' eyes; to these, the slain stag's tears,
The unctuous dewlaps of a snail;   45
The broke-heart of a nightingale
O'ercome in music; with a wine
Ne'er ravished from the flattering vine.
But gently pressed from the soft side
Of the most sweet and dainty bride,   50
Brought in a dainty daisy, which
He fully quaffs up to bewitch
His blood to height; this done, commended
Grace by his priest; the feast is ended.

~❧~

From *Noble Numbers*

(1648)

HIS LITANY TO THE HOLY SPIRIT

In the hour of my distress,
When temptations me oppress,
And when I my sins confess,
        Sweet Spirit, comfort me!

---

34. *well-bestrutted:* swollen.

When I lie within my bed,
Sick in heart and sick in head,
And with doubts discomforted,
    Sweet Spirit, comfort me!   5

When the house doth sigh and weep,
And the world is drowned in sleep,
Yet mine eyes the watch do keep,   10
    Sweet Spirit, comfort me!

When the artless doctor sees
No one hope, but of his fees,
And his skill runs on the lees,
    Sweet Spirit, comfort me!   15

When his potion and his pill
Has or none or little skill,
Meet for nothing but to kill,
    Sweet Spirit, comfort me!   20

When the passing bell doth toll,
And the furies in a shoal
Come to fright a parting soul,
    Sweet Spirit, comfort me!

When the tapers now burn blue,   25
And the comforters are few,
And that number more than true,
    Sweet Spirit, comfort me!

When the priest his last hath prayed,
And I nod to what is said,   30
'Cause my speech is now decayed,
    Sweet Spirit, comfort me!

When, God knows, I'm tossed about,
Either with despair, or doubt,
Yet before the glass be out,   35
    Sweet Spirit, comfort me!

When the tempter me pursu'th
With the sins of all my youth,
And half damns me with untruth,
    Sweet Spirit, comfort me!   40

HIS LITANY: 13. *artless:* skilless.

When the flames and hellish cries
Fright mine ears, and fright mine eyes,
And all terrors me surprise,
  Sweet Spirit, comfort me!

When the judgment is revealed,   45
And that opened which was sealed,
When to thee I have appealed,
  Sweet Spirit, comfort me!

ANOTHER GRACE FOR A CHILD

Here a little child I stand,
Heaving up my either hand;
Cold as paddocks though they be,
Here I lift them up to thee,
For a benison to fall   5
On our meat, and on us all. *Amen.*

Thomas Carew

THE SPRING
(1640)

Now that the winter's gone, the earth hath lost
Her snow-white robes, and now no more the frost
Candies the grass, or casts an icy cream
Upon the silver lake or crystal stream;
But the warm sun thaws the benumbèd earth,   5
And makes it tender; gives a sacred birth
To the dead swallow; wakes in hollow tree
The drowsy cuckoo and the humble-bee.

ANOTHER GRACE FOR A CHILD: 3. *paddocks:* frogs or toads.

Now do a choir of chirping minstrels bring
In triumph to the world the youthful spring.   10
The valleys, hills, and woods in rich array
Welcome the coming of the longed-for May.
Now all things smile, only my love doth lour;
Nor hath the scalding noonday sun the power
To melt that marble ice, which still doth hold   15
Her heart congealed, and makes her pity cold.
The ox, which lately did for shelter fly
Into the stall, doth now securely lie
In open fields; and love no more is made
By the fireside, but in the cooler shade   20
Amyntas now doth with his Chloris sleep
Under a sycamore, and all things keep
Time with the season; only she doth carry
June in her eyes, in her heart January.

᭲᭜

ASK ME NO MORE
(1640)

Ask me no more where Jove bestows,
When June is past, the fading rose;
For in your beauty's orient deep
These flowers, as in their causes, sleep.

Ask me no more whither doth stray   5
The golden atoms of the day;
For in pure love heaven did prepare
Those powders to enrich your hair.

Ask me no more whither doth haste
The nightingale when May is past;   10
For in your sweet dividing throat
She winters, and keeps warm her note.

Ask me no more where those stars light
That downwards fall in dead of night;

ASK ME NO MORE: 3. *orient:* eastern, rising like the sun, lustrousness of a
pearl. 4. *causes:* Aristotle's material cause. 11. *dividing:* melodic.

For in your eyes they sit, and there 15
Fixèd become as in their sphere.

Ask me no more if east or west
The phœnix builds her spicy nest;
For unto you at last she flies,
And in your fragrant bosom dies. 20

❧

MEDIOCRITY IN LOVE REJECTED
(1640)

Give me more love or more disdain:
  The torrid or the frozen zone
Bring equal ease unto my pain,
  The temperate affords me none;
Either extreme of love or hate 5
Is sweeter than a calm estate.

Give me a storm; if it be love,
  Like Danaë in that golden shower,
I swim in pleasure; if it prove
  Disdain, that torrent will devour 10
My vulture-hopes; and he's possessed
Of heaven, that's but from hell released.
  Then crown my joys or cure my pain;
  Give me more love or more disdain.

❧

TO MY INCONSTANT MISTRESS
(1640)

When thou, poor excommunicate
  From all the joys of love, shalt see
The full reward and glorious fate
  Which my strong faith shall purchase me,
Then curse thine own inconstancy. 5

---

16. *sphere:* the eighth of the concentric spheres in the Ptolemaic system was
that of the fixed stars. 18. *phoenix:* mythological oriental bird which
burned itself every 500 years in a spicy fire and arose anew from the ashes.

A fairer hand than thine shall cure
  That heart which thy false oaths did wound;
And to my soul, a soul more pure
  Than thine shall by love's hand be bound,
  And both with equal glory crowned.   10

Then shalt thou weep, entreat, complain
  To love, as I did once to thee;
When all thy tears shall be as vain
  As mine were then, for thou shalt be
  Damned for thy false apostasy.   15

DISDAIN RETURNED
(1632)

He that loves a rosy cheek,
  Or a coral lip admires,
Or from star-like eyes doth seek
  Fuel to maintain his fires;
As old time makes these decay,   5
So his flames must waste away.

But a smooth and steadfast mind,
  Gentle thoughts and calm desires,
Hearts with equal love combined,
  Kindle never-dying fires.   10
Where these are not, I despise
Lovely cheeks, or lips, or eyes.

No tears, Celia, now shall win
  My resolved heart to return;
I have searched thy soul within,   15
  And find nought but pride and scorn;
I have learned thy arts, and now
Can disdain as much as thou.
  Some power, in my revenge, convey
  That love to her I cast away.   20

MARIA WENTWORTH

(1632)

And here the precious dust is laid,
Whose purely tempered clay was made
So fine that it the guest betrayed.

Else the soul grew so fast within
It broke the outward shell of sin,   5
And so was hatched a cherubin.

In height it soared to God above;
In depth it did to knowledge move,
And spread in breadth to general love.

Before, a pious duty shined   10
To parents, courtesy behind;
On either side an equal mind,

Good to the poor, to kindred dear,
To servants kind, to friendship clear,
To nothing but herself severe.   15

So, though a virgin, yet a bride
To every grace, she justified
A chaste polygamy, and died.

Learn from hence, reader, what small trust
We owe this world, where virtue must,   20
Frail as our flesh, crumble to dust.

❧

AN ELEGY UPON THE DEATH OF DOCTOR DONNE, DEAN OF PAUL'S

(1633)

Can we not force from widowed poetry,
Now thou art dead, great Donne, one elegy

MARIA WENTWORTH: *Title:* Second daughter of Thomas, Earl of Cleveland. She died in 1632 and these lines were her epitaph.

To crown thy hearse? Why yet did we not trust,
Though with unkneaded dough-baked prose, thy dust,
Such as th' unscissored lect'rer from the flower   5
Of fading rhet'ric, short-lived as his hour,
Dry as the sand that measures it, might lay
Upon the ashes, on the funeral day?
Have we nor tune nor voice? Didst thou dispense
Through all our language both the words and sense?   10
'Tis a sad truth. The pulpit may her plain
And sober Christian precepts still retain;
Doctrines it may, and wholesome uses, frame,
Grave homilies and lectures, but the flame
Of thy brave soul, that shot such heat and light   15
As burnt our earth and made our darkness bright,
Committed holy rapes upon the will,
Did through the eye the melting heart distil,
And the deep knowledge of dark truths so teach
As sense might judge where fancy could not reach,   20
Must be desired forever. So the fire
That fills with spirit and heat the Delphic choir,
Which, kindled first by thy Promethean breath,
Glowed here a while, lies quenched now in thy death.
The Muses' garden, with pedantic weeds   25
O'erspread, was purged by thee; the lazy seeds
Of servile imitation thrown away,
And fresh invention planted; thou didst pay
The debts of our penurious bankrupt age;
Licentious thefts, that make poetic rage   30
A mimic fury, when our souls must be
Possessed, or with Anacreon's ecstasy,
Or Pindar's, not their own; the subtle cheat
Of sly exchanges, and the juggling feat
Of two-edged words, or whatsoever wrong   35
By ours was done the Greek or Latin tongue,
Thou hast redeemed, and opened us a mine
Of rich and pregnant fancy; drawn a line
Of masculine expression, which had good
Old Orpheus seen, or all the ancient brood   40
Our superstitious fools admire, and hold

AN ELEGY: 5. *unscissored lect'rer:* unshorn reader; "lect'rer," from the
1640 edition, replaced "Churchman" in the first appearance of the Elegy in
Donne's *Poems,* 1633.

Their lead more precious than thy burnished gold,
Thou hadst been their exchequer, and no more
They each in other's dung had searched for ore.
Thou shalt yield no precedence, but of time   45
And the blind fate of language, whose tuned chime
More charms the outward sense; yet thou mayst claim
From so great disadvantage greater fame,
Since to the awe of thy imperious wit
Our troublesome language bends, made only fit   50
With her tough thick-ribbed hoops to gird about
Thy giant fancy, which had proved too stout
For their soft melting phrases. As in time
They had the start, so did they cull the prime
Buds of invention many a hundred year,   55
And left the rifled fields, besides the fear
To touch their harvest; yet from those bare lands
Of what was only thine, thy only hands,
And that their smallest work, have gleanèd more
Than all those times and tongues could reap before.   60
    But thou art gone, and thy strict laws will be
Too hard for libertines in poetry;
They will recall the goodly exiled train
Of gods and goddesses, which in thy just reign
Was banished nobler poems; now with these,   65
The silenced tales i' th' *Metamorphoses,*
Shall stuff their lines, and swell the windy page,
Till verse, refined by thee in this last age,
Turn ballad-rhyme, or those old idols be
Adored again with new apostasy.   70
    Oh, pardon me, that break with untuned verse
The reverend silence that attends thy hearse,
Whose solemn awful murmurs were to thee,
More than these rude lines, a loud elegy,
That did proclaim in a dumb eloquence   75
The death of all the arts; whose influence,
Grown feeble, in these panting numbers lies,
Gasping short-winded accents, and so dies.
So doth the swiftly turning wheel not stand
In th' instant we withdraw the moving hand,   80
But some short time retain a faint weak course,
By virtue of the first impulsive force;
And so, whilst I cast on thy funeral pile
Thy crown of bays, oh, let it crack awhile,

And spit disdain, till the devouring flashes   85
Suck all the moisture up, then turn to ashes.
   I will not draw the envy to engross
All thy perfections, or weep all the loss;
Those are too numerous for one elegy,
And this too great to be expressed by me.   90
Let others carve the rest; it shall suffice
I on thy grave this epitaph incise:
   Here lies a king that ruled as he thought fit
   The universal monarchy of wit;
   Here lies two flamens, and both those the best,   95
   Apollo's first, at last the true God's priest.

❧

George Herbert

From *The Temple*

(1633)

JORDAN [1]

Who says that fictions only and false hair
Become a verse? Is there in truth no beauty?
Is all good structure in a winding stair?
May no lines pass except they do their duty
   Not to a true, but painted chair?   5

Is it no verse except enchanted groves
And sudden arbors shadow coarse-spun lines?
Must purling streams refresh a lover's loves?
Must all be veiled, while he that reads, divines,
   Catching the sense at two removes?   10

Shepherds are honest people; let them sing.
Riddle who list for me, and pull for prime;
I envy no man's nightingale or spring,

---

95. *flamens:* priests.
   JORDAN [1]: 12. *Riddle . . . prime:* Whoever please may make riddles
for all of me; we shall see who draws (*pull*) the winning card (*prime*).

Nor let them punish me with loss of rhyme,
Who plainly say, My God, my King.   15

~<

VANITY

The fleet astronomer can bore
And thread the spheres with his quick-piercing mind.
He views their stations, walks from door to door,
   Surveys as if he had designed
To make a purchase there. He sees their dances,   5
      And knoweth long before
Both their full-eyed aspects and secret glances.

The nimble diver with his side
Cuts through the working waves, that he may fetch
His dearly-earned pearl, which God did hide   10
   On purpose from the venturous wretch;
That he might save his life, and also hers
      Who with excessive pride
Her own destruction and his danger wears.

The subtle chymic can divest   15
And strip the creature naked, till he find
The callow principles within their nest.
   There he imparts to them his mind,
Admitted to their bed-chamber, before
      They appear trim and dressed   20
To ordinary suitors at the door.

What hath not man sought out and found,
But his dear God? who yet His glorious law
Embosoms in us, mellowing the ground
   With showers and frosts, with love and awe,
So that we need not say, "Where's this command?"
      Poor man, thou searchest round
To find out death, but missest life at hand.

~<

VANITY: 15. *chymic*: alchemist. 16. *creature*: any created thing.

THE QUIP

The merry world did on a day
  With his train-bands and mates agree
To meet together where I lay,
  And all in sport to jeer at me.

First Beauty crept into a rose;   5
  Which when I plucked not, "Sir," said she,
"Tell me, I pray, whose hands are those?"
  But Thou shalt answer, Lord, for me.

Then Money came, and chinking still,
  "What tune is this, poor man?" said he;   10
"I heard in music you had skill."
  But Thou shalt answer, Lord, for me.

Then came brave Glory puffing by
  In silks that whistled, who but he?
He scarce allowed me half an eye.   15
  But Thou shalt answer, Lord, for me.

Then came quick Wit and Conversation,
  And he would needs a comfort be,
And, to be short, make an oration.
  But Thou shalt answer, Lord, for me.   20

Yet when the hour of Thy design
  To answer these fine things shall come,
Speak not at large; say I am Thine;
  And then they have their answer home.

❦

REDEMPTION

Having been tenant long to a rich Lord,
  Not thriving, I resolvèd to be bold,

THE QUIP: 2. *train-bands:* fellow soldiers.

And make a suit unto him to afford
A new small-rented lease and cancel th' old.
In heaven at his manor I him sought.   5
   They told me there that he was lately gone
   About some land which he had dearly bought
Long since on earth, to take possession.
I straight returned, and knowing his great birth,
   Sought him accordingly in great resorts,   10
   In cities, theaters, gardens, parks, and courts.
At length I heard a ragged noise and mirth
   Of thieves and murderers; there I him espied,
   Who straight, Your suit is granted, said, and died.

NATURE

Full of rebellion, I would die,
Or fight, or travel, or deny
That thou hast aught to do with me.
   O tame my heart!
   It is thy highest art   5
To captivate strongholds to thee.

If thou shalt let this venom lurk
And in suggestions fume and work,
My soul will turn to bubbles straight,
   And thence by kind   10
   Vanish into a wind,
Making thy workmanship deceit.

O smooth my rugged heart, and there
Engrave thy rev'rend law and fear!
Or make a new one, since the old   15
   Is sapless grown,
   And a much fitter stone
To hide my dust than thee to hold.

NATURE: 10. *by kind:* because of its nature.

THE PEARL

I know the ways of learning: both the head
And pipes that feed the press, and make it run;
What reason hath from nature borrowèd,
Or of itself, like a good housewife, spun
In laws and policy; what the stars conspire;   5
What willing nature speaks, what forced by fire;
Both th'old discoveries and the new-found seas,
The stock and surplus, cause and history;
All these stand open, or I have the keys,—
        Yet I love thee.   10

I know the ways of honor: what maintains
The quick returns of courtesy and wit;
In vies of favors whether party gains
When glory swells the heart and moldeth it
To all expressions both of hand and eye,   15
Which on the world a true-love-knot may tie,
And bear the bundle wheresoe'er it goes;
How many drams of spirit there must be
To sell my life unto my friends or foes,—
        Yet I love thee.   20

I know the ways of pleasure: the sweet strains,
The lullings and the relishes of it;
The propositions of hot blood and brains;
What mirth and music mean; what love and wit
Have done these twenty hundred years and more;   25
I know the projects of unbridled store;
My stuff is flesh, not brass; my senses live,
And grumble oft that they have more in me
Than he that curbs them, being but one to five,—
        Yet I love thee.   30

I know all these and have them in my hand;
Therefore not seelèd but with open eyes

THE PEARL: *Title:* Based on St. Matthew xiii, 45—"Again, the kingdom of heaven is likened unto a merchant man, seeking goodly pearls, who, when he had found one pearl of great price, went and sold all that he had, and bought it." 26. *store:* wealth. 32. *seelèd:* sewn shut, like the lids of a young hawk in training.

I fly to thee, and fully understand
Both the main sale and the commodities;
And at what rate and price I have thy love,   35
With all the circumstances that may move.
Yet through the labyrinths, not my groveling wit,
But thy silk twist let down from heav'n to me
Did both conduct and teach me how by it
        To climb to thee.   40

LOVE

Love bade me welcome, yet my soul drew back,
  Guilty of dust and sin.
But quick-eyed Love, observing me grow slack
  From my first entrance in,
Drew nearer to me, sweetly questioning   5
  If I lacked anything.

A guest, I answered, worthy to be here.
  Love said, You shall be he.
I, the unkind, the ungrateful? ah, my dear,
  I cannot look on thee.   10
Love took my hand and smiling did reply,
  Who made the eyes but I?

Truth, Lord, but I have marred them; let my shame
  Go where it doth deserve.
And know you not, says Love, who bore the blame?   15
  My dear, then I will serve.
You must sit down, says Love, and taste my meat.
  So I did sit and eat.

DEATH

Death, thou wast once an uncouth hideous thing,
  Nothing but bones,
The sad effect of sadder groans;
The mouth was open but thou couldst not sing.

For we consider'd thee as at some six   5
   Or ten years hence,
After the loss of life and sense,
Flesh being turn'd to dust, and bones to sticks.

We lookt on this side of thee, shooting short;
   Where we did find   10
The shells of fledge souls left behind,
Dry dust, which sheds no tears but may extort.

But since our Saviour's death did put some blood
   Into thy face,
Thou art grown fair and full of grace,   15
Much in request, much sought for as a good.

For we do now behold thee gay and glad,
   As at dooms-day;
When souls shall wear their new array,
And all thy bones with beauty shall be clad.   20

Therefore we can go die as sleep, and trust
   Half that we have
Unto an honest faithfull grave,
Making our pillows either down or dust.

❧

THE PULLEY

   When God at first made man,
Having a glass of blessings standing by,
Let us, said he, pour on him all we can.
Let the world's riches, which dispersèd lie,
   Contract into a span.   5

   So strength first made a way,
Then beauty flowed, then wisdom, honor, pleasure.
When almost all was out, God made a stay,
Perceiving that alone of all his treasure
   Rest in the bottom lay.   10

   For if I should, said he,
Bestow this jewel also on my creature,
He would adore my gifts instead of me,
And rest in nature, not the God of nature;
   So both should losers be.   15

Yet let him keep the rest,
But keep them with repining restlessness.
Let him be rich and weary, that at least,
If goodness lead him not, yet weariness
   May toss him to my breast.   20

THE COLLAR

I struck the board and cried, No more!
        I will abroad.
What? Shall I ever sigh and pine?
My lines and life are free, free as the road,
   Loose as the wind, as large as store.   5
       Shall I be still in suit?
  Have I no harvest but a thorn
  To let me blood, and not restore
What I have lost with cordial fruit?
       Sure there was wine   10
  Before my sighs did dry it; there was corn
    Before my tears did drown it.
  Is the year only lost to me?
    Have I no bays to crown it?
No flowers, no garlands gay? All blasted?   15
      All wasted?
  Not so, my heart! But there is fruit,
    And thou hast hands.
    Recover all thy sigh-blown age
On double pleasures. Leave thy cold dispute   20
Of what is fit and not. Forsake thy cage,
      Thy rope of sands,
Which petty thoughts have made, and made to thee
  Good cable, to enforce and draw,
      And be thy law,   25
  While thou didst wink and wouldst not see.
      Away! Take heed!
      I will abroad.
Call in thy death's head there. Tie up thy fears.
      He that forbears   30
    To suit and serve his need
      Deserves his load.
But as I raved and grew more fierce and wild
      At every word,

Me thoughts I heard one calling, Child!
And I replied, My Lord.   3⁵

❧

VIRTUE

Sweet day, so cool, so calm, so bright,
The bridal of the earth and sky;
The dew shall weep thy fall to-night,
     For thou must die.

Sweet rose, whose hue angry and brave   5
Bids the rash gazer wipe his eye;
Thy root is ever in its grave,
     And thou must die.

Sweet spring, full of sweet days and roses,
A box where sweets compacted lie;   10
My music shows ye have your closes,
     And all must die.

Only a sweet and virtuous soul,
Like seasoned timber, never gives;
But though the whole world turn to coal,   15
     Then chiefly lives.

❧

Henry Vaughan

From *Silex Scintillans*

(1650, 1655)

MAN

Weighing the steadfastness and state
Of some mean things which here below reside,
Where birds like watchful clocks the noiseless date

VIRTUE: 5. *angry:* red; *brave:* showy. 11. *closes:* end of a musical phrase.
15. *coal:* ashes, at Judgment Day.
SILEX SCINTILLANS: sparkling flint.

And intercourse of times divide,
Where bees at night get home and hive, and flowers   5
    Early, as well as late,
Rise with the sun, and set in the same bowers;

  I would, said I, my God would give
The staidness of these things to man! for these
To his divine appointments ever cleave,   10
    And no new business breaks their peace;
The birds nor sow nor reap, yet sup and dine,
    The flowers without clothes live,
Yet Solomon was never dressed so fine.

  Man hath still either toys or care,   15
He hath no root, nor to one place is tied,
But ever restless and irregular
    About this earth doth run and ride;
He knows he hath a home, but scarce knows where,
    He says it is so far   20
That he hath quite forgot how to go there.

  He knocks at all the doors, strays and roams,
Nay, hath not so much wit as some stones have,
Which in the darkest nights point to their homes
    By some hid sense their maker gave;   25
Man is the shuttle, to whose winding quest
    And passage through these looms
God ordered motion, but ordained no rest.

PEACE

  My soul, there is a country
    Far beyond the stars,
  Where stands a wingèd sentry
    All skilful in the wars.
There, above noise and danger,   5
    Sweet Peace sits crowned with smiles,
And One born in a manger
    Commands the beauteous files.
He is thy gracious friend,
    And—O my soul, awake!—   10
Did in pure love descend

To die here for thy sake.
If thou canst get but thither,
    There grows the flower of peace,
The rose that cannot wither,   15
    Thy fortress and thy ease.
Leave, then, thy foolish ranges;
    For none can thee secure
But One who never changes,
    Thy God, thy life, thy cure.   20

❧

THE RETREAT

Happy those early days when I
Shined in my angel-infancy!
Before I understood this place
Appointed for my second race,
Or taught my soul to fancy aught   5
But a white celestial thought;
When yet I had not walked above
A mile or two from my first love,
And looking back at that short space,
Could see a glimpse of his bright face;   10
When on some gilded cloud or flower
My gazing soul would dwell an hour,
And in those weaker glories spy
Some shadows of eternity;
Before I taught my tongue to wound   15
My conscience with a sinful sound,
Or had the black art to dispense
A sev'ral sin to ev'ry sense;
But felt through all this fleshly dress
Bright shoots of everlastingness.   20
    Oh, how I long to travel back
And tread again that ancient track!
That I might once more reach that plain
Where first I left my glorious train,
From whence th' enlightened spirit sees   25
That shady city of palm trees.
But, ah, my soul with too much stay

Is drunk, and staggers in the way.
Some men a forward motion love,
But I by backward steps would move,   30
And when this dust falls to the urn,
In that state I came, return.

∾

THE WORLD

I saw eternity the other night
Like a great ring of pure and endless light,
    All calm as it was bright;
And round beneath it, time in hours, days, years,
        Driv'n by the spheres,   5
Like a vast shadow moved, in which the world
    And all her train were hurled:
The doting lover in his quaintest strain
        Did there complain;
Near him his lute, his fancy, and his flights,   10
        Wit's sour delights,
With gloves and knots, the silly snares of pleasure,
        Yet his dear treasure,
All scattered lay, while he his eyes did pore
        Upon a flower.   15

The darksome statesman, hung with weights and woe,
Like a thick midnight fog moved there so slow
    He did not stay, nor go;
Condemning thoughts, like sad eclipses, scowl
        Upon his soul,   20
And clouds of crying witnesses without
    Pursued him with one shout;
Yet digged the mole, and lest his ways be found
        Worked underground,
Where he did clutch his prey, but One did see   25
        That policy;
Churches and altars fed him; perjuries
        Were gnats and flies;
It rained about him blood and tears, but he
        Drank them as free.   30

The fearful miser on a heap of rust
Sat pining all his life there, did scarce trust
   His own hands with the dust,
Yet would not place one piece above, but lives
    In fear of thieves.   35
Thousands there were as frantic as himself,
    And hugged each one his pelf:
The downright epicure placed heav'n in sense,
    And scorned pretense;
While others, slipped into a wide excess,   40
    Said little less;
The weaker sort slight trivial wares enslave,
    Who think them brave;
And poor despisèd truth sat counting by
    Their victory.   45

Yet some, who all this while did weep and sing,
And sing and weep, soared up into the ring;
   But most would use no wing.
O fools, said I, thus to prefer dark night
    Before true light,   50
To live in grots and caves, and hate the day
   Because it shows the way,
The way which from this dead and dark abode
    Leads up to God,
A way where you might tread the sun, and be   55
    More bright than he.
But as I did their madness so discuss,
    One whispered thus:
This ring the bridegroom did for none provide
    But for his bride.   60

THEY ARE ALL GONE

They are all gone into the world of light!
   And I alone sit lingering here;
Their very memory is fair and bright,
   And my sad thoughts doth clear.

It glows and glitters in my cloudy breast   5
   Like stars upon some gloomy grove,

Or those faint beams in which this hill is dressed
    After the sun's remove.

I see them walking in an air of glory,
    Whose light doth trample on my days,   10
My days, which are at best but dull and hoary,
    Mere glimmering and decays.

O holy hope and high humility,
    High as the heavens above!
These are your walks, and you have showed them me   15
    To kindle my cold love.

Dear, beauteous death! the jewel of the just!
    Shining no where but in the dark;
What mysteries do lie beyond thy dust,
    Could man outlook that mark!   20

He that hath found some fledged bird's nest may know
    At first sight if the bird be flown;
But what fair well or grove he sings in now,
    That is to him unknown.

And yet, as angels in some brighter dreams   25
    Call to the soul when man doth sleep,
So some strange thoughts transcend our wonted themes,
    And into glory peep.

If a star were confined into a tomb,
    Her captive flames must needs burn there;   30
But when the hand that locked her up gives room,
    She'll shine through all the sphere.

O Father of eternal life, and all
    Created glories under thee,
Resume thy spirit from this world of thrall   35
    Into true liberty!

Either disperse these mists which blot and fill
    My perspective, still, as they pass,
Or else remove me hence unto that hill
    Where I shall need no glass.   40

❧

THEY ARE ALL GONE: 35. *Resume:* take back. 38. *perspective:* telescope.

Andrew Marvell

THE GARDEN
(1681)

How vainly men themselves amaze
To win the palm, the oak, or bays,
And their uncessant labors see
Crowned from some single herb or tree,
Whose short and narrow vergèd shade   5
Does prudently their toils upbraid;
While all flowers and all trees do close
To weave the garlands of repose.

Fair quiet, have I found thee here,
And innocence, thy sister dear!   10
Mistaken long, I sought you then
In busy companies of men;
Your sacred plants, if here below,
Only among the plants will grow.
Society is all but rude,   15
To this delicious solitude.

No white nor red was ever seen
So am'rous as this lovely green.
Fond lovers, cruel as their flame,
Cut in these trees their mistress' name;   20
Little, alas, they know or heed
How far these beauties hers exceed!
Fair trees! wheres' e'er your barks I wound,
No name shall but your own be found.

When we have run our passion's heat,   25
Love hither makes his best retreat.
The gods that mortal beauty chase,
Still in a tree did end their race:
Apollo hunted Daphne so,
Only that she might laurel grow;   30

THE GARDEN: 1. *amaze*: perplex and drive oneself stupid. 17. *white nor red*: of a lady's face. 28. *Still*: always.

And Pan did after Syrinx speed,
Not as a nymph, but for a reed.

What wond'rous life in this I lead!
Ripe apples drop about my head;
The luscious clusters of the vine   35
Upon my mouth do crush their wine;
The nectarine and curious peach
Into my hands themselves do reach;
Stumbling on melons as I pass,
Ensnared with flowers, I fall on grass.   40

Meanwhile the mind from pleasure less
Withdraws into its happiness;
The mind, that ocean where each kind
Does straight its own resemblance find,
Yet it creates, transcending these,   45
Far other worlds and other seas,
Annihilating all that's made
To a green thought in a green shade.

Here at the fountain's sliding foot,
Or at some fruit tree's mossy root,   50
Casting the body's vest aside,
My soul into the boughs does glide;
There like a bird it sits and sings,
Then whets, then combs its silver wings;
And till prepared for longer flight,   55
Waves in its plumes the various light.

Such was that happy garden-state,
While man there walked without a mate;
After a place so pure and sweet,
What other help could yet be meet!   60
But 'twas beyond a mortal's share
To wander solitary there;
Two paradises 'twere, in one,
To live in paradise alone.

How well the skillful gard'ner drew   65
Of flowers and herbs this dial new,
Where, from above, the milder sun
Does through a fragrant zodiac run;

---

37. *curious:* delicate. 41. *pleasure less:* lesser pleasure.

And as it works, th' industrious bee
   Computes its time as well as we.
How could such sweet and wholesome hours   70
   Be reckoned but with herbs and flowers?

THE MOWER AGAINST GARDENS
(1681)

Luxurious man, to bring his vice in use,
   Did after him the world seduce,
And from the fields the flowers and plants allure,
   Where nature was most plain and pure.
He first enclosed within the garden's square   5
   A dead and standing pool of air;
And a more luscious earth for them did knead,
   Which stupefied them while it fed.
The pink grew then as double as his mind;
   The nutriment did change the kind.   10
With strange perfumes he did the roses taint;
   And flowers themselves were taught to paint.
The tulip, white, did for complexion seek,
   And learned to interline its cheek;
Its onion root they then so high did hold   15
   That one was for a meadow sold.
Another world was searched, through oceans new,
   To find the marvel of Peru.
And yet these rarities might be allowed
   To man, that sov'reign thing and proud,   20
Had he not dealt between the bark and tree,
   Forbidden mixtures there to see.
No plant now knew the stock from which it came;
   He grafts upon the wild the tame,
That the uncertain and adult'rate fruit   25
   Might put the palate in dispute.
His green seraglio has its eunuchs too,
   Lest any tyrant him outdo;

THE MOWER AGAINST GARDENS: 16. *sold:* tulip bulbs were sold in Holland in the 1630's by the weight, like gems. 18. *marvel of Peru:* an exotic flower.

And in the cherry he does nature vex,
  To procreate without a sex.   30
'Tis all enforced, the fountain and the grot,
  While the sweet fields do lie forgot,
Where willing nature does to all dispense
  A wild and fragrant innocence;
And fauns and fairies do the meadows till   35
  More by their presence than their skill.
Their statues, polished by some ancient hand,
  May to adorn the gardens stand;
But howsoe'er the figures do excel,
  The gods themselves with us do dwell.   40

❧

THE MOWER TO THE GLOW-WORMS
(1681)

Ye living lamps, by whose dear light
The nightingale does sit so late,
And studying all the summer night,
Her matchless songs does meditate;

Ye county comets that portend   5
No war nor prince's funeral,
Shining unto no higher end
Than to presage the grass's fall;

Ye glow-worms, whose officious flame
To wand'ring mowers shows the way,   10
That in the night have lost their aim,
And after foolish fires do stray;

Your courteous lights in vain you waste,
Since Juliana here is come,
For she my mind hath so displaced   15
That I shall never find my home.

❧

---

29. *vex:* alter by force.
  THE MOWER TO THE GLOW-WORMS: 5. *county:* country. 9. *officious:* helpful.

A DIALOGUE BETWEEN THE SOUL AND BODY
(1681)

Soul

Oh, who shall from this dungeon raise
A soul enslaved so many ways?
With bolts of bones; that fettered stands
In feet, and manacled in hands;
Here blinded with an eye, and there   5
Deaf with the drumming of an ear;
A soul hung up, as 'twere, in chains
Of nerves and arteries and veins;
Tortured, besides each other part,
In a vain head and double heart.   10

Body

Oh, who shall me deliver whole
From bonds of this tyrannic soul?
Which, stretched upright, impales me so
That mine own precipice I go;
And warms and moves this needless frame,   15
A fever could but do the same.
And, wanting where its spite to try,
Has made me live to let me die.
A body that could never rest,
Since this ill spirit it possessed.   20

Soul

What magic could me thus confine
Within another's grief to pine?
Where whatsoever it complain,
I feel, that cannot feel, the pain.
And all my care itself employs,   25
That to preserve which me destroys.
Constrained not only to endure
Diseases, but, what's worse, the cure;
And ready oft the port to gain,
Am shipwrecked into health again.

Body

But physic yet could never reach
The maladies thou me dost teach:
Whom first the cramp of hope does tear,
And then the palsy shakes of fear;
The pestilence of love does heat,   35
Or hatred's hidden ulcer eat.
Joy's cheerful madness does perplex,
Or sorrow's other madness vex;
Which knowledge forces me to know,
And memory will not forgo.   40
What but a soul could have the wit
To build me up for sin so fit?
So architects do square and hew
Green trees that in the forest grew.

BERMUDAS

(1681)

Where the remote Bermudas ride
In th' ocean's bosom unespied,
From a small boat that rowed along,
The list'ning winds received this song:
    What should we do but sing his praise   5
That led us through the wat'ry maze
Unto an isle so long unknown,
And yet far kinder than our own?
Where he the huge sea-monsters wracks,
That lift the deep upon their backs,   10
He lands us on a grassy stage,
Safe from the storms and prelates' rage.
He gave us this eternal spring
Which here enamels everything,
And sends the fowls to us in care,   15
On daily visits through the air.
He hangs in shades the orange bright,
Like golden lamps in a green night;
And does in the pomegranates close

Jewels more rich than Ormus shows.   20
He makes the figs our mouths to meet
And throws the melons at our feet,
But apples plants of such a price,
No tree could ever bear them twice.
With cedars, chosen by his hand,   25
From Lebanon, he stores the land,
And makes the hollow seas that roar
Proclaim the ambergris on shore.
He cast, of which we rather boast,
The Gospel's pearl upon our coast,   30
And in these rocks for us did frame
A temple, where to sound his name.
Oh, let our voice his praise exalt,
Till it arrive at heaven's vault;
Which thence, perhaps, rebounding, may   35
Echo beyond the Mexic Bay.
   Thus sung they in the English boat
An holy and a cheerful note,
And all the way, to guide their chime,
With falling oars they kept the time.   40

❦

THE DEFINITION OF LOVE

(1681)

My love is of a birth as rare   5ems
As 'tis for object strange and high;
It was begotten by despair
Upon impossibility.

Magnanimous despair alone   5
Could show me so divine a thing,
Where feeble hope could ne'er have flown,
But vainly flapped its tinsel wing.

And yet I quickly might arrive
Where my extended soul is fixed,   10

BERMUDAS: 20. *Ormus:* proverbially wealthy trading port near the entrance of the Persian Gulf. 23. *apples:* pineapples.

But fate does iron wedges drive,
And always crowds itself betwixt.

For fate with jealous eye does see
Two perfect loves, nor lets them close;
Their union would her ruin be,   15
And her tyrannic power depose.

And therefore her decrees of steel
Us as the distant poles have placed,
Though love's whole world on us doth wheel,
Not by themselves to be embraced;   20

Unless the giddy heaven fall,
And earth some new convulsion tear,
And, us to join, the world should all
Be cramped into a planisphere.

As lines, so loves, oblique may well   25
Themselves in every angle greet;
But ours so truly parallel,
Though infinite, can never meet.

Therefore the love which us doth bind,
But fate so enviously debars,   30
Is the conjunction of the mind,
And opposition of the stars.

❧

TO HIS COY MISTRESS

(1681)

Had we but world enough, and time,
This coyness, lady, were no crime.
We would sit down and think which way
To walk, and pass our long love's day;
Thou by the Indian Ganges' side   5
Shouldst rubies find; I by the tide
Of Humber would complain. I would

THE DEFINITION OF LOVE: 24. *planisphere:* a flattened globe, or sphere projected on a plane.

TO HIS COY MISTRESS: 7. *Humber:* estuary of the Ouse and Trent rivers in
eastern England; Marvell's town of Hull is on it.

Love you ten years before the Flood;
And you should, if you please, refuse
Till the conversion of the Jews.   10
My vegetable love should grow
Vaster than empires, and more slow.
An hundred years should go to praise
Thine eyes, and on thy forehead gaze;
Two hundred to adore each breast,   15
But thirty thousand to the rest;
An age at least to every part,
And the last age should show your heart.
For, lady, you deserve this state,
Nor would I love at lower rate.   20
   But at my back I always hear
Time's wingèd chariot hurrying near;
And yonder all before us lie
Deserts of vast eternity.
Thy beauty shall no more be found,   25
Nor in thy marble vault shall sound
My echoing song; then worms shall try
That long preserved virginity,
And your quaint honor turn to dust,
And into ashes all my lust.   30
The grave's a fine and private place,
But none, I think, do there embrace.
   Now therefore, while the youthful hue
Sits on thy skin like morning glew,
And while thy willing soul transpires   35
At every pore with instant fires,
Now let us sport us while we may;
And now, like am'rous birds of prey,
Rather at once our time devour,
Than languish in his slow-chapped power.   40
Let us roll all our strength, and all
Our sweetness, up into one ball;
And tear our pleasures with rough strife
Thorough the iron gates of life.

---

11. *vegetable:* containing life. 19. *state:* princely manner. 20. *rate:* implied valuation. 29. *quaint:* fastidious, prim, with a possible play on the older meaning of "female private parts." 34. *glew:* glow, sometimes emended to "dew" or "lew" (warmth). 35. *transpires:* comes out. 36. *instant:* eager. 40. *-chapped:* chopped, jawed.

Thus, though we cannot make our sun   45
Stand still, yet we will make him run.

❧

AN HORATIAN ODE UPON CROMWELL'S
RETURN FROM IRELAND
(1681)

The forward youth that would appear
Must now forsake his muses dear,
   Nor in the shadows sing
   His numbers languishing.
'Tis time to leave the books in dust,   5
And oil th' unusèd armor's rust,
   Removing from the wall
   The corslet of the hall.
So restless Cromwell could not cease
In the inglorious arts of peace,   10
   But through advent'rous war
   Urgèd his active star.
And like the three-forked lightning, first
Breaking the clouds where it was nursed,
   Did through his own side   15
   His fiery way divide.
For 'tis all one to courage high,
The emulous or enemy;
   And with such to enclose
   Is more than to oppose.   20
Then burning through the air he went,
And palaces and temples rent;
   And Cæsar's head at last
   Did through his laurels blast.
'Tis madness to resist or blame   25
The force of angry heaven's flame;
   And if we would speak true,
   Much to the man is due,

AN HORATIAN ODE: *Title:* Cromwell returned from Ireland late in May,
1650, to direct the campaign in Scotland. 1. *forward:* ambitious; *appear:*
win fame. 15. *side:* party; Cromwell went beyond the Presbyterians in his
opposition to Charles. 20. *more:* worse.

Who from his private gardens where
He lived reservèd and austere, 30
  As if his highest plot
  To plant the bergamot,
Could by industrious valor climb
To ruin the great work of time,
  And cast the kingdom old 35
  Into another mold,
Though justice against fate complain,
And plead the ancient rights in vain;
  But those do hold or break
  As men are strong or weak. 40
Nature that hateth emptiness
Allows of penetration less,
  And therefore must make room
  Where greater spirits come.
What field of all the civil wars 45
Where his were not the deepest scars?
  And Hampton shows what part
  He had of wiser art,
Where, twining subtile fears with hope,
He wove a net of such a scope 50
  That Charles himself might chase
  To Carisbrooke's narrow case,
That thence the royal actor borne
The tragic scaffold might adorn,
  While round the armèd bands 55
  Did clap their bloody hands.
He nothing common did or mean
Upon that memorable scene,
  But with his keener eye
  The axe's edge did try; 60
Nor called the gods with vulgar spite
To vindicate his helpless right,
  But bowed his comely head
  Down as upon a bed.
This was that memorable hour 65
Which first assured the forcèd power.

---

32. *bergamot:* a species of pear. 42. *penetration:* occupation of the same place by two bodies at the same time. 47. *Hampton:* Court Palace, from where Charles fled to Carisbrooke on the Isle of Wight. 49. *subtile:* finely woven. 52. *case:* plight and trap.

So when they did design
The Capitol's first line,
A bleeding head, where they begun,
Did fright the architects to run;   70
And yet in that the state
Foresaw its happy fate.
And now the Irish are ashamed
To see themselves in one year tamed;
So much one man can do   75
That does both act and know.
They can affirm his praises best,
And have, though overcome, confessed
How good he is, how just,
And fit for highest trust;   80
Nor yet grown stiffer with command,
But still in the republic's hand;
How fit he is to sway
That can so well obey.
He to the Commons' feet presents   85
A kingdom for his first year's rents;
And, what he may, forbears
His fame, to make it theirs,
And has his sword and spoils ungirt,
To lay them at the public's skirt.   90
So when the falcon high
Falls heavy from the sky,
She, having killed, no more does search
But on the next green bough to perch,
Where, when he first does lure,   95
The falc'ner has her sure.
What may not then our isle presume
While victory his crest does plume!
What may not others fear
If thus he crown each year!   100
A Cæsar he ere long to Gaul,
To Italy an Hannibal,
And to all states not free,
Shall climacteric be.

67-70: the architects of the temple of Jupiter at Rome were said to have un-
covered a human head (*caput*), which was interpreted as a sign of good
fortune and led to naming the building the Capitol.

The Pict no shelter now shall find   105
Within his parti-colored mind;
        But from this valor sad
        Shrink underneath the plaid,
Happy if in the tufted brake
The English hunter him mistake,   110
        Nor lay his hounds in near
        The Caledonian deer.
But thou, the war's and fortune's son,
March indefatigably on;
        And for the last effect   115
        Still keep thy sword erect;
Besides the force it has to fright
The spirits of the shady night,
        The same arts that did gain
        A power, must it maintain.   120

❧

---

105. *Pict:* Scots. 106. *parti-colored:* a pun on the supposed derivation of
Pict from *pingere,* "to paint." 116. *sword erect:* like a cross.

Selected Seventeenth Century Poems

❧

George Wither

SHALL I WASTING IN DESPAIR
(1622)

Shall I wasting in despair
Die because a woman's fair?
Or make pale my cheeks with care
'Cause another's rosy are?
Be she fairer than the day,   5
Or the flow'ry meads in May,
    If she be not so to me,
    What care I how fair she be?

Shall my heart be grieved or pined
'Cause I see a woman kind?   10
Or a well-disposèd nature
Joinèd with a lovely feature?
Be she meeker, kinder, than
Turtle-dove or pelican,
    If she be not so to me,   15
    What care I how kind she be?

SHALL I WASTING IN DESPAIR: 14. *pelican:* believed to feed her young on her own blood.

Shall a woman's virtues move
Me to perish for her love?
Or her well-deserving known
Make me quite forget mine own?   20
Be she with that goodness blest
Which may gain her name of best,
   If she be not such to me,
    What care I how good she be?

'Cause her fortune seems too high,   25
Shall I play the fool and die?
Those that bear a noble mind,
Where they want of riches find,
Think what with them they would do
That without them dare to woo;   30
   And unless that mind I see,
    What care I how great she be?

Great, or good, or kind, or fair,
I will ne'er the more despair;
If she love me, this believe,   35
I will die ere she shall grieve;
If she slight me when I woo,
I can scorn and let her go;
   For if she be not for me,
    What care I for whom she be?   40

Edmund Waller

ON A GIRDLE
(1645, 1664)

That which her slender waist confined
Shall now my joyful temples bind;
No monarch but would give his crown
His arms might do what this has done.

It was my heaven's extremest sphere,   5
The pale which held that lovely deer.
My joy, my grief, my hope, my love,
Did all within this circle move!

A narrow compass, and yet there
Dwelt all that's good and all that's fair; 10
Give me but what this riband bound,
Take all the rest the sun goes round.

❧

GO, LOVELY ROSE
(1645, 1664)

Go, lovely rose!
Tell her that wastes her time and me
That now she knows,
When I resemble her to thee,
How sweet and fair she seems to be. 5

Tell her that's young
And shuns to have her graces spied,
That hadst thou sprung
In deserts where no men abide,
Thou must have uncommended died. 10

Small is the worth
Of beauty from the light retired;
Bid her come forth,
Suffer herself to be desired,
And not blush so to be admired. 15

Then die, that she
The common fate of all things rare
May read in thee;
How small a part of time they share
That are so wondrous sweet and fair! 20

❧

Sir John Suckling

OH! FOR SOME HONEST LOVER'S GHOST
(1646)

Oh! for some honest lover's ghost,
 Some kind unbodied post

Sent from the shades below!
I strangely long to know
Whether the nobler chaplets wear,
Those that their mistress' scorn did bear,
Or those that were used kindly.

For whatsoe'er they tell us here
To make those sufferings dear,
'Twill there, I fear, be found
That to the being crowned
'I' have loved alone will not suffice,
Unless we also have been wise
And have our loves enjoyed.

What posture can we think him in,
That here unloved again
Departs, and 's thither gone
Where each sits by his own?
Or how can that Elysium be,
Where I my mistress still must see
Circled in other's arms?

For there the judges all are just,
And Sophonisba must
Be his whom she held dear,
Not his who loved her here;
The sweet Philoclea, since she died,
Lies by her Pirocles his side,
Not by Amphialus.

Some bays, perchance, or myrtle bough,
For difference crowns the brow
Of those kind souls that were
The noble martyrs here;
And if that be the only odds,
(As who can tell?) ye kinder gods,
Give me the woman here.

5

10

15

20

25

30

35

❧

OH! FOR SOME HONEST LOVER'S GHOST: 23. *Sophonisba:* daughter of Hasdrubal, the Carthaginian general. She was betrothed to Prince Masinissa, but her father married her to Syphax for political reasons. Masinissa defeated Syphax and was about to marry Sophonisba when Scipio [his Roman superior] ordered her imprisoned. To save her from captivity, Masinissa sent her poison, with which she committed suicide. 26-28. *Philoclea, Pirocles, Amphialus:* characters in Sidney's *Arcadia.*

CONSTANCY
(1659)

Out upon it! I have loved
  Three whole days together;
And am like to love three more,
  If it prove fair weather.

Time shall moult away his wings,   5
  Ere he shall discover
In the whole wide world again
  Such a constant lover.

But the spite on 't is, no praise
  Is due at all to me;   10
Love with me had made no stays,
  Had it any been but she.

Had it any been but she,
  And that very face,
There had been at least ere this   15
  A dozen dozen in her place.

WHY SO PALE AND WAN
(1646)

Why so pale and wan, fond lover?
  Prithee, why so pale?
Will, when looking well can't move her,
  Looking ill prevail?
  Prithee, why so pale?   5

Why so dull and mute, young sinner?
  Prithee, why so mute?
Will, when speaking well can't win her,
  Saying nothing do 't?
  Prithee, why so mute?   10

Quit, quit, for shame, this will not move,
   This cannot take her.
If of herself she will not love,
   Nothing can make her.
   The devil take her!   15

              From *Aglaura*

A BALLAD UPON A WEDDING
(1646, 1648)

I tell thee, Dick, where I have been,
Where I the rarest things have seen,
   Oh, things without compare!
Such sights again cannot be found
In any place on English ground,   5
   Be it at wake or fair.

At Charing Cross, hard by the way
Where we, thou know'st, do sell our hay,
   There is a house with stairs;
And there did I see coming down   10
Such folk as are not in our town,
   Vorty at least, in pairs.

Amongst the rest, one pest'lent fine,
His beard no bigger though than thine,
   Walked on before the rest;   15
Our landlord looks like nothing to him,
The King, God bless him, 'twould undo him
   Should he go still so dressed.

At course-a-park, without all doubt,
He should have first been taken out   20
   By all the maids i' th' town;
Though lusty Roger there had been,
Or little George upon the Green,
   Or Vincent of the Crown.

A BALLAD UPON A WEDDING: 19. *course-a-park:* a country game in which a girl called out a boy to chase her.

But wot you what? the youth was going   25
To make an end of all his wooing,
  The parson for him stayed;
Yet by his leave, for all his haste,
He did not so much wish all past,
  Perchance, as did the maid.   30

The maid—and thereby hangs a tale:
For such a maid no Whitsun ale
  Could ever yet produce;
No grape that's kindly ripe could be
So round, so plump, so soft as she,   35
  Nor half so full of juice.

Her finger was so small the ring
Would not stay on, which they did bring,
  It was too wide a peck;
And to say truth, for out it must,   40
It looked like the great collar, just,
  About our young colt's neck.

Her feet beneath her petticoat,
Like little mice, stole in and out,
  As if they feared the light;   45
But oh, she dances such a way!
No sun upon an Easter day
  Is half so fine a sight.

He would have kissed her once or twice,
But she would not, she was nice,   50
  She would not do't in sight;
And then she looked as who should say,
I will do what I list to-day,
  And you shall do't at night.

Her cheeks so rare a white was on,   55
No daisy makes comparison,
  Who sees them is undone;
For streaks of red were mingled there,
Such as are on a Katherne pear,
  The side that's next the sun.   60

Her lips were red, and one was thin,
Compared to that was next her chin,

    Some bee had stung it newly;
But Dick, her eyes so guard her face
    I durst no more upon them gaze   65
      Then on the sun in July.

Her mouth so small, when she does speak
Thou'dst swear her teeth her words did break,
    That they might passage get;
But she so handled still the matter,   70
They came as good as ours, or better,
    And are not spent a whit.

If wishing should be any sin,
The parson himself had guilty been,
    She looked that day so purely;   75
And did the youth so oft the feat
At night, as some did in conceit,
    It would have spoiled him surely.

Passion o' me, how I run on!
There's that that would be thought upon,   80
    I trow, besides the bride.
The business of the kitchen's great,
For it is fit that man should eat,
    Nor was it there denied.

Just in the nick the cook knocked thrice,   85
And all the waiters in a trice
    His summons did obey;
Each serving-man, with dish in hand,
Marched boldly up like our trained band,
    Presented, and away.   90

When all the meat was on the table,
What man of knife or teeth was able
    To stay to be entreated?
And this the very reason was—
Before the parson could say grace,   95
    The company was seated.

Now hats fly off, and youths carouse,
Healths first go round, and then the house,
    The bride's came thick and thick;

---

77. *conceit:* imagination.

And when 'twas named another's health,   100
Perhaps he made it hers by stealth,
    And who could help it, Dick?

O' th' sudden up they rise and dance,
Then sit again and sigh and glance,
    Then dance again, and kiss;   105
Thus several ways the time did pass,
Whilst ev'ry woman wished her place,
    And ev'ry man wished his.

By this time all were stolen aside
To counsel and undress the bride,   110
    But that he must not know;
But yet 'twas thought he guessed her mind,
And did not mean to stay behind
    Above an hour or so.

When in he came, Dick, there she lay   115
Like new-fallen snow melting away
    ('Twas time, I trow, to part);
Kisses were now the only stay,
Which soon she gave, as who would say,
    God b' w' ye, with all my heart.   120

But just as heavens would have, to cross it,
In came the bridesmaids with the posset;
    The bridegroom eat in spite,
For, had he left the women to 't,
It would have have cost two hours to do 't,   125
    Which were too much that night.

At length the candle's out, and now
All that they had not done they do;
    What that is, who can tell?
But I believe it was no more   130
Than thou and I have done before
    With Bridget and with Nell.

❧

---

122. *posset*: hot milk curdled with ale or wine and spiced.

Richard Lovelace

TO ALTHEA, FROM PRISON
(1649)

When Love with unconfinèd wings
  Hovers within my gates,
And my divine Althea brings
  To whisper at the grates;
When I lie tangled in her hair,   5
  And fettered to her eye,
The gods that wanton in the air
  Know no such liberty.

When flowing cups run swiftly round
  With no allaying Thames,   10
Our careless heads with roses bound,
  Our hearts with loyal flames;
When thirsty grief in wine we steep,
  When healths and draughts go free,
Fishes that tipple in the deep   15
  Know no such liberty.

When, like committed linnets, I
  With shriller throat shall sing
The sweetness, mercy, majesty,
  And glories of my King;   20
When I shall voice aloud, how good
  He is, how great should be,
Enlargèd winds that curl the flood
  Know no such liberty.

Stone walls do not a prison make,   25
  Nor iron bars a cage;
Minds innocent and quiet take
  That for an hermitage;
If I have freedom in my love,
  And in my soul am free,   30
Angels alone that soar above
  Enjoy such liberty.

TO LUCASTA, GOING TO THE WARS
(1649)

Tell me not, sweet, I am unkind,
   That from the nunnery
Of thy chaste breast and quiet mind,
   To war and arms I fly.

True, a new mistress now I chase,   5
   The first foe in the field;
And with a stronger faith embrace
   A sword, a horse, a shield.

Yet this inconstancy is such
   As you too shall adore;   10
I could not love thee, dear, so much,
   Loved I not honor more.

John Cleveland

MARK ANTONY
(1677)

Whenas the nightingale chanted her vespers,
And the wild forester couched cn the ground,
Venus invited me in th' evening whispers
Unto a fragrant field with roses crowned,
   Where she before had sent   5
   My wishes' complement;
   Unto my heart's content
   Played with me on the green.
     Never Mark Antony
     Dallied more wantonly   10
     With the fair Egyptian Queen.

First on her cherry cheeks I mine eyes feasted,
Thence fear of surfeiting made me retire;

Next on her warmer lips, which when I tasted,
My duller spirits made active as fire.   15
   Then we began to dart,
   Each at another's heart,
   Arrows that knew no smart,
   Sweet lips and smiles between.
      Never Mark, &c.   20

Wanting a glass to plait her amber tresses,
Which like a bracelet rich deckèd mine arm,
Gaudier than Juno wears whenas she graces
Jove with embraces more stately than warm;
   Then did she peep in mine   25
   Eyes' humor crystalline;
   I in her eyes was seen,
   As if we one had been.
      Never Mark, &c.

Mystical grammar of amorous glances;   30
Feeling of pulses, the physic of love;
Rhetorical courtings and musical dances;
Numb'ring of kisses arithmetic prove;
   Eyes like astronomy;
   Straight-limbed geometry;   35
   In her art's ingeny
   Our wits were sharp and keen.
      Never Mark Antony
      Dallied more wantonly
      With the fair Egyptian Queen.   40

❧

John Hall

AN EPICUREAN ODE
(1646)

Since that this thing we call the world
By chance on atoms is begot,

MARK ANTONY: 36. *ingeny:* ingenuity, wit.

Which though in daily motions hurled
    Yet weary not,
      How doth it prove   5
Thou art so fair, and I in love?

Since that the soul doth only lie
Immersed in matter, chained in sense,
How can, Romira, thou and I
      With both dispense?   10
      And thus ascend
In higher flights than wings can lend.

Since man's but pasted up of earth,
And ne'er was cradled in the skies,
What *terra lemnia* gave thee birth?   15
      What diamond, eyes?
      Or thou alone,
To tell what others were, came down?

❧

John Webster

CALL FOR THE ROBIN REDBREAST
(1612)

Call for the robin redbreast and the wren,
Since o'er shady groves they hover,
And with leaves and flowers do cover
The friendless bodies of unburied men.
Call unto his funeral dole   5
The ant, the field-mouse, and the mole,
To rear him hillocks that shall keep him warm,
And, when gay tombs are robbed, sustain no harm;
But keep the wolf far thence, that's foe to men,
For with his nails he'll dig them up again.   10
                        From *The White Devil*

❧

AN EPICUREAN ODE: 15. *terra lemnia:* a medicinal earth from the island of Lemnos.

HARK, NOW EVERYTHING IS STILL
(1623)

Hark, now everything is still;
The screech-owl and the whistler shrill
Call upon our dame aloud,
And bid her quickly don her shroud;
Much you had of land and rent,   5
Your length in clay's now competent.
A long war disturbed your mind;
Here your perfect peace is signed.
Of what is 't fools make such vain keeping?
Sin their conception, their birth weeping,   10
Their life a general mist of error,
Their death a hideous storm of terror.
Strew your hair with powders sweet,
Don clean linen, bathe your feet,
And, the foul fiend more to check,   15
A crucifix let bless your neck;
'Tis now full tide, 'tween night and day,
End your groan and come away.

From *The Duchess of Malfi*

❧

ALL THE FLOWERS OF THE SPRING
(1623)

All the flowers of the spring
Meet to perfume our burying;
These have but their growing prime,
And man does flourish but his time.
Survey our progress from our birth—   5
We are set, we grow, we turn to earth,
Courts adieu, and all delights,
All bewitching appetites!
Sweetest breath and clearest eye,
Like perfumes go out and die;   10
And consequently this is done

As shadows wait upon the sun.
Vain the ambition of kings
Who seek by trophies and dead things
To leave a living name behind,   15
And weave but nets to catch the wind.

From *The Devil's Law Case*

James Shirley

THE GLORIES OF OUR BLOOD AND STATE
(1659)

The glories of our blood and state
 Are shadows, not substantial things;
There is no armor against fate;
 Death lays his icy hand on kings.
  Scepter and crown   5
  Must tumble down,
And in the dust be equal made
With the poor crooked scythe and spade.

Some men with swords may reap the field,
 And plant fresh laurels where they kill;   10
But their strong nerves at last must yield,
 They tame but one another still.
  Early or late,
  They stoop to fate,
And must give up their murmuring breath,   15
When they, pale captives, creep to death.

The garlands wither on your brow,
 Then boast no more your mighty deeds;
Upon death's purple altar now,
 See where the victor-victim bleeds.   20
  Your heads must come
  To the cold tomb;
Only the actions of the just
Smell sweet and blossom in their dust.

From *The Contention of Ajax and Ulysses*

Henry King

THE EXEQUY
(1657)

Accept, thou shrine of my dead saint,
Instead of dirges, this complaint;
And for sweet flowers to crown thy hearse,
Receive a strew of weeping verse
From thy grieved friend, whom thou might'st see   5
Quite melted into tears for thee.

Dear loss! since thy untimely fate
My task hath been to meditate
On thee, on thee; thou art the book,
The library whereon I look,   10
Though almost blind. For thee, loved clay,
I languish out, not live, the day,
Using no other exercise
But what I practise with mine eyes;
By which wet glasses I find out   15
How lazily time creeps about
To one that mourns; this, only this,
My exercise and business is.
So I compute the weary hours
With sighs dissolvèd into showers.   20

Nor wonder if my time go thus
Backward and most preposterous;
Thou hast benighted me; thy set
This eve of blackness did beget,
Who wast my day, though overcast   25
Before thou hadst thy noon-tide passed;
And I remember must in tears,
Thou scarce hadst seen so many years
As day tells hours. By thy clear sun
My love and fortune first did run;   30
But thou wilt never more appear

THE EXEQUY: *Title:* Written in memory of King's first wife, Anne, who died about 1624.

Folded within my hemisphere,
Since both thy light and motïon
Like a fled star is fall'n and gone;
And 'twixt me and my soul's dear wish   35
An earth now interposèd is,
Which such a strange eclipse doth make
As ne'er was read in almanac.

I could allow thee for a time
To darken me and my sad clime;   40
Were it a month, a year, or ten,
I would thy exile live till then,
And all that space my mirth adjourn,
So thou wouldst promise to return,
And putting off thy ashy shroud,   45
At length disperse this sorrow's cloud.

But woe is me! the longest date
Too narrow is to calculate
These empty hopes; never shall I
Be so much blest as to descry   50
A glimpse of thee, till that day come
Which shall the earth to cinders doom,
And a fierce fever must calcine
The body of this world like thine,
My little world. That fit of fire   55
Once off, our bodies shall aspire
To our souls' bliss; then we shall rise
And view ourselves with clearer eyes
In that calm region where no night
Can hide us from each other's sight.   60

Meantime, thou hast her, earth; much good
May my harm do thee. Since it stood
With heaven's will I might not call
Her longer mine, I give thee all
My short-lived right and interest   65
In her whom living I loved best;
With a most free and bounteous grief,
I give thee what I could not keep.
Be kind to her, and prithee look
Thou write into thy doomsday book   70
Each parcel of this rarity
Which in thy casket shrined doth lie.

See that thou make thy reck'ning straight,
And yield her back again by weight;
For thou must audit on thy trust   75
Each grain and atom of this dust,
As thou wilt answer Him that lent,
Not gave thee, my dear monument.

So close the ground, and 'bout her shade
Black curtains draw, my bride is laid.   80

Sleep on, my love, in thy cold bed,
Never to be disquieted!
My last good-night! Thou wilt not wake
Till I thy fate shall overtake;
Till age, or grief, or sickness must   85
Marry my body to that dust
It so much loves, and fill the room
My heart keeps empty in thy tomb.
Stay for me there, I will not fail
To meet thee in that hollow vale.   90
And think not much of my delay;
I am already on the way,
And follow thee with all the speed
Desire can make, or sorrows breed.
Each minute is a short degree,   95
And ev'ry hour a step towards thee.
At night when I betake to rest,
Next morn I rise nearer my west
Of life, almost by eight hours' sail,
Than when sleep breathed his drowsy gale.   100

Thus from the sun my bottom steers,
And my day's compass downward bears;
Nor labor I to stem the tide
Through which to thee I swiftly glide.

'Tis true, with shame and grief I yield,   105
Thou like the van first tookst the field,
And gotten hath the victory
In thus adventuring to die
Before me, whose more years might crave
A just precedence in the grave.   110
But hark! my pulse like a soft drum

---

101. *bottom:* ship.

Beats my approach, tells thee I come;
And slow howe'er my marches be,
I shall at last sit down by thee.

The thought of this bids me go on,   115
And wait my dissolution
With hope and comfort. Dear, forgive
The crime, I am content to live
Divided, with but half a heart,
Till we shall meet and never part.   120

SIC VITA

(1657)

Like to the falling of a star,
Or as the flights of eagles are,
Or like the fresh spring's gaudy hue,
Or silver drops of morning dew,
Or like a wind that chafes the flood,   5
Or bubbles which on water stood:
Even such is man, whose borrowed light
Is straight called in, and paid to night.
    The wind blows out, the bubble dies;
    The spring entombed in autumn lies;   10
    The dew dries up, the star is shot;
    The flight is past, and man forgot.

A CONTEMPLATION UPON FLOWERS

(1657)

Brave flowers, that I could gallant it like you
And be as little vain!
You come abroad and make a harmless show,
And to your beds of earth again;
You are not proud, you know your birth,   5
For your embroidered garments are from earth.

You do obey your months and times, but I
Would have it ever spring;
My fate would know no winter, never die
Nor think of such a thing;   10
Oh, that I could my bed of earth but view
And smile, and look as cheerfully as you.

Oh, teach me to see death and not to fear,
But rather to take truce;
How often have I seen you at a bier,   15
And there look fresh and spruce;
You fragrant flowers, then teach me that my breath
Like yours may sweeten, and perfume my death.

❧

Richard Crashaw

From THE FLAMING HEART
(1648, 1652)

*Upon the book and picture of the seraphical Saint Teresa,
as she is usually expressed with a seraphim beside her*

.   .   .   .

O heart, the equal poise of love's both parts,   75
Big alike with wounds and darts,
Live in these conquering leaves; live all the same,
And walk through all tongues one triumphant flame;
Live here, great heart, and love and die and kill,
And bleed and wound, and yield and conquer still.   80
Let this immortal life, where'er it comes,
Walk in a crowd of loves and martyrdoms.
Let mystic deaths wait on 't, and wise souls be
The love-slain witnesses of this life of thee.
O sweet incendiary! show here thy art,   85
Upon this carcass of a hard cold heart,

THE FLAMING HEART: 76. *darts:* In St. Teresa's autobiography, *The Flaming Heart* (translated into English in 1642), is an account of a vision in which an angel repeatedly pierced her heart with a gold dart, inflaming her with divine love and agony.

Let all thy scattered shafts of light, that play
Among the leaves of thy large books of day,
Combined against this breast, at once break in
And take away from me my self and sin;   90
This gracious robbery shall thy bounty be,
And my best fortunes such fair spoils of me.
O thou undaunted daughter of desires!
By all thy dower of lights and fires,
By all the eagle in thee, all the dove,   95
By all thy lives and deaths of love,
By thy large draughts of intellectual day,
And by thy thirsts of love more large than they,
By all thy brim-filled bowls of fierce desire,
By thy last morning's draught of liquid fire,   100
By the full kingdom of that final kiss
That seized thy parting soul and sealed thee his,
By all the heav'ns thou hast in him,
Fair sister of the seraphim!
By all of him we have in thee,   105
Leave nothing of myself in me:
Let me so read thy life that I
Unto all life of mine may die.

❧

Thomas Traherne

WONDER

How like an angel came I down!
    How bright are all things here!
When first among his works I did appear,
    Oh, how their glory did me crown!
The world resembled his eternity,   5
        In which my soul did walk;
        And ev'rything that I did see
        Did with me talk.

The skies in their magnificence,
    The lovely lively air,   10
Oh, how divine, how soft, how sweet, how fair!
    The stars did entertain my sense,

WONDER: Traherne's poems first published by Bertram Dobell in 1903.

And all the works of God so bright and pure,
 So rich and great, did seem,
As if they ever must endure   15
 In my esteem.

A native health and innocence
 Within my bones did grow,
And while my God did all his glories show,
 I felt a vigor in my sense   20
That was all spirit; I within did flow
 With seas of life like wine;
 I nothing in the world did know,
 But 'twas divine.

Harsh rugged objects were concealed; 25
 Oppressions, tears, and cries,
Sins, griefs, complaints, dissensions, weeping eyes,
 Were hid, and only things revealed
Which heavenly spirits and the angels prize:
 The state of innocence   30
 And bliss, not trades and poverties,
 Did fill my sense.

The streets seemed paved with golden stones,
 The boys and girls all mine—
To me how did their lovely faces shine! 35
 The sons of men all holy ones,
In joy and beauty then appeared to me;
 And ev'rything I found,
 While like an angel I did see,
 Adorned the ground.   40

Rich diamonds, and pearl, and gold
 Might ev'rywhere be seen;
Rare colors, yellow, blue, red, white, and green,
 Mine eyes on ev'ry side behold;
All that I saw a wonder did appear, 45
 Amazement was my bliss,
 That and my wealth met ev'rywhere;
 No joy to this!

Cursed, ill-devised proprieties,
 With envy, avarice,   50
And fraud, those fiends that spoil ev'n paradise,
 Were not the object of mine eyes;
Nor hedges, ditches, limits, narrow bounds,

I dreamt not aught of those,
But in surveying all men's grounds 55
I found repose.

For property itself was mine,
And hedges, ornaments,
Walls, houses, coffers, and their rich contents,
To make me rich combine. 60
Clothes, costly jewels, laces, I esteemed
My wealth, by others worn,
For me they all to wear them seemed,
When I was born.

Bibliographical References

ANTHOLOGIES

Metaphysical Lyrics and Poems of the Seventeenth Century, ed. H. J. C. Grierson, Oxford, 1925.

Minor Poems of the Caroline Period, ed. G. Saintsbury, Oxford, 1905-21.

Minor Poets of the 17th Century, ed. R. G. Howarth, Everyman, 1931.

Oxford Book of Sixteenth Century Verse, ed. E. K. Chambers, Oxford, 1932.

Oxford Book of Seventeenth Century Verse, ed. H. J. C. Grierson and G. Bullough, Oxford, 1934.

Poetry of the English Renaissance, ed. J. W. Hebel and H. H. Hudson, New York, 1929.

Rare Poems of the Seventeenth Century, ed. L. B. Marshall, Cambridge, 1936.

GENERAL CRITICISM

Owen Barfield, *Poetic Diction,* London, 1925, rev. 1953.

F. W. Bateson, *English Poetry and the English Language,* Oxford, 1934.

Joan Bennett, *Four Metaphysical Poets,* Cambridge, 1934.

John Berdan, *Early Tudor Poetry,* New York, 1920.

Cleanth Brooks, *The Well Wrought Urn,* New York, 1947.

W. Bowden, *The English Dramatic Lyric, 1603-42,* Yale, 1951.

Douglas Bush, *English Literature in the Earlier Seventeenth Century,* Oxford, 1945.

————, *Mythology and the Renaissance Tradition in English Poetry,* Minneapolis, 1932.

L. B. Campbell, *Divine Poetry and Drama in Sixteenth-Century England,* Cambridge and Calif., 1959.

Determinations, ed. F. R. Leavis, London, 1934.

E. C. Dunn, *Literature of Shakespeare's England,* New York, 1936.

T. S. Eliot, *Selected Essays,* New York, 1932.

————, *Elizabethan Essays,* London, 1934.

William Empson, *Seven Types of Ambiguity,* London, 1930, New York, 1948.

————, *Some Versions of Pastoral,* London, 1935; *English Pastoral Poetry,* New York, 1938.

The Explicator (passim, and annual checklist of explications).

Elizabeth Holmes, *Aspects of Elizabethan Imagery,* New York, 1929.

H. H. Hudson, *The Epigram in the English Renaissance,* Princeton, 1947.

L. C. Johns, *Elizabethan Sonnet Sequences,* New York, 1938.

A. Kernan, *The Cankered Muse: Satire of the English Renaissance,* Yale, 1959.

F. R. Leavis, *Revaluations.* London, 1936, New York, 1947.

J. B. Leishman, *Metaphysical Poets,* Oxford, 1934.

C. S. Lewis, *The Allegory of Love*, Oxford, 1936.
————, *English Literature in the Sixteenth Century, excluding Drama*, Oxford, 1954.
L. L. Martz, *The Poetry of Meditation, a Study in English Religious Literature of the Seventeenth Century*, Yale, 1954.
Herbert Read, *Reasons and Romanticism*, London, 1926.
H. D. Rix, *Rhetoric in Spenser's Poetry*, Penn. State College Studies 7, 1940.
V. L. Rubel, *Poetic Diction in the English Renaissance*, New York, 1941.
M. A. Rugoff, *Donne's Imagery*, New York, 1939.
G. H. W. Ryland, *Words and Poetry*, London, 1920.
J. G. Scott, *Les sonnets elizabethains*, Paris, 1928.
Seventeenth Century Studies Presented to Sir Herbert Grierson, Oxford, 1938.
R. L. Sharp, *From Donne to Dryden*, Chapel Hill, 1940.
H. Smith, *Elizabethan Poetry*, Harvard, 1952.
W. Sypher, *Four Stages of Renaissance Style*, New York, 1955.
Allen Tate, *Reactionary Essays*, New York, 1936.
E. M. W. Tillyard, *Poetry Direct and Oblique*, London, 1934.
Rosamond Tuve, *Elizabethan and Metaphysical Imagery*, Chicago, 1947.
R. Wallerstein, *Studies in Seventeenth-Century Poetic*, Madison, 1950.
Henry W. Wells, *Poetic Imagery, Illustrated from Elizabethan Literature*, New York, 1924.
Helen C. White, *Metaphysical Poets*, New York, 1936.
Basil Willey, *The Seventeenth Century Background*, London, 1934.
George Williamson, *The Donne Tradition*, Cambridge, Mass., 1930.

INDIVIDUAL POETS

BALLADS. The popular or folk ballad is a fairly short narrative designed to be sung. Since ballads were composed and transmitted orally, their date of composition cannot be determined. Some of those in this volume may go back very far, but they are associated with the fifteenth century, and the versions recorded are generally from the eighteenth or later. The themes are commonly of basic human relationships and values: unhappy love affairs, border heroism, domestic comedy or tragedy, the supernatural. The conventional literary methods reflect the popular oral origin of the ballad. The common stanza is a quatrain with alternating four-foot and three-foot lines, rhyming a b c b or a b a b. It may include a refrain, and make use of incremental repetition, in which the story is advanced by the variation of a verbal pattern. The narrative is largely implied rather than complete, and the structure is usually dramatic. *English & Scottish Popular Ballads,* ed. F. J. Child, Boston, 1882-98; abridged by H. C. Sargent and G. L. Kittridge, Boston, 1904.

CAMPION, THOMAS (1567-1620), was born into a prosperous London family and was educated at Cambridge, at Gray's Inn, and as a physician, but he devoted himself to poetry and music. His first *Book of Airs* was published in 1601, and it was followed by others (c. 1613, 1617) for which he composed both words and music.

MODERN EDITIONS AND CRITICISM: *Works*, ed. by P. Vivian, Oxford, 1909; *The English School of Lutenist Song-Writers*, ed. by E. H. Fellowes, London (Second Series), 1926; M. W. Kastendiek, *England's Musical Poet: Thomas Campion*, New York, 1938.

CAREW, THOMAS (1594/95-1639?), was educated at Oxford (B.A. 1611) and the Middle Temple, was secretary to the English ambassador Sir Dudley Carleton at Venice (1613) and the Hague (1616), and was attached to the household of Lord Herbert of Cherbury, ambassador to France in 1619. After 1628 he served at the court of Charles I.

MODERN EDITIONS AND CRITICISM: *Poems*, with his masque, *Coelum Britannicum*, ed by Rhodes Dunlap, Oxford, 1949. G. Williamson, *The Donne Tradition;* F. R. Leavis, *Revaluations;* R. A. Blanshard, "Thomas Carew and the Cavalier Poets," *Transactions of Wisconsin Academy*, XLII (1954), 97-106; "Carew and Jonson," *SP*, LII (1955), 195-211; "Thomas Carew's Master Figures," *BSUE*, III (1957), 214-27; W. Selig, *The Flourishing Wreath: A Study of Thomas Carew's Poetry*, Yale, 1958.

CLEVELAND, JOHN (1613-1658), son of a Yorkshire preacher, was at Cambridge with Milton (B.A., 1631; M.A., 1635) and was a fellow and Reader in Rhetoric at St. John's College (1634). A Royalist, he moved to Oxford in 1643; he died at Gray's Inn.

MODERN EDITIONS AND CRITICISM: *Poems*, ed. by J. M. Berdan, Yale, 1911; Williamson, *The Donne Tradition;* J. L. Kimmey, "John Cleveland and the Satiric Couplet in the Restoration," *PQ*, 37 (1958), 410-23.

CRASHAW, RICHARD (1613-1649), was born in London, the son of an Anglican preacher. He was educated at Charterhouse, Cambridge (B.A., 1634), and in 1635 he became a fellow of the high-church Peterhouse College. He was ordained by 1639; he left Cambridge in 1643 in advance of the Puritans. He was thereafter in exile abroad with other Royalists, including Cowley. After his conversion to Catholicism, probably in 1645, he served Cardinal Pallotta, who in 1649 gave him a benefice at the Shrine of Loretto, where he died.

MODERN EDITIONS AND CRITICISM: *The Poems*, ed. by L. C. Martin, Oxford, 1957; R. C. Wallerstein, *Richard Crashaw*, U. of Wisconsin, 1935; Austin Warren, *Richard Crashaw, A Study in Baroque Sensibility*, Louisiana State U., 1939; R. Wellek, "The Concept of Baroque in Literary Scholarship," *JAAC*, V (1946), 77-109; K. Neill, "Structure and Symbol in Crashaw's *Hymn in the Nativity*," *PMLA* (1948), 101-13; S. Manning, "The Meaning of 'The Weeper,'" *ELH*, XXII (1955), 34-47; R. M. Adams, "Taste and Bad Taste in Metaphysical Poetry: Richard Crashaw and Dylan Thomas," *Hud. Rev.*, VIII (1955), 61-77.

DANIEL, SAMUEL (1563?-1619), entered Oxford in 1581, left without a degree, was in Paris in 1586, and traveled in Italy with Sir Edward Dymoke (1591?), where he visited Guarini. He became tutor to William Herbert, and through him a member of the Countess of Pembroke's literary circle; upon the accession of James to the throne, he entered the service of his consort, Queen Anne. In 1618 he was dismissed; a year later he died on his farm in Somerset.

MODERN EDITIONS AND CRITICISM: *Poems* and *A Defence of Ryme*, ed. by A. C. Sprague, Harvard, 1930; *The Civil Wars*, ed. with intro. and notes by Laurence Michel, Yale, 1958; E. H. Miller, "Samuel Daniel's Revisions in *Delia*," *JEGP*, LIII (1954), 58-68; C. Seronsy, "Well-languaged Daniel: A Reconsideration," *Modern Language Review*, LII (1957), 481-97.

DEKKER, THOMAS (1572?-1632), was a London playwright and a prolific author of miscellaneous prose.
MODERN EDITIONS AND CRITICISM: M. L. Hunt, *Thomas Dekker*, Columbia, 1911; *The Dramatic Works*, ed. by F. Bowers, Cambridge University Press, 1953-.

DONNE, JOHN (1572-1631), was born in London and brought up a Catholic. He attended Oxford and Cambridge, and studied law at Thavies Inn (1591) and Lincoln's Inn (1592-4), but was more interested in the humanities and theology. He traveled abroad and volunteered with the Earl of Essex on the expeditions against Cadiz in 1596 and the Azores in 1597. Most of his satirical and love poems appeared to have been written during the 1590's. He became secretary to the Lord Keeper, Sir Thomas Egerton, but his career was interrupted in 1601 by his secret marriage with Egerton's niece, Anne More. Her father had Donne dismissed and imprisoned. After much urging and self-questioning he was ordained in the Church of England in 1615, and in 1621 he was made Dean of St. Paul's. His wife died in 1617, having borne twelve children and lost five; he himself died in 1631 shortly after it had been decided to make him a bishop.
MODERN EDITIONS AND CRITICISM: *The Poems*, ed. by H. J. C. Grierson, Oxford, 1912; *Complete Poems*, ed. by R. Bennett, Chicago, 1942; *The Sermons of John Donne*, ed., with Intros. and Critical Apparatus, by G. M. Potter and E. M. Simpson, California University Press, 1953-; *A Garland for John Donne*, ed. by T. Spencer and M. Van Doren, Harvard, 1939 (which lists criticism published 1912-38); William White, *John Donne Since 1900: A Bibliography of Periodical Articles*, Boston, 1942; V. Harris, *All Coherence Gone*, Chicago, 1949; L. Unger, *Donne's Poetry and Modern Criticism*, Chicago, 1950; D. Louthan, *The Poetry of John Donne, A Study in Explication*, New York, 1951; J. B. Leishman, *The Monarch of Wit*, London, 1951; C. Hunt, *Donne's Poetry*, Yale, 1954; R. C. Bald, *Donne and the Drurys*, Cambridge University Press, 1959.

DRAYTON, MICHAEL (1563-1631), was born in Warwickshire, and divided his life between the country and London, where he had a wide circle of literary acquaintances and a succession of patrons. He was a voluminous and competent writer in almost all the popular literary forms of his time.

MODERN EDITIONS AND CRITICISM: *Works,* ed. by J. W. Hebel and others, Oxford, 1931-1941; B. H. Newdigate, *Michael Drayton and His Circle,* Oxford, 1941.

DYER, SIR EDWARD (d. 1607), was educated at Oxford, held various positions at court, and was a friend of Sidney and Greville.
MODERN EDITIONS AND CRITICISM: *The Courtly Poets from Raleigh to Montrose,* ed. by J. Hannah, London, 1870; R. M. Sargent, *At the Court of Queen Elizabeth: The Life and Lyrics of Sir Edward Dyer,* Oxford, 1935.

GREENE, ROBERT (1558-1592), born at Norwich, was educated at Cambridge (B.A., 1578; M.A., 1583), and lived a bohemian life in London, where he wrote romances, plays and pamphlets of various kinds, many autobiographical.
MODERN EDITIONS AND CRITICISM: *Plays and Poems,* ed. by J. C. Collins, Oxford, 1905; U. Ellis-Fermor, "Marlowe and Greene: A Note on Their Relations as Dramatic Artists," *Studies in Honor of T. W. Baldwin* (University of Illinois Press, 1958), 136-49.

GREVILLE, FULKE, first Lord Brooke (1554-1628), was a friend from boyhood of Sir Philip Sidney, was educated at Cambridge, become wealthy and prominent at court under Elizabeth and James, and was friend and patron to many of the leading thinkers and writers of his time.
MODERN EDITIONS AND CRITICISM: *Caelica in Elizabethan Sonnet Cycles,* ed. M. F. Crow, London, 1898; *Poems and Dramas,* ed. by G. Bullough, London, 1939; M. W. Croll, *The Works of Fulke Greville,* Philadelphia, 1903; William Frost, *Fulke Greville's Caelica,* Pleasantville, N. Y., 1942.

HALL, JOHN (1627-56), educated at Cambridge, was an essayist in the manner of Bacon, pamphleteer for Cromwell, translator of Longinus, and minor poet.
MODERN EDITIONS AND CRITICISM: Saintsbury, *Minor Poets of the Caroline Period.*

HERBERT, GEORGE (1593-1633), younger brother of Lord Herbert of Cherbury, came from an old and distinguished Welsh family, and was educated at Westminster School and Cambridge (B.A., 1612; M.A., 1616), where he was Reader in Rhetoric and Public Orator (1620-27). His mother was a friend of Donne's. He was ordained deacon about 1626, married in 1629, and was ordained priest and appointed rector of Bemerton in 1630. During his final illness he sent his poems, which had circulated in manuscript, to Nicholas Ferrar, a merchant who had established a Protestant monastic community at Little Gidding; they appeared in 1633 under the title *The Temple.*
MODERN EDITIONS AND CRITICISM: *Works,* ed. by F. E. Hutchinson, Oxford, 1941; M. M. Ross, "George Herbert and the Humanist Tradition," *UTQ,* XVI (1947), 169-82; R. Tuve, *A Reading of George Herbert,* London, 1952; J. H. Summers, *George Herbert: His Religion and Art,*

Harvard, 1954; L. L. Martz, *The Poetry of Meditation*, Yale, 1954; M. Chute, *Two Gentle Men: The Lives of George Herbert and Robert Herrick*, New York, 1959.

HERRICK, ROBERT (1591-1674), son of a London goldsmith, was apprenticed to his uncle, also a goldsmith, in 1607, but left in 1613 for Cambridge (B.A., 1617; M.A., 1620). After a time in London, he turned to the church, and in 1629 became vicar of Dean Prior in Exeter. He was ejected by the Puritans in 1647 and lived in London until he was restored to his vicarship in 1662.
MODERN EDITIONS AND CRITICISM: *Poetical Works*, ed. F. W. Moorman, Oxford, 1915; *Poetical Works*, ed. with introductions, notes, and commentary by L. C. Martin, Oxford, 1956; Moorman, *Robert Herrick*, Oxford, 1910; F. Delattre, *Robert Herrick*, Paris, 1912; M. Chute (see Herbert); T. R. Whitaker, "Herrick and the Fruits of the Garden," *ELH*, XXII (1955), 16-33.

JONSON, BEN (1572-1637), posthumous son of a minister and stepson of a master bricklayer, was educated at Westminster School under William Camden; though not a university man, he was one of the most learned writers of his time. By 1597 he was a London actor and a noted playwright. Shakespeare played in his *Everyman in his Humour* (1598); in the same year Jonson was convicted of killing an actor, and while in prison was converted to Catholicism. Under King James, he became the official composer of court masques, and from 1603-14 his greatest plays were produced. In 1612-13 he was abroad as tutor to young Walter Ralegh. He collected and published his best writings up to 1612 in the folio *Works* of 1616, and became the literary dictator of his time.
MODERN EDITIONS AND CRITICISM: *Works*, ed. by C. H. Herford and P. Simpson, Oxford, 1925-52; *Poems*, ed. by B. H. Newdigate, Oxford, 1936; *Ben Jonson*, ed. by H. Levin, New York, 1938; M. Castelain, *Ben Jonson*, Paris, 1907; R. S. Walker, "Ben Jonson's Lyric Poetry," *Criterion*, XIII, 1933-4; G. B. Johnston, *Ben Jonson: Poet*, New York, 1945; M. Van Deusen, "Criticism and Ben Jonson's 'To Celia,'" *EIC*, VII (1957), 95-103; and see Volume II.

KING, HENRY (1592-1669), son of a bishop (who ordained Donne), was educated at Westminster School and Oxford (B.A., 1611; M.A., 1614), and rose in the church to the bishopric of Chichester (1642), from which he was expelled in 1643 by the Puritans and to which he returned after the Restoration. He was Donne's closest friend, executor of his will, and perhaps the editor of the 1633 edition of his poems. King's wife, the mother of six children, died about 1624 in her early twenties; this was the occasion for "The Exequy."
MODERN EDITIONS AND CRITICISM: *Poems*, ed. by J. Sparrow, London, 1925; R. Gleckner, "Henry King: A Poet of His Age," *Transactions Wisconsin Academy*, LXV (1956), 149-67.

LODGE, THOMAS (1558?-1625), son of a Lord Mayor of London, was educated at Merchant Taylors' School and Oxford (B.A., 1577). He left the law for literature, writing a *Defence of Poetry* (1580) and a variety of plays, lyrics, romances, and satires. In 1600 and 1602 Lodge took an M.D. at Avignon (where he became a Catholic) and Oxford, and practiced successfully thereafter in London.

MODERN EDITIONS AND CRITICISM: *Works*, ed. by E. Gosse, Glasgow, 1883; N. B. Paradise, *Thomas Lodge*, New Haven, 1931; E. A. Tenney, *Thomas Lodge*, Ithaca, 1935; P. M. Ryan, Jr., *Thomas Lodge. Gentleman*, Hamden, Conn., 1959.

LOVELACE, RICHARD (1618-1656/7), son of a Kentish knight, was educated at Charterhouse and Oxford (M.A., 1636). He was early noted for his gallant appearance and behavior. He composed "To Althea, from Prison" while confined for seven weeks in 1642 for presenting to Parliament the Kentish petition in favor of the Bishops. He was abroad in 1643-6, serving with the King's armies, and this may have been the occasion for the farewells to Lucasta. On his return he was again imprisoned and lost most of his fortune because of his Royalist leanings.

MODERN EDITIONS AND CRITICISM: *Poems*, ed. by C. H. Wilkinson, Oxford, 1925, 1930; C. H. Hartmann, *The Cavalier Spirit, and Its Influence on the Life and Works of Richard Lovelace*, London, 1925.

LYLY, JOHN (1554-1606), the grandson of the humanist William Lyly, was educated at Oxford (B.A., 1573; M.A., 1575), and spent his life in London and at court, where his patron was the Earl of Oxford. He was famous for his court comedies and his two books on Euphues, the latter introducing an elaborate prose style that was considerably imitated.

MODERN EDITIONS AND CRITICISM: *Works*, ed. by R. W. Bond, Oxford, 1902; *Euphues*, ed. by Croll and Clemens, London, 1916; J. R. Moore, "The Songs in Lyly's Plays," *PMLA*, XLII (1927), 623-40.

MARLOWE, CHRISTOPHER (1564-1593). For biographical sketch, see Volume II.

MODERN EDITIONS AND CRITICISM: *Works*, gen. ed., R. H. Case, London, 1931; P. W. Miller, "A Function of Myth in Marlowe's 'Hero and Leander,'" *SP*, L (1953), 158-167; T. W. Baldwin, "Marlowe's Musaeus," *JEGP*, LIV (1955), 478-485; M. T. Williams, "The Temptations in Marlowe's *Hero and Leander*," *MLQ*, XVI (1955), 226-231; R. A. Fraser, "The Art of *Hero and Leander*," *JEGP*, LVII (1958), 743-54.

MARVELL, ANDREW (1621-1678), the son of a Calvinist preacher, studied at Cambridge (1633-41), traveled abroad (1642-46), tutored the daughter of Lord Fairfax (1651-52), and (1653) a ward of Cromwell's, whom he had come to admire. He was assistant in the Latin secretaryship (1657-59) to John Milton, who had recommended him and who may have protected him during the Restoration. He served in Parliament from Hull from 1659 until his death.

MODERN EDITIONS AND CRITICISM: *Poems and Letters*, ed. by H. M. Margoliouth, Oxford, 1927; P. Legouis, *Andrew Marvell*, Paris, 1928; *Tercentenary Tributes*, ed. by W. H. Bagguley, Oxford, 1922; M. C.

Bradbrook and M. G. Lloyd Thomas, *Andrew Marvell,* New York, 1940; C. Brooks, "Criticism and Literary History: Marvell's Horatian Ode," *English Institute Essays* (1946), 127-58; M. Klonsky, "A Guide Through the Garden," *Sewanee Review,* LVIII (1950), 16-35; D. Bush, "Marvell's 'Horatian Ode,'" *Sewanee Review,* LX (1952), 363-76; J. H. Summers, "Marvell's Nature," *ELH,* XX (1953), 121-35.

NASHE, THOMAS (1567-1601), son of a minister, was educated at Cambridge (B.A., 1586) and lived in London, associated with the so-called University Wits—Marlowe, Greene, Peele, and wrote in a variety of forms, frequently satiric in nature.
MODERN EDITIONS AND CRITICISM: *Works,* ed. by R. B. McKerrow, London, 1904-10; repr. with corrections and supplementary notes by F. P. Wilson, Oxford, 1958.

PEELE, GEORGE (1558?-1597?), born in London and educated at Oxford (B.A., 1577; M.A., 1579), was one of the London University Wits, and author of plays, pageants, and occasional poems.
MODERN EDITIONS AND CRITICISM: *Works,* ed. by A. H. Bullen, London, 1888; *The Life and Minor Works,* ed. by D. H. Horne (*The Life and Works,* Vol. I, gen. ed., C. T. Prouty), Yale, 1952.

RALEGH, SIR WALTER (1552-1618), after attending Oxford and fighting in France and Ireland, was from 1580 to 1592 one of the leading figures at the court of Elizabeth. While confined by King James on trumped-up charges (1603-1618), he developed his scientific, philosophic, and literary interests, which find their fullest expression in his *History of the World* (1614).
MODERN EDITIONS AND CRITICISM: *Poems,* ed. by A. M. C. Latham, London, 1929; rev. ed., 1950; M. C. Bradbrook, *The School of Night,* Cambridge, 1936; E. G. Clark, *Ralegh and Marlowe,* New York, 1941; E. A. Strathmann, *Sir Walter Ralegh: A Study in Elizabethan Skepticism,* New York, 1950; W. M. Wallace, *Sir Walter Ralegh,* Princeton, 1959.

SHAKESPEARE, WILLIAM (1564-1616). For biographical sketch, see Volume II.
MODERN EDITIONS AND CRITICISM: *The Sonnets, A New Variorum Edition,* ed. by H. E. Rollins, Philadelphia, 1944; E. Hubler, *The Sense of Shakespeare's Sonnets,* Princeton, 1952; J. M. Davis and J. E. Grant, "A Critical Dialogue on Shakespeare's Sonnet 71," *Texas Studies in Language and Literature,* I (1959), 214-32.

SHIRLEY, JAMES (1596-1666), chiefly a dramatist, was born in London and educated at Oxford and Cambridge; he was by turns Anglican and Catholic.
MODERN EDITIONS AND CRITICISM: *Poems,* ed. by R. L. Armstrong, New York, 1941; E. S. Ownbey, "Shirley's *The Glories of Our Blood and State,*" *Explicator,* X (1952), item 10.

SIDNEY, SIR PHILIP (1554-1586), was born at Penshurst, the Kentish country place of his father, thrice lord deputy of Ireland. His mother was the sister of the Earl of Leicester. He attended Shrewsbury School with Fulke Greville, and spent three years at Oxford, leaving in 1572 to join the train of the English ambassador to France. In France he met leading writers and became acquainted with the difficulties of the Huguenot Protestants, many of whom were massacred on St. Bartholomew's Day, August 23. He visited Germany, Hungary, the Netherlands, and Italy (where he met Tintoretto and sat for Paolo Veronese) before returning to his uncle's reception for Queen Elizabeth at Kenilworth Castle in July 1575. He followed the Queen to the castle of the Earl of Essex, where he is supposed to have first met Essex's daughter, Penelope Devereux, aged thirteen, the Stella of his sonnets. He was thereafter prominent in literary and courtly circles and performed important services for the Queen until 1580, when he displeased her by opposing her projected marriage to the Duke of Anjou. Retiring to the home of his sister, the Countess of Pembroke, he wrote the early draft of a long pastoral romance, *Arcadia,* and in 1583(?) his *Defence of Poesy* against the puritanical attack of Stephen Gosson. He was knighted in 1583 and married Frances Walsingham. While planning an expedition to America with Drake in 1585, he was appointed Governor of Flushing, where he received a fatal wound during a skirmish.

MODERN EDITIONS AND CRITICISM: *Works,* ed. by A. Feuillerat, Cambridge, 1912-26; K. O. Myrick, *Sir Philip Sidney as a Literary Craftsman,* Harvard, 1935; Mona Wilson, *Sir Philip Sidney,* London, 1931; Theodore Spencer, "The Poetry of Sir Philip Sidney," *ELH,* 12 (1945), 251-78; R. B. Young, "English Petrarke: A Study of Sidney's *Astrophel and Stella,*" in *Three Studies in the Renaissance,* Yale, 1958.

SPENSER, EDMUND (1552?-1599), was educated at Merchant Taylors' School, where Richard Mulcaster was headmaster, and at Pembroke Hall, Cambridge (B.A., 1569-1573; M.A., 1576), where he was a friend of Gabriel Harvey, with whom he discussed classical and English meters. In 1578 he became secretary to John Young, master of Pembroke, Bishop of Rochester, and member of the Privy Council. The following year he entered the service of Robert Dudley, Earl of Leicester, favorite of the Queen; and in the same year he married nineteen-year-old Machabeus Chyld, who bore him a son and a daughter and died in 1591. In 1580 he left for Ireland as secretary to the new Lord Deputy, Lord Grey. Six years later he leased the 3,000-acre-estate of Kilcomnan, where Ralegh visited him in 1589 and brought him back to London to publish the first three books of the *Faerie Queene* in 1590. He returned to Kilcomnan in 1591, having been granted an annual pension of £50, and three years later married Elizabeth Boyle, which occasioned the writing of the *Epithalamion* (1595). During this period he finished three more books of the *Faerie Queene,* which appeared in 1596, and while in London wrote the *Prothalamion* (1596). Tyrone's rebellion broke out in 1598, a year after Spenser's return to Ireland. His estate was captured, and he died January 13, 1599, in Westminster.

MODERN EDITIONS AND CRITICISM: *Variorum Edition,* ed. by C. G.

Osgood, F. M. Padelford and others, Johns Hopkins, 1932-49; *Poetical Works*, ed. by E. de Selincourt, Oxford, 1916; H. S. V. Jones, *A Spenser Handbook*, New York, 1930; A. C. Judson, *Life of Edmund Spenser*, Johns Hopkins, 1945; W. T. Renwick, *Edmund Spenser*, London, 1925; Janet Spens, *Spenser's Faerie Queen*, London, 1934; C. S. Lewis, *The Allegory of Love*, Oxford, 1936; Josephine Bennett, *The Evolution of the Faerie Queen*, Chicago, 1942; Leicester Bradner, *Edmund Spenser and the Faerie Queen*, Chicago, 1948; W. B. C. Watkins, *Shakespeare and Spenser*, Princeton, 1950; D. S. Norton, "The Tradition of Prothalamia," *University of Virginia Studies*, IV (1951), 223-41; *That Soveraine Light: Essays in Honor of Spenser*, ed. by W. R. Mueller and D. C. Allen, Johns Hopkins, 1952; T. H. Greene, "Spenser and the Epithalamic Convention," *Comparative Literature*, IX (1957), 215-28; H. Berger, *The Allegorical Temper: Vision and Reality in Book II of Spenser's "Faerie Queene,"* Yale, 1957; J. N. Smith, "Spenser's *Prothalamion:* A New Genre," *RES*, X (1959), 173-78.

SUCKLING, SIR JOHN (1609-42), born near Twickenham of an old Norfolk family, was educated at Cambridge and Gray's Inn. He was abroad in 1628-30, knighted on his return, and served the following year under Gustavus Adolphus. He was the most famous gallant and gamester of his time, and died abroad, perhaps by suicide, after taking part in the attempt to rescue Strafford from the tower.

MODERN EDITIONS AND CRITICISM: *Works*, ed. by A. H. Thompson, London, 1910; F. O. Henderson, "Traditions of *Précieux* and *Libertin* in Suckling's Poetry," *ELH*, 4, 1937.

TRAHERNE, THOMAS (1636-1674), son of a Hereford shoemaker, was educated at Oxford (B.A., 1656; M.A., 1661; B.D., 1669); off and on during the same period he was rector of Credenhill in Herefordshire and chaplain to Sir Orlando Bridgeman. When Sir Orlando retired in 1672, Traherne followed him to his house in Teddington. Manuscripts of Traherne's poetry and prose meditations first appeared in a London bookstall in 1897 and were printed in 1903 and 1908 by Bertram Dobell, who determined their authorship.
MODERN EDITIONS AND CRITICISM: *Poems*, ed. by G. I. Wade, Oxford, 1932; *Centuries, Poems, and Thanksgivings*, ed. by H. M. Margoliouth, Oxford, 1958; Wade, *Thomas Traherne*, Princeton, 1944; A. H. Gilbert, "Thomas Traherne as Artist," *MLQ*, VIII (1947), 319-41, 435-47; J. M. Wallace, "Thomas Traherne and the Structure of Meditation," *ELH*, XXV (1958), 79-89.

VAUGHAN, HENRY (1622-1695), was born in Brecknockshire, South Wales, and signed himself "Silurist" from the Roman name for the district. He attended Oxford and studied law in London until the Civil War, in which he served on the Royalist side. During the rest of his life he was a country doctor at Newton-by-Usk, near Brecknock.
MODERN EDITIONS AND CRITICISM: *Works*, ed. by L. C. Martin, Oxford, 1914; 2nd ed., 1957; *The Secular Poems*, ed. by E. L. Marilla, Harvard, 1958; E. L. Marilla, *A Comprehensive Bibliography of Henry*

Vaughan, U. of Alabama Studies, 3, 1948; R. Durr, "Vaughan's Theme and Its Pattern: Regeneration," *SP,* LIV (1957), 14-28.

WALLER, EDMUND (1606-1687), son of a wealthy country family, studied at Cambridge, and early entered Parliament. His plot to seize London for the King was exposed in 1643, and he was fined and banished, spending seven years abroad. He was pardoned in 1651 and returned to Parliament in 1661.
MODERN EDITIONS AND CRITICISM: *Poems,* ed. by G. Thorn-Drury, London, 1905.

WEBSTER, John (1580?- 1625?). For biographical sketch, see Volume II.
MODERN EDITIONS AND CRITICISM: *Works,* ed. by F. L. Lucas, London, 1927.

WITHER, GEORGE (1588-1667), was born in Hampshire and studied at Oxford. He was imprisoned in 1614 because of the satiric *Abuses Stript and Whipt.* He wrote religious verse, was a Puritan officer, and composed voluminously until his death.
MODERN EDITIONS AND CRITICISM: *Poetry,* ed. by F. Sidgwick, London, 1902.

WOTTON, SIR HENRY (1568-1639), was educated at Winchester, Oxford, and the Middle Temple, and spent much of his life abroad as secretary to the Earl of Essex and ambassador to Venice. He was provost of Eton (1624-39). Izaak Walton finished the biography he had begun of his friend John Donne.
MODERN EDITIONS AND CRITICISM: *Poems,* ed. by A. Dyce, London, 1842; L. P. Smith, *Life and Letters of Sir Henry Wotton,* Oxford, 1907; F. Hard, "Sir Henry Wotton: Renaissance Englishman," *Pacific Spec.,* VII (1953), 364-79.

WYATT, SIR THOMAS (1503?-1542), was educated as a courtier and at the new St. John's College, Cambridge. He served Henry VIII in important posts, including assignments in France, Spain, and Italy (1527). He paraphrased and imitated many French and Italian lyric and satiric forms, particularly those used by Petrarch, Serafino, Aretino, and Alamanni. His poems circulated in manuscript, and 97 were published in Tottell's *Songs and Sonnets,* 1557.
MODERN EDITIONS AND CRITICISM: *The Poems,* ed. by A. K. Foxwell, London, 1913; E. M. W. Tillyard, *The Poetry of Sir Thomas Wyatt.* London, 1929; *Collected Poems,* ed. by K. Muir, London, 1949; A. K. Foxwell, *A Study of Sir Thomas Wyatt's Poems,* London, 1909; J. M. Berdan, *Early Tudor Poetry,* New York, 1920; E. K. Chambers, *Sir Thomas Wyatt . . . ,* London, 1933; D. W. Harding, "The Rhythmical Intention of Wyatt's Poetry," *Scrutiny,* XIV (1946), 90-102; H. Smith, "The Art of Sir Thomas Wyatt," *HLQ,* IX (1946), 323-355; R. O. Evans, "Some Aspects of Wyatt's Metrical Technique," *JEGP,* LIII (1954), 197-213; D. G. Rees, "Sir Thomas Wyatt's Translations from Petrarch," *Comparative Literature,* VII (1955), 15-24; P. Thomson, "The First English Petrarch," *HLO.* XXII (1959), 85-105.